25.00

THE CAMBRIDGE COMPANION TO
MALCOLM X

Malcolm X is one of the most important figures in the twentieth-century struggle for racial equality in America. With the passing of time, and changing attitudes to race and religion in American society, the significance of a public figure like Malcolm X continues to evolve and to challenge. This Companion presents new perspectives on Malcolm X's life and legacy in a series of specially commissioned essays by prominent scholars from a range of disciplines. As a result, this is an unusually rich analysis of this important African American leader, orator, and cultural icon. Intended as a source of information on his life, career and influence and as an innovative substantive scholarly contribution in its own right, the book also includes an introduction, a chronology of the life of Malcolm X, and a guide to further reading.

ROBERT E. TERRILL teaches in the Department of Communication and Culture at Indiana University, Bloomington. He is the author of *Malcolm X: Inventing Radical Judgment* (2004), which won the Kohrs-Campbell Prize in Rhetorical Criticism, 2005.

D0927321

Cambridge Companions to American Studies

This series of Companions to key figures in American history and culture is aimed at students of American studies, history, and literature. Each volume features newly commissioned essays by experts in the field, with a chronology and guide to further reading.

Volumes published:

The Cambridge Companion to Frederick Douglass edited by Maurice Lee

The Cambridge Companion to Bob Dylan edited by Kevin Dettmar

The Cambridge Companion to W. E. B. Du Bois edited by Shamoon Zamir

The Cambridge Companion to Benjamin Franklin edited by Carla Mulford

The Cambridge Companion to Thomas Jefferson edited by Frank Shuffelton

The Cambridge Companion to Malcolm X edited by Robert Terrill*

THE CAMBRIDGE
COMPANION TO
MALCOLM X

EDITED BY
ROBERT E. TERRILL

CAMBRIDGE
UNIVERSITY PRESS

CAMBRIDGE UNIVERSITY PRESS
Cambridge, New York, Melbourne, Madrid, Cape Town, Singapore,
São Paulo, Delhi, Dubai, Tokyo

Cambridge University Press
The Edinburgh Building, Cambridge CB2 8RU, UK

Published in the United States of America by Cambridge University Press, New York

www.cambridge.org
Information on this title: www.cambridge.org/9780521731577

© Cambridge University Press 2010

First published 2010

Printed in the United States of America

A catalogue record for this publication is available from the British Library.

ISBN 978-0-521-51590-0 Hardback
ISBN 978-0-521-73157-7 Paperback

CONTENTS

CONTRIBUTORS

MOLEFI KETE ASANTE is professor in the Department of African American Studies at Temple University, Philadelphia. He is the author of sixty-seven books, including *Malcolm X as Cultural Hero & Other Afrocentric Essays* (1994) and *Erasing Racism: The Survival of the American Nation* (2003). He is the editor of the *Journal of Black Studies*.

CLAUDE CLEGG is professor of history at Indiana University, Bloomington. He is the author of *An Original Man: The Life and Times of Elijah Muhammad* (1997) and *The Price of Liberty: African Americans and the Making of Liberia* (2004), as well as several articles and book chapters. Presently, he is writing a book about a lynching that took place in early twentieth-century North Carolina.

ANGELA D. DILLARD is associate professor in the Center for Afroamerican and African Studies and the Residential College at the University of Michigan, Ann Arbor. She is author of *Guess Who's Coming to Dinner Now?: Multicultural Conservatism in America* (2001) and *Faith in the City: Preaching Radical Social Change in Detroit* (2007).

KEVIN GAINES is professor in the Department of History at the University of Michigan, Ann Arbor. He is the author of *American Africans in Ghana: Black Expatriates in the Civil Rights Era* (2006) and *Uplifting the Race: Black Leadership, Politics and Culture During the Twentieth Century* (1996), winner of the John Hope Franklin Book Prize of the American Studies Association, 1997.

ALEX GILLESPIE is lecturer in Social Psychology at the University of Stirling (UK). His theoretical focus concerns dialogue, intersubjectivity, and identity, which has led to a range of empirical studies including a number of case studies of identity development. He has published *Becoming Other: From Social Interaction to Self-Reflection* (2006).

JEFFREY B. LEAK is associate professor of English at the University of North Carolina, Charlotte. He is the author of *Racial Myths and Masculinity in African*

American Literature (2005) and is completing a biography of Henry Dumas, a writer associated with the Black Arts Movement of the 1960s.

MARK LAWRENCE McPHAIL is professor and chair of Corporate Communication and Public Affairs at Southern Methodist University, Dallas, Texas. He is the author of *Zen in the Art of Rhetoric: An Inquiry into Coherence* (1996) and *The Rhetoric of Racism Revisited: Reparations or Separation?* (2002). As an undergraduate student at Emerson College, Boston, Massachusetts, he served as the president of the Norfolk Prison Debate Society, and had the opportunity to speak in the same spaces in which Malcolm X once debated.

BRIAN NORMAN is in the English Department at Loyola College in Maryland. He is the author of *The American Protest Essay and National Belonging* (2007) and the co-editor of *Representing Segregation*, a special issue of *African American Review*. His current book project concerns Jim Crow in post–civil rights American literature.

SHEILA RADFORD-HILL is Executive Director of the Luther College Diversity Center, Decorah, Iowa. She holds a Master of Arts in American Studies from the University of Pennsylvania, Philadelphia, a graduate certificate in Community Development from the University of Illinois, Urbana, and a Ph.D. in Humanities with a specialization in education from Columbia Commonwealth University, Missoula, Montana. She is the author of *Further to Fly: Black Women and the Politics of Empowerment* (2000).

WILLIAM W. SALES, JR. is associate professor and past chair of the Department of African American Studies, and Director of the Center for African American Studies, at Seton Hall University, South Orange, New Jersey. He is the author of *From Civil Rights to Black Liberation: Malcolm X and the Organization of Afro-American Unity* (1994), *Southern Africa/Black America: Same Struggle, Same Fight* (1977), and numerous articles in the field of African American Studies.

JAMES SMETHURST teaches in the Department of Afro-American Studies at the University of Massachusetts, Amherst. He is the author of *The New Red Negro: The Literary Left and African American Poetry, 1930–1946* (1999) and *The Black Arts Movement: Literary Nationalism in the 1960s and 1970s* (2005). He is also the co-editor of *Left of the Color Line: Race, Radicalism and Twentieth-Century Literature of the United States* (2006) and *Radicalism in the South Since Reconstruction* (2006).

ROBERT E. TERRILL teaches in the Department of Communication and Culture at Indiana University, Bloomington. His scholarship has focused on rhetorical analysis of important speeches by African American orators. His *Malcolm X: Inventing Radical Judgment* (2004), was awarded the Kohrs-Campbell Prize in Rhetorical Criticism, 2005.

RICHARD BRENT TURNER is coordinator of the African American Studies Program and Associate Professor of Religious Studies at the University of Iowa, Iowa City. He is the author of *Islam in the African-American Experience* (1997) and *Jazz Religion, the Second Line, and Black New Orleans* (2009).

JAMES TYNER is professor of geography at Kent State University, Ohio. His research interests include political geography, mass violence, genocide, and radical politics. He is the author of nine books, including *The Geography of Malcolm X: Black Radicalism and the Remaking of American Space* (2005).

CHRONOLOGY

1925   Malcolm Little is born on May 19 in Omaha, Nebraska, to Earl and Louise Little. Malcolm is Earl's seventh child, and Louise's fourth (Earl had three children from a previous marriage). Both Earl and Louise are members of Marcus Garvey's Universal Negro Improvement Association.

1929   On November 7, the Littles' home in Lansing, Michigan, is burned to the ground. In his autobiography, Malcolm calls this his "earliest vivid memory," and suggests that the fire was started by the "Black Legion," a local white-supremacy group.

1931   Earl Little is killed on September 28, when he is run over by a streetcar in Lansing. In his autobiography, Malcolm suggests that his father was attacked by whites and then laid across the streetcar tracks.

1939   On January 9, Louise Little is declared insane and committed to the state mental asylum in Kalamazoo, Michigan. Her eight children are divided among several different foster homes, and Malcolm eventually is made a ward of the state and sent to a group home for boys in Mason, Michigan.

1940   Malcolm is elected class president at Mason Junior High, and earns high grades; his English teacher, Mr. Ostrowski, tells him he should consider becoming a carpenter because that is a "realistic goal for a nigger."

1941   Malcolm finishes the eighth grade and leaves Lansing, and school, for Boston, to live with his half-sister Ella.

1942   On December 18, Elijah Muhammad is sentenced to five years in prison for draft evasion.

1943   Malcolm is rejected by the draft board as unfit for service.

1946   Malcolm is arrested on January 12, in Boston, for burglary, and is sentenced to eight to ten years in prison, which is an unusually heavy sentence. In his autobiography, Malcolm speculates that he also was being punished for consorting with white women in his burglary gang. On August 24, Elijah Muhammad is released from prison.

1948   In March, Malcolm is transferred from Concord Reformatory to Norfolk Prison Colony. His younger brother Reginald introduces him to the Nation of Islam. Malcolm begins corresponding by letter with Elijah Muhammad.

1952   On August 7, Malcolm is paroled, and goes to live with his eldest brother Wilfred in Detroit. He meets Elijah Muhammad and joins the Nation of Islam.

1953   Recognizing Malcolm's considerable gifts, Elijah Muhammad promotes him to Assistant Minister of Detroit Temple Number 1.

1954   After establishing new Temples in Philadelphia and Boston, Malcolm is appointed Minister of the key Temple Number 7, in Harlem, and would remain associated with it for the remainder of his tenure with the Nation of Islam. On May 17, the United States Supreme Court hands down the decision in *Brown v. Board of Education of Topeka, Kansas*.

1955   Emmett Till is lynched after whistling at a white woman in Money, Mississippi. On December 1, Rosa Parks is arrested in Montgomery, Alabama, for refusing to give up her seat on a bus to a white person. On December 5, African Americans began a boycott of the buses in Montgomery that would last for over a year.

1957   Hinton X (Johnson), a member of Temple Number 7, is beaten and arrested on April 14. Malcolm leads a contingent of his followers to the police station, and negotiates medical treatment. The incident brings the Nation of Islam increased visibility and respect in Harlem.

1958   On January 14, Malcolm marries Betty X (Sanders). Their first daughter, Attallah, is born on November 16.

1959   The first segment of "The Hate That Hate Produced" airs on Mike Wallace's *News Beat* show on WNTA-TV, on July 13. It is the first time that most white Americans have heard of the Nation of Islam, Elijah Muhammad, and Malcolm X. Later that year, Malcolm travels to the Middle East and Africa, but does not visit Mecca. His passport lists his name as Malcolm X, also known as Malik El-Shabazz.

1960   In February, in Greensboro, North Carolina, four young African Americans "sit in" at a whites-only Woolworth's lunch counter. On April 21, the Civil Rights Act of 1960 passes the US Congress. In September, Malcolm meets Fidel Castro, who is staying at the

Theresa Hotel in Harlem. Malcolm's daughter Qubilah is born on Christmas Day. *Muhammad Speaks* is launched.

1961 In January, Malcolm meets with members of the Ku Klux Klan, in Atlanta, Georgia. The KKK was considering procuring land for the Nation of Islam because they perceived a common interest in the separation of the races, and because they thought that if the Nation of Islam became more influential it would draw attention away from the integrationist civil-rights movement.

1962 On April 27, Ronald X (Stokes), a member of the Los Angeles Mosque, is shot to death by police. Malcolm flies out to L.A. to preach at the funeral and seems tempted to organize a protest in response, but Elijah Muhammad does not allow it. On July 22, Malcolm's daughter Ilyasah is born.

1963 Early this year, Malcolm begins working with Alex Haley on his *Autobiography*, which will be published posthumously in 1965. In April, Malcolm confronts Elijah Muhammad about his adultery. In May, a widely-read interview that Haley conducts with Malcolm X appears in *Playboy*. In August, Dr. Martin Luther King, Jr. delivers his famous "I Have a Dream" speech during the March on Washington, DC. In November, President John F. Kennedy is assassinated in Dallas, Texas; on December 1, Malcolm calls this a case of the "chickens coming home to roost," and is subsequently "silenced" by Elijah Muhammad.

1964 In February, Malcolm visits Cassius Clay while he is training for his championship bout with Sonny Liston; after the fight, Malcolm announces that Clay will be receiving his "X" and joining the Nation of Islam. On March 8, Malcolm announces that he is leaving the Nation of Islam, and, on the 12th, that he is founding a new organization, the Muslim Mosque, Inc. On March 26, Malcolm X and King meet for the only time when they are both observing the Senate debate over the 1964 Civil Rights Bill. In April and May, *Muhammad Speaks*, the official organ of the Nation of Islam, which Malcolm had helped to establish, carries a series of essays highly critical of Malcolm. On April 13, Malcolm begins his journey to Mecca to perform the hajj, a ritual pilgrimage to Islamic holy sites that is required of all muslims who can afford it. He also delivers speeches in Beirut, Nigeria, and Ghana. He returns home to New York on May 21, bearing the name El-Hajj Malik El-Shabazz. On June 28, he announces the founding of the Organization of Afro-American Unity. On July 9, Malcolm again travels to Africa, and submits a written address to the Organization of African Unity, meeting in Cairo. He returns to New York on November 24, twelve days after his mother Louise is finally released from the mental hospital in Kalamazoo. On November 30, he leaves to participate in a debate at Oxford, England. Malcolm returns to the States on December 14; a fourth daughter is born, Gamilah Lamumbah, on December 4.

1965   On February 5, Malcolm leaves for Europe, where he plans to address the Council of African Organizations in London and the Federation of African Students in France; however, he is denied entry into France. On February 12, lawyers working for the Nation of Islam attempt to have Malcolm and his family evicted from their house, owned by the Nation. On February 13, he returns to New York for the final time. In the early hours of February 14, his house is firebombed, and Malcolm blames the Nation of Islam. Malcolm X is assassinated on February 21, in New York, as he is about to begin his address at the Audubon Ballroom.

In the early hours of February 23, Harlem Mosque Number 7 burns to the ground. Malcolm is buried in Ferncliff Cemetery on February 27. In March, Betty Shabazz participates in the pilgrimage to Mecca, taking the name Hajj Bahiyah Betty Shabazz. On March 11, a grand jury indicts Talmadge Hayer, Norman 3X Butler, and Thomas 15X Johnson for the murder of Malcolm X.

On September 30, twin daughters Malaak and Malikah are born.

ACKNOWLEDGMENTS

Any book is a collective effort, at least to some degree, but a project of this scope simply could not have been completed without the assistance and support of a great many individuals. I cannot list them all, but I would like to acknowledge at least a few. At home, my family continues to be extraordinarily accepting of the ongoing distractions and minor crises that accompany an academic life. At Cambridge University Press, I thank Ray Ryan for inviting me into the project, and Maartje Scheltens for helping it move forward. Lindeth Vasey possesses a keen eye, and the manuscript was much improved through her copy-editing. And Christina Sarigiannidou guided me with expertise and patience through the final stages of production. At Indiana University, my department chair, Greg Waller, supported my request for a leave during which a part of this project was completed, and I thank my colleagues for their interest in my work. And, of course, I thank the contributors to this volume for their fine essays, each of which makes a substantive contribution to our understanding of Malcolm X.

Robert E. Terrill

ROBERT E. TERRILL

Introduction

Mention Malcolm X, and you are almost certain to receive a reaction. Many admire him, many loathe him, but even now, more than four decades after his death, few lack an opinion about him. A polarizing figure, in death as in life, Malcolm X continues to haunt American national consciousness like few other figures. His name is known around the world, his autobiography is on American high school and college reading lists around the country, his life was the subject of a blockbuster Hollywood film, hundreds of websites are dedicated to his legacy, and he has even appeared on a United States postage stamp. And yet he resists now, as he did then, being fully accepted – or co-opted, depending on your point of view – by the culture that he spent his life critiquing. Malcolm X will forever speak to all of us from the margins, pointing out our collective failure to live according to the ideals we proclaim, taking us to task for the inconsistencies and hypocrisies that riddle our politics, revealing our complicity and reviling our complacency. He will always speak in the voice of the marginalized, a voice that cannot be placated or patronized, a voice both self-righteous and self-educated, passionate and cerebral, angry and eloquent. As a passionate advocate for his people, a persistent critic of inequity, a widely emulated and appropriated cultural icon, and an extraordinarily gifted orator, Malcolm X will have few equals.

Scholars, it seems, are as susceptible to the allure of Malcolm X as anyone else. The tremendous flood of words that he produced during his lifetime – his speeches, press releases, public letters, television appearances, campus debates, radio interviews, newspaper columns, and of course his *Autobiography* – has been more than matched by a formidable torrent of scholarly work. Library shelves and the pages of academic journals are laden with cultural and psychological biographies; memoirs of his children, and of those who knew him and worked with him; critical analyses of Malcolm's oratory and *Autobiography*; explorations of his influence on, and representation in, art, music, and politics; comparisons between Malcolm X and other revolutionary leaders, including his contemporaries, his antecedents, and his ideological progeny; efforts to align him with various political categories or organizations; and speculations about what he might have said or thought or done had he lived longer. The scholarly attention focused on Malcolm X began as soon as he and the Nation of Islam rose to national prominence and has continued unabated.

The vitality and breadth of this scholarly work reflects the complexities of the man. Malcolm X lived multiple lives – overachieving Midwestern school-kid, anxious foster child, teenaged hoodlum, unskilled service worker, petty criminal, small-time hustler, convicted felon, zealous religious convert, Muslim minister, respected orator, civil rights leader, international celebrity, and martyr – each of which has attracted scholarly attention, and sometimes multiple analytical approaches. The resulting riot of academic work indicates a healthy and vigorous area of study, one untroubled by calcifying orthodoxy but also without a clear center of gravity. On the one hand, this is an entirely fitting state of affairs for an iconoclast who often vehemently rejected efforts to define himself or his position. On the other hand, however, this scholarly diversity can make it difficult to tease out the central questions and themes that animate and integrate all this work.

This book is intended as an introduction and as a contribution to the scholarship on Malcolm X; it also represents the range of this work in an interdisciplinary microcosm. Just as the scholarship on Malcolm X is produced by scholars trained in a variety of disciplines, so too are the essays in this volume. The latter come from men and women of different ethnic backgrounds, from younger and more established scholars. But perhaps most significantly, just as there are themes that recur throughout the scholarship, despite its diversity and variety, so too there are for these essays. For the researcher in the early stages of their work, this volume should provide a starting point that not only presents some of the most important scholarly approaches to Malcolm X but also – through the guide for further reading as well as the endnotes for each essay – directions for further study. For the more established researcher, these new essays both draw upon and contribute to established scholarship.

In the first essay, Claude Clegg provides an overview of the complex, mutually dependent, and eventually destructive relationship between Malcolm X and Elijah Muhammad. That his essay also provides a condensed biography of Malcolm X is a testament not only to Clegg's skill, but also to the fact that the rise and fall of Malcolm X are tied so intimately to the relationship between these two men. There could have been no Malcolm X without Elijah Muhammad, of course; but also, and no less substantively, there could have been no Elijah Muhammad – at least not as we know him – without Malcolm X. And more broadly, as their connection flourished, matured, and finally soured, it can be understood as an extended analogy to the generational and ideological tensions that arose in the civil rights movements of the 1960s. Clegg, then, rightly gives this relationship a central place in our understanding of both Malcolm X and of the history of that time.

The Autobiography of Malcolm X occupies a similar status, being both the fundamental text at the center of all studies of Malcolm X and a vital record of one man's experience of mid-twentieth-century America. In this literary masterpiece we see not only the shattering transformations that Malcolm underwent during his lifetime, but also, through his eyes, the world in which and against which he wrought those changes. The *Autobiography* was largely complete at the time of Malcolm's death, and he was able to proofread the text. However, Haley convinced Malcolm not to revise the sections that deal with his early devotion to Elijah Muhammad, and as a result the text is something of a palimpsest, less a narrative of complete transformation than an evolution of an identity in which traces of all previous identities are retained. Alex Gillespie argues that the *Autobiography* draws upon cultural expectations, or "narrative resources," in its construction and as such should not be misunderstood as a transparent portrait of the man and his times. In fact, as Gillespie discusses, the *Autobiography* itself is an important element of the life that it chronicles: that it constitutes Malcolm X at least as much as it represents him. That is, the *Autobiography* might be seen as not merely a record of transformations, but also as itself a transformative moment in the life of Malcolm X.

It was inevitable, perhaps, that a story with such far-reaching significance and narrative appeal eventually would be brought to Hollywood, but it is not widely known that the first efforts to do so involved commissioning the African American writer James Baldwin to write a screenplay. Brian Norman takes Baldwin's work as an example of a "closet screenplay," published in book form but never produced as a film. The work of adapting the life of an iconoclast like Malcolm X to a medium that largely traffics in icons is inevitably rife with difficulty and compromise, and Norman attends carefully to the differences between Baldwin's failed screenplay and Spike Lee's successful and critically-acclaimed film. The script is more experimental in form, for example, breaking up the linear narrative of transformation that governs the *Autobiography* and thus self-consciously presenting a multi-layered personality that is in some ways analogous to the one that Gillespie describes. By resisting the heroic narrative arc that commonly shapes blockbuster biopics, Norman argues, Baldwin also resisted providing Malcolm's story with a definitive ending: Malcolm's work remains unfinished. Significantly, Norman also argues that Baldwin resisted the hypermasculine stance often ascribed to Malcolm X by inserting into his screenplay proto-feminist and queer subtexts that were not part of Lee's film.

Jeffrey Leak specifically explores the implications of the *Autobiography* for understanding African American masculinity. He sees the text as a narrative representation of a process of change, as does Gillespie, and argues that Malcolm does not present a static icon of black masculinity, but rather an evolving process that points toward, even if it does not fully define, a more progressive masculine stance. While the close relationship between Malcolm X and Elijah Muhammad, as explored by Clegg, helped to define Malcolm X, Leak notes that the close collaboration between Malcolm X and Alex Haley shaped the *Autobiography*. Further, he points out, this relationship between two African American men models a collaborative and mutually supportive form of black masculinity that is not often portrayed in public culture. Malcolm's relationships with women, as presented in the *Autobiography*, offer further evidence of an evolving rather than static presentation of black manhood. Comparing Malcolm's portrayal of his mother to the more complex portrayal of his half-sister Ella, Leak finds a potentially progressive portrayal of African American manhood that is nonetheless undermined by a consistent suspicion of strong black women.

Indeed, Malcolm's public statements about black women, including those in the *Autobiography*, have been almost uniformly described as misogynist. But Sheila Radford-Hill argues for "womanizing" Malcolm X, attending to the roles that women played in his life rather than exclusively to what he said, and thus shifting the focus toward female agency. This form of feminist critique, she suggests, helps to illuminate how women helped to shape Malcolm X. Supplementing their limited portrayals within the *Autobiography*, Radford-Hill explores Malcolm's personal relationships with his mother and with Ella, as well as those with his other sisters, his girlfriends, his wife Betty, and his professional collaboration with female civil-rights leaders such as Fannie Lou Hamer. The portrait that emerges is subtle and complex, a constructive response to, rather than a full repudiation of, other feminist critiques: in contrast to his statements, Malcolm's actual relationships and attitudes toward African American women draw upon a less restricted emotional palate and a more equitable gender sensibility. Radford-Hill then builds on her analysis to explore the gender norms that inform Malcolm's intellectual and ideological descendents, from Black Power forward, and finds that Malcolm's more progressive tendencies do have some degree of continued presence in contemporary black nationalist gender critique.

The Black Arts Movement flourished during the 1960s and 1970s and consisted of politically engaged artists and art institutions that were aligned ideologically with Black Power. And, as James Smethurst argues, this movement also was strongly influenced by Malcolm X, beginning with his rise to prominence with the Nation of Islam and extending beyond his death. Smethurst points out that a part of Malcolm's influence on the Black Arts Movement stemmed directly from his speeches and statements: his persistent message of racial pride and his fluid, eloquent, markedly African American rhetorical artistry served as a model and inspiration. But in addition, Malcolm's influence also came from his actions: he frequently took time to talk with the rank-and-file members of grass-roots organizations who later participated in or aligned themselves with the Black Arts Movement. Smethurst notes that Malcolm X offered a unique combination that attracted many young activist artists: a core of black nationalism together with an insistence that the African American freedom struggle must be understood within a global context. The multiple points of contact between Malcolm X and the Black Arts Movement illuminate a dense network of association and influence, and it was within this nourishing environment, and especially after his death, that artists began the process of appropriating Malcolm's words and image into a wide variety of media.

Throughout his life, Malcolm X held a special attraction for young people. Though he actually was a few years older than Dr. Martin Luther King, Jr., Malcolm often aligned himself with youth and characterized the more mainstream civil-rights leaders as older and out of touch. It is not surprising, then, that youth culture has been especially active in its appropriation of Malcolm's words and image; somewhat analogous to his presence in Black Arts Movement poetry, Malcolm is a prominent presence in rap music and hip-hop culture. Indeed, for the latter, he is so ubiquitous a presence in their multi-mediated world – his ideas, his likeness, his words, his attitudes, his struggles, his martyrdom – that sweeping or general surveys may miss much of the subtlety of Malcolm's influence. Richard Turner concentrates on a particular site of this appropriation: Malcolm's effect on African American Muslim youth in university communities. This focus allows Turner to provide a very fine-grained analysis, utilizing textual analysis and personal interviews, to flesh out the meanings and connotations that are associated with Malcolm X within a specific community. Taking as starting points the two organizations that Malcolm founded after his split with the Nation of Islam and his conversion to Sunni Islam – the Organization for Afro-American Unity and the Muslim Mosque, Inc. – Turner explores the multiple inventional resources that Malcolm X presents for these young contemporary artists and audiences.

Among the less obvious audiences for whom Malcolm's legacy has offered resources for identity and legitimacy in recent years have been black conservatives. His endorsement of traditional gender roles and pull-yourself-up-by-your-bootstraps, self-help, free-market capitalism, especially while he was affiliated with the Nation of Islam, seem to fit easily with contemporary conservative views. But such an appropriation of Malcolm X is uneasy at best, while calling for neither a cynical dismissal nor an uncritical acceptance. Angela Dillard explores the terrain upon which black nationalism and black conservatism intersect, and some of the ways that Malcolm's ideas were themselves influenced by these intersections. Her analysis thus provides the historical and ideological context that enables a more careful and nuanced assessment regarding the degree to which Malcolm X might legitimately be called "conservative." As is so often the case with regard to him, and as Smethurst also argues regarding his appeal in the Black Arts Movement, Dillard's assessment shows that Malcolm X presented a uniquely complex mixture of many influences and traditions. Attempts at appropriation that force Malcolm into artificially narrow confines necessarily ignore his fundamental complexity and thus diminish our understanding of the liberatory potential of his words and ideas.

Mark McPhail takes up one aspect of this potential, arguing that Malcolm's public speeches and statements present a manifestation of the "rhetorical ideal," in which style and ornamentation are appreciated as substantive, rather than superfluous. In contrast to the age-old attack on rhetoric as a form of obfuscation and mystification that protects those in power, McPhail argues that Malcolm's was a specifically African American rhetorical ideal, which challenged the norms of the dominant culture from within, utilizing the tropes and figures of traditional rhetoric to critique racial hierarchy. Eschewing the "sweet talk" that had characterized so much of the discourse about race relations in the United States, Malcolm X offered instead a searing indictment that deployed analogy, metaphor, synecdoche, and irony to sharpen rather than sweeten his argument. Ultimately, McPhail concludes that the collapse of the style/content opposition in Malcolm's discourse renders his rhetorical practice analogous to jazz, an indigenous American art form rooted firmly in African and African American stylistic traditions. The improvisational impulse that is fundamental to jazz suggests not only Malcolm's own use of an extemporaneous speech delivery, but also the flexible and inventive political style that he invited his audiences to adopt. As McPhail puts it, Malcolm X provides for his audiences *"equipment for living together."*

In my own essay I take another approach to exploring the sort of rhetorical "equipment" that Malcolm X provides for his audiences. Because Malcolm's concrete legacy consists primarily of his public address, I argue that understanding that legacy is best grounded in close attention to those texts. I analyze two speeches from the last year of his life, after his split with the Nation of Islam, a time in which his ideas were undergoing especially rapid change. Taken together, these texts illustrate a shift in Malcolm's thought, from the straightforward call for African Americans to identify themselves primarily as Africans that characterized his rhetoric immediately after he cast off the limitations of Elijah Muhammad's Nation of Islam, to a more complex call to occupy a sort of ideological middle ground, where African Americans would be suspended between domestic and global perspectives. From this interstitial space, his audience is able to critique the oppressive practices in both places without being co-opted and thus silenced by either. Through the performative artistry of his public address, then, Malcolm X is modelling for his audiences a tactic of interpretive judgment that he would have them take up and emulate.

The sustained effort, especially in his last year, that Malcolm X made to broaden his audience's horizons, and then to help them to understand the connections and parallels between their struggles in the United States and those of oppressed peoples across the globe, can be understood as geographic in scope. Malcolm encouraged his listeners to see their familiar landscape in a new way, as a part of a contiguous and international whole rather than as an isolated backwater. James Tyner situates Malcolm's "geographical imagination," his effort to remake the spaces occupied by his audiences, within a tradition of dystopian literature, and thus highlights the special qualities of Malcolm's social critique. Though his speeches and statements clearly were not intended as fictions, Tyner argues that their critical potentials were in some ways similar to that of dystopian fiction. Because a person's sense of self emanates, in part, from their perception of the environment with which they interact, by altering his audience's perception of their environment Malcolm X was able to alter their perception of themselves. He was empowering his audiences to read, and to critique, the oppressive landscapes in which they lived their everyday lives.

The specific perspective that Malcolm X was working to provide for his audiences has much in common with that now called *Afrocentric*. While he did not seek to replace all European ways of thinking and being with African ways, as the paradigmatic Afrocentrist might, Malcolm certainly was attempting to supplant those that were inauthentic and thus dysfunctional. Malcolm was among the first, for example, to insist that the terms "black" or "Afro-American" replace "Negro," because that word offered no connection to African culture. Molefi Kete Asante shows that Malcolm consistently schooled his audiences not only on the importance of Africa but on understanding themselves as African, not only to have pride in Africa but also in themselves as peoples of African descent. Asante argues that Malcolm understood that knowledge of, and practice of, cultural traditions that reinforced his audience's African identity were a powerful source of resistance, and that his project entailed the reconstruction and maintenance of culture in the face of a domination that would negate that culture.

Malcolm X spent much of his last year, after his split with the Nation of Islam, outside of the United States, exploring important connections between Africans and African Americans. No serious study could exclude both an account of his international presence during that time and an assessment of the global scope of his legacy. Kevin Gaines argues that not only were Malcolm's international experiences important to the formation of his evolving thought, but also that they have had a significant impact on the way that he is remembered, at home and abroad. Malcolm worked to help his African American audiences see their connection to the African diaspora, he urged his global audiences to recognize their stake in the African American freedom struggle, and on a personal level, he reached out to leaders and movements around the world – working toward bringing into concrete manifestation the ideological breadth of scope that so many have noted as a key component of his thought.

William Sales, in the final essay, offers a detailed survey of the legacy of Malcolm X, arguing that Malcolm X was central to the restoration of an African American resistance tradition extending back at least to Martin Delany, whom many consider to be the father of black nationalism. In the last year of his life, Sales notes, Malcolm founded the Organization of Afro-American Unity on the principles that he believed would enable it to become an umbrella organization under which black nationalist groups and ideas could be developed and coordinated. This was to be a democratic body in which women were to hold leadership roles, and it was to be politically independent yet not politically inert; the organization would participate in electoral politics but on its own terms. While the Organization of Afro-American Unity did not perhaps achieve the sort of high-profile political activity that Malcolm seems to have hoped for, Sales finds the political legacy and continuing influence of Malcolm X is especially evident in academia, in archival library and museum institutions, in popular culture, and in political thought and action. He provides thorough yet efficient summaries of each of these areas; though each site necessarily privileges particular facets of this most multifaceted man, in practice there is considerable overlap among academia and archive, popular and political culture.

When I contacted the contributors, I told them that I wanted their help in producing a book that would be "a fitting contribution to the legacy of this most extraordinary man." And I hope that we have fulfilled that promise, because, as Sales points out, while Malcolm X remains a vigorous presence in American and African American life, maintaining that vigor requires a proactive and coordinated effort. By bringing together scholars from diverse backgrounds and academic disciplines, this volume is intended both to represent and to encourage the continuing, overlapping, and interdisciplinary interest in Malcolm X that is helping to keep his legacy alive. From the rise of politically conservative African American "mega-churches" to the rolling back of civil liberties in post-9/11 America, Malcolm's spirit and ideas face continuing resistance. Throughout his many transformations, for example, he never abandoned his commitment to Islam, a religion that has been denigrated repeatedly since the attacks on the World Trade Center and the Pentagon. Though he softened his views somewhat on many issues, he never wavered on his insistence that violence was justified in self-defense; he never endorsed simple assimilation; he never described the political system in the United States as anything other than thoroughly and institutionally corrupt; and he never publically imagined that America could one day throw back the cloak of racism and emerge as a society characterized by justice, equity, and brotherhood. His speeches and statements, his ideas and his condemnations, sound as breathtakingly fearless, compelling, perceptive – and yes, to some, as dangerous – today as they were when he first uttered them. Yet they persist, for as long as there remains a racial hierarchy, the model of personal and political development that Malcolm X presents will remain relevant. Young people searching for their own identities will recognize themselves in the *Autobiography*; artists seeking an authentic and original vision will be inspired; politicians and public figures of all ideological stripes will feel compelled to embrace him, to shun him, or to answer to him. And, I hope, we will continue to find within him something to feed our individual souls and our collective selves.

I

CLAUDE CLEGG

Malcolm X and Elijah Muhammad

Elijah Muhammad rarely granted press interviews. His reluctance to indulge reporters was at least partially due to a history of unflattering news coverage of his organization, the Nation of Islam, which was routinely characterized in the media as racist, extremist, and un-American. Moreover, Muhammad's modest formal education and advanced age – he was in his early sixties when his group became the object of dubious press scrutiny in 1959 – further discouraged active engagement with news organizations that were largely in the hands of whites hostile to his message. His last significant encounter with newsmen took place in January 1972 in the comfort of his Chicago mansion. It was a far-reaching exploration of topics, ranging from matters of theology (he reaffirmed a decades-long commitment to a racially exclusivist iteration of Islam) to his own reaction to dissenters within the Nation (he summarily dismissed their influence as negligible). A press inquiry about one apostate in particular did elicit specific comments from Muhammad, even though the individual in question had died several years earlier. When asked about Malcolm X, a former national minister of the Nation, Muhammad appeared roiled by the query. "I would not lose any time with a man that has been talked and talked about for years," Muhammad shot back, before veering away into other subject matter.[1]

The unwillingness of Muhammad to countenance a discussion of Malcolm X was not a new development. He had avoided extended public commentary on the topic since the mid-1960s, when he and his former lieutenant grappled for months in an open conflict that ultimately resulted in Malcolm's assassination in February 1965. Even after death, the reverence that Malcolm's brand of black nationalism still evoked among the Black Power generation of African American activists continued to annoy Muhammad. Malcolm's posthumously published autobiography, detailing a fascinating personal journey through social alienation and self-destructiveness to political awakening and self-realization, conferred more longevity upon his views and relevance than he would have likely predicted during his thirty-nine years of life. While he indeed sought to marginalize Malcolm's legacy with both damning criticism and self-aggrandizing portrayals of his own leadership, Muhammad had eventually to coexist with a canonized Malcolm X, whose credibility as an icon of militant protest was inscribed in stone at the very moment of his murder before a Harlem crowd of supporters.[2]

To be sure, the rancor and rivalry that existed between Muhammad and Malcolm, both in life and death, had not been the distinguishing feature of their relationship over two decades of acquaintance. During his sojourn in the Muslim movement of Muhammad, Malcolm participated in a matrix of complex encounters, collaborations, and interactions with the man to whom he would attribute his spiritual salvation and public notoriety. Fundamentally, their relationship was that of mentor and protégé, with Malcolm having been brought into the fold of the Nation of Islam during a nearly seven-year stint in prison in the 1940s and 1950s. Further, the association between the men had familial qualities, not unlike that between father and son. Having lost his own father during his early childhood, Malcolm – and many others – engaged a paternal dimension of Muhammad's personality and patriarchal-leadership style that was arguably part of his appeal as the steward of the Nation of Islam, but also characteristic of the group's autocratic, hierarchical dynamics and structural limitations. The connection between Muhammad and Malcolm, given the latter's prominent roles as an organizer of local mosques, a gifted fundraiser, and eventually, national spokesman, revealed a corporatist bent, with the older man – as titular head of the Nation and custodian of its finances – cast as chief executive officer alongside the younger man's role as a sort of senior vice president.

The finer point here is that these relationships were not unidirectional, one dimensional, or static, which was understood by both Muhammad and Malcolm, as well as the keener observers around them. Illustratively, Malcolm could take on the role of father figure, teacher, and public face of the Nation at various points, whether through debating scholars on Ivy League campuses, jostling for advantage with journalists on television, or exercising paternal influence and intellectual guidance over younger talents – such as Louis Farrakhan and Cassius Clay – who found the Nation's message irresistibly alluring. Malcolm advised Muhammad as well as sought his counsel, and his imprimatur was indelibly pressed upon a number of institutional assets, including local mosques that he had been instrumental in founding, along with the Nation's organ, *Muhammad Speaks*.[3]

Just as the personal and organizational collaboration of Muhammad and Malcolm was marked by complexity and fluidity, these patterns of contact, cooperation, and resultant synergies also disclosed their boundaries and contradictions. Malcolm was the ultimate insider of the Nation, but still an outsider to Muhammad's family and Chicago inner circle, as would become painfully clear to him once differences between himself and Muhammad – on both matters of doctrine and practice – were exploited by some of his detractors. Likewise, what Malcolm and Muhammad may have shared on a spiritual or personal level was not easily convertible into a political currency that was acceptable to both men, particularly given Malcolm's more avid interest in civil rights activism and anticolonial struggles and Muhammad's essential conservatism and concern for the fiscal well-being of the Nation, particularly the "royal family" that he headed. Viewed all together as a holistic phenomenon, the multilayered, richly alloyed, and incessantly shifting relationship between the two men makes more intelligible the generational cleavages among black activists during the 1960s and 1970s, the personality politics inherent in autocratic black organizations, and the ideological and doctrinal slippages that both fueled and fractured the African American protest tradition of the twentieth century.[4]

Salvation and ascent: the making of an original man

Elijah Muhammad first became acquainted with Malcolm Little through his brothers, Philbert and Reginald Little, who had become members of the Nation of Islam during the 1940s. The initial contact between the two men was a 1949 letter Malcolm had written while serving his sentence for breaking and entering and larceny in Norfolk Prison Colony, Massachusetts. At first glance, Malcolm seemed quite similar to other incarcerated converts of the postwar period. In common with many of these believers, he had grown up in an impoverished, broken home. His father had been killed when he was quite young, and his mother had been committed to a mental institution in 1939. His formal education through the eighth grade had not served him particularly well, and by his late teenage years, he had become a fixture in the urban underworlds of Detroit, Boston, and Harlem. In these environments, he procured women for prostitution, used narcotics, and participated in burglary rings. When his criminal exploits finally caught up with him in February 1946, Malcolm had become an extreme skeptic regarding all forms of authority and entered prison an avowed atheist, despite his Baptist upbringing. Scarcely literate and dependent upon various drugs, the teachings of the Nation of Islam found him in his most desperate hour.

On the advice of his brothers, Malcolm quit smoking and eating pork and even abandoned the profane colloquialisms that had marked his verbal interactions with others. Reading and writing skills were improved through painstaking practice, and correspondence courses and prison debates bolstered his growing fascination with etymology and elocution. His most significant inspiration toward self-reform came from the letters and other printed literature that family members sent him regarding the Nation of Islam and its leader, Elijah Muhammad. These teachings seemed to situate his entire life within a larger, more meaningful framework.[5]

The spiritual nourishment that Malcolm received from the Nation of Islam had been substantially conditioned by the life experiences of Elijah Poole, a Georgia-born migrant who first encountered the message of the Nation in the early 1930s, after migrating to Detroit. His mentor, W. D. Fard, whom he would later revere as "Allah in Person," offered a heterodox brand of Islam to blacks in the Depression-stricken Motor City that stressed, among many other things, that blacks were the "Original People" who had created the universe and ruled it for trillions of years; a black scientist named Yacub had created the white race which was by nature evil and inferior to blacks; and whites would rule the earth for six thousand years, before being annihilated in the late twentieth century by a spaceship called the Mother Plane. Following this destruction, black people would again rule the earth under Allah's right-eous guidance. In addition to its own version of history and cosmology, the Nation of Islam proffered a message of moral uplift. Members of the group were advised to give up drinking, smoking, fornicating, eating swine, dan-cing, and a number of other alleged vices. They were also to relinquish European names in exchange for an "original" (typically Arabic) name or an X, which had a dual meaning that symbolized both the lost ancestral names of African Americans and the adherent's moral re-emergence as an ex-smoker, ex-thief, ex-prostitute, and so forth.[6]

In the aftermath of the disappearance of W. Fard Muhammad (formerly W. D. Fard) in 1934, the newly dubbed "Elijah Muhammad" (Poole) assumed the reins of the Nation of Islam and shifted its headquarters to Chicago. Along with constant bickering and infighting between his Nation of Islam and other quasi-Islamic black groups, Muhammad faced incessant harassment from law enforcement agencies, which had become increasingly suspicious of African American organizations during the social and economic upheavals of the Depression years. Muhammad and a number of his fol-lowers would serve federal prison sentences during World War II for failing to register for the draft. For Muhammad in particular, his persecution for what he believed to be principled objections to fighting a war on behalf of a racially oppressive white America simply reified his own notions of mission and destiny as the "Messenger of Allah" and confirmed his view of the innate incapacity of whites to deal justly with non-whites. Memories of firsthand experiences with lynch mobs in his native Georgia further illuminated, in his opinion, the fundamental truths behind the Nation's racialized demonology, as well as the need for blacks to organize their own schools, businesses, and other resources for their survival – at least until Allah's retribution could be decisively visited upon the "white devils." When Muhammad left prison in August 1946, he first set out to rebuild the infrastructure and membership of his organization, which had suffered grievously during his three and a half years of incarceration. Additionally, he resolved to cast his recruitment net over the growing black inmate population of the United States, which might prove amenable to his message.

From Malcolm's vantage point, the past grandeur of the original black man, his fall from grace with the birth of the white man, the African experience in American slavery, and his own ill-fated peregrinations through urban cesspools appeared to be a continuum that flowed logically together. All of the tragedies that he, his parents, and every other black person had endured were a result, directly or indirectly, of the actions of whites. All of the wickedness that he had indulged in while in Harlem and other places was perpetrated in open view of a Christian America that in many ways had limited his chances for success in life while counseling him "to be realistic about being a nigger." His drug dealing, his mother's mental difficulties, and his father's death possibly at the hands of white racists could no longer be satisfactorily explained as simple misfortune or coincidence. To Malcolm, his brother Reginald perhaps described the situation best during one of his many visits to the prison in 1948: "The white man is the devil." As Malcolm would later write, this assertion was "a perfect echo of ... [his] lifelong experience."[7]

Malcolm corresponded with Muhammad frequently until his parole on August 7, 1952. Three weeks later, he was among a number of Muslims who traveled to Temple Number 2, the Nation's headquarters in Chicago, to hear Muhammad speak. The two hundred people in attendance were indicative of the size of the movement, which had largely been populated by Southern migrants who had been affiliated with the group prior to the war. Nonetheless, the same pageantry and military pomp that would mark the mass meetings of the 1960s were evident here among these few believers who congregated to praise their leader and his vision. Accompanied by bodyguards and topped with a gold-embroidered fez, Muhammad entered the room to adulation and assumed his place behind the rostrum. His speech touched on staple themes that had become typical of these sorts of public presentations, including his persecution and incarceration during the war, the impact of the white man's treachery on the "so-called Negro," and how "the true knowledge of ourselves would lift up the black man." During a pause in the lecture, Muhammad, without glancing in his direction, requested that Malcolm Little stand up. Put on the spot, the convert rose and was recognized by his teacher for his dutiful correspondence and the fortitude that he had demonstrated while behind bars. Muhammad also issued a challenge to the twenty-seven-year-old Muslim. Comparing him to the biblical Job, Muhammad told the congregation: "Well, now, our good brother Malcolm's hedge [prison cell] is removed and we will see how he does … I believe that he is going to remain faithful." This expression of confidence in his sincerity left Malcolm without words, as he felt "the eyes of two hundred Muslims upon me."[8]

Stationed in Detroit, Malcolm busied himself with recruiting prospective converts. Mainly through his efforts, temple services attracted larger, and younger, crowds. Knowledge of Malcolm's productive work to draw African Americans to the Nation reached Chicago where Muhammad immediately recognized the benefits that this particular convert had brought to the organization. Over the following months, the interactions between Malcolm and his mentor became more regular, resulting in a relationship of a familial nature. By the summer of 1953, Muhammad had dubbed him "Malcolm X" and appointed him assistant minister of Detroit's Temple No. 1 following a series of inspired sermons.[9]

Malcolm's work convinced Muhammad to send him on other missions to start new temples and revitalize older ones that were in decline. Accordingly, he was first dispatched to Boston to organize among blacks in Roxbury where he had hustled before his incarceration in 1946. After three months of meetings in the home of a local member, the small congregation of Boston Muslims was able to finance a tiny temple with rented chairs. When it appeared that the new group could stand on its own under the leadership of the newly appointed minister, Ulysses X, Muhammad sent Malcolm to Philadelphia in March 1954 where he organized Temple Number 12 in three months. Again, Muhammad acknowledged the value of Malcolm's talents and contributions, rewarding him with yet another promotion. In June, he was appointed minister of Temple Number 7 in New York City, a metropolis that offered over one million African Americans as potential converts.[10]

Crucial to the expansion of the Nation of Islam during the 1950s and 1960s was the public image that the organization crafted for its audiences. Aside from its message of moral reform, black economic self-sufficiency, and racial separatism, the propagators were as significant to its appeal as the message itself. Better than anyone else, Malcolm X represented those elements of style and charisma that resonated with curious youths and persuaded many to join the Nation so that they, too, could be elevated from "so-called Negroes" to "Original People." A lean, towering man of 6' 3", with light ruddy skin and a youthful countenance, Malcolm had a well-cultivated gift for eloquence and was an energetic recruiter for the movement. Having formerly been involved for years in street life, the New York minister understood the plight and mannerisms of urban African Americans, and over time he became just as conversant with the political premises and social values of the intellectuals and middle-class individuals whom he debated on some of America's most prestigious college campuses. The demographic texture of the Nation reflected and accentuated his appeal among the membership, which by 1960 was predominately male and between the ages of seventeen and thirty-five. Even among the group's ministerial cadre, men of Malcolm's age and younger were becoming commonplace, and some patterned their leadership style after his. In a period when the televised image was beginning to inform people's understanding of almost every public event and personality, the Nation greatly benefited from Malcolm's service. While recruiting and organizing were his favorite activities, entrancing orations wrapped in inescapable logic were his speciality.[11]

In important ways, Malcolm X was to Elijah Muhammad what the latter had been to W. Fard Muhammad. The New York minister was the intermediary between the "Messenger of Allah" and young blacks who were put off by the strategies and objectives of the civil rights movement. As Muhammad had glorified his teacher as "Allah in Person," Malcolm lionized his mentor as "the Honorable Elijah Muhammad." His fidelity and talent garnered him the position of ambassador during the movement's "Goodwill Tour" (recruitment drive) in Atlanta in the late summer of 1956. Most of the Muslims' preliminary efforts to publicize their ideals in newspapers and magazines were spearheaded by Malcolm X, who wrote the editorial column, "God's Angry Men," for the *Los Angeles Herald Dispatch* and helped launch the short-lived publications, the *Messenger Magazine* and the *Islamic News*. His influence may have also helped shape Muhammad's own printed message, "Mr. Muhammad Speaks," which appeared in weekly newspapers such as the *Pittsburgh Courier* and the *Amsterdam News*. Undoubtedly, Malcolm was behind the founding of the official organ of the Nation, *Muhammad Speaks*, in 1960. As Fard Muhammad had done in 1934, Elijah Muhammad was slowly fading into the background while his talented protégé delivered the message of the Nation to the public.[12]

Malcolm was both Muhammad's cudgel against detractors and main drawing card within the organization. When Muhammad unsuccessfully invited Dr. Martin Luther King, Jr. to speaking engagements to explore the merits of integration, it was Malcolm X who informed the world just how much of "a traitor to the black people" the reverend was. The disciplined vigil of Malcolm and five hundred Muslims outside the 123rd Street Police precinct to protest the April 1957 beating of Johnson Hinton by New York law officers underscored the reputation of the Nation for action, though the demonstration itself was much more staid than Muslim–police encounters of the 1930s. Ultimately, when it came to fund raising, Malcolm X was without peer and regularly excelled rival temples in generating donations. Despite unpleasant rumors about ambitions harbored by Malcolm and innuendo regarding Muhammad's private life, the two men constantly tried to repay the debts that they owed each other. Muhammad had saved Malcolm from irrelevance and given him "the wings" to fly. In return, Malcolm X had substantially revitalized the Nation's message and membership through refracting its conservative trajectory in a more militant and youthful direction. Into the early 1960s, teacher and pupil rode the crest of the Nation's popularity together, though storm clouds were gathering on the horizon.[13]

Pushing against the hedges: a relationship under stress

From the time when the Nation of Islam first attracted national media attention via a sensationalist exposé entitled "The Hate That Hate Produced," televised in July 1959, Malcolm X and Muhammad's inner circle – which included close advisers, Chicago-based officials, and a number of relatives – competed for influence in the organization. The rivalry waxed and waned depending upon the health of Muhammad and other variables, but did not cease to embitter relations between the New York minister and other power brokers in the movement. The tensions were principally over Malcolm's prominent role in the group and his image in the media as the key figure in the Nation. Malcolm regularly dismissed assertions by reporters and others that he was Muhammad's successor or the vice messenger of the group. However, the minister's passionate oratory and photogenic countenance, which so readily attracted the press, conveyed a different impression. Although he would later be preoccupied with Malcolm's stature in the Nation and the media, Muhammad favored him above all other ministers and routinely designated him as the organization's spokesman regarding a range of matters. As mentioned earlier, the relationship between the two men was akin to a father-son dynamic, and it would not be inaccurate to characterize it as a loving friendship.[14]

This closeness between the two men worsened the envy and jealousy of Chicago-based officials who curried Muhammad's favor. Particularly among family members and certain associates, there was a sense that Malcolm's relationship with Muhammad was depriving them of both his paternal attention and the kind of influence that Malcolm wielded in the organization. Also, apparent philosophical differences repelled some of the Chicago leadership away from the New York minister. As Malcolm contemplated a more activist black nationalism that might inspire the Nation to participate more militantly in the civil rights movement, many Chicago officials, complacent in their affluence and their largely rhetorical program of racial separatism, avoided any political agitation that might negatively impact the economic wherewithal (and tax-exempt status) of the organization. The Muslim leadership, including Muhammad, embraced the doctrinal hard-line of emphasizing divine solutions for the black man's problems. Malcolm and others viewed more politicized protest, along with the practical application of the Muslims' belief in self-defense, as proper strategies in the face of intransigent opposition to black civil rights.[15]

At no time during his leadership of Mosque Number 7 was Malcolm in open rebellion against Elijah Muhammad or his critics at the Chicago headquarters.[16] If anything, he seemed more ingratiating toward Muhammad as the animosity of Muslim national officials grew. When he was told to decline speaking invitations, he did so. He raised and channeled annually to Chicago more donations than most mosques could ever hope to collect. In July 1962, he even honored Muhammad by naming his third daughter "Ilyasah," a feminized Arabic version of Elijah. Muhammad was aware that the efforts of Malcolm X had been largely responsible for the popularity of the Nation among African Americans, and despite resistance from some around him, named him national minister in 1963. Yet, Muhammad was also cognizant, as were other top officials, of the fact that any proactive attempt by Malcolm to gain control of the Nation – particularly in the event of his death – could be irreparably divisive and thus sought to bind his influence. As early as 1961, he made local captains of the Fruit of Islam, the security detail drawn from the male membership of each mosque, directly responsible to him, a change that Malcolm would find hard to digest over time. A year later, Malcolm began disappearing from the pages of *Muhammad Speaks*. If he had not entirely engineered these measures, Muhammad at least acquiesced to them as a means to reduce the influence of the New York minister and to appease his advisers and selected members of the first family in Chicago.[17]

The conflict between Malcolm and the Chicago nerve center was inflamed even more by the issue of succession. Complicating matters further was Muhammad's health. A severe case of bronchial asthma had compelled him to buy a home in Phoenix, Arizona, in the early 1960s to escape the debilitating Chicago winters. By the time he turned sixty-five in October 1962, and as his condition worsened, open talk of a successor coursed through the Nation for months. Given that Muhammad had always declared a divine right to rule the Nation, discourse regarding his death and its aftermath was always awkward at best. Moreover, plans for a contingency arrangement were not helped by his own refusal to name publicly a successor and his oft-repeated assertion that after his death "come God himself." Notwithstanding Muhammad's official stance on succession, it appeared that his seventh child, Wallace, was being groomed to assume his father's mantle, but this was not without obstacles. Like his father, Wallace, who was the minister of the Philadelphia mosque, had refused to obey Selective Service orders to register for the draft and was sentenced to three years of imprisonment at the Federal Correctional Institution at Sandstone, Minnesota. He would not be released until January 1963. Unlike his father, he had begun to question openly the theological foundations of the Nation of Islam, and these doubts raised the stakes regarding the succession crisis. Alone, Wallace's flirtation with Sunni Islam would have been problematic enough for his father. However, other crises emerged during this time that rattled the organization and its long-time leader.[18]

By this time, Malcolm had gone far afield ideologically from the rest of the leadership of the Nation of Islam. He was beginning to dabble in an activist philosophy and agenda that envisaged a more prominent role for the organization in the civil rights movement. Malcolm had a keen interest in the anticolonial struggles of people around the world, an internationalist perspective that was not nurtured by the religious strictures of the Nation. As the struggle for black rights intensified across the South and other regions, Malcolm found it increasingly difficult to sit on the sidelines and carp about the tactical inadequacies of civil disobedience or the shortcomings of individual organizations and leaders without offering a viable alternative model of direct action against racial oppression and social exclusion. Malcolm was particularly appalled when Muhammad counseled patience and forbearance as politicians and law enforcement agencies assailed Muslims, under the pretext of rooting out subversion, in places such as California, Louisiana, and even Chicago during the early 1960s. "We spout our militant revolutionary rhetoric and we preach Armageddon," Malcolm indignantly noted to New York associates following a savage attack by Los Angeles policemen upon unarmed Nation of Islam members. "[But] when our own brothers are brutalized or killed, we do nothing ... We just sit on our hands."[19]

As Malcolm would have known, these actions against the Nation were part of a broader pattern of state surveillance and repression of the Muslims and other groups that had been deemed subversive and un-American by the Federal Bureau of Investigation, local law enforcement officials, red-baiting politicians, and others, at least some of whom were opposed to vocal advocacy of first-class citizenship for African Americans. Over time, it became increasingly clear to him that Muhammad and many of those around him were not prepared to take on the local and national appendages of state power if the outcome might be the utter destruction of the Nation of Islam and perhaps stiff prison sentences – or worse – for its leaders. By the 1960s, Muhammad had become much more preoccupied with fiscal concerns and business propositions that might pay off for the Nation, and more specifically for his "royal family," than launching any overt challenge to the racial status quo in the United States. At his advanced age and affluence, he had become more conservative and adverse to risk than he had ever been, along with those in Chicago who depended upon the Nation's coffers for their sustenance.[20]

This creeping conservatism bred complacency, insularity, and corruption, as well as a willingness to indulge in personal behaviors that were off limits to rank-and-file members of the organization. Whether one considers the nepotistic divvying up of Nation of Islam business enterprises among relatives of Muhammad, lavish spending on homes and cars, or the leader's affairs and resultant offspring with a number of unmarried women, it was increasingly hard to imagine Muhammad joining Malcolm on an uncertain and potentially perilous path of politically radicalizing the Nation. Given the leader's illnesses, damaging government-sponsored counterintelligence offensives, and the vexing issue of succession, aggressively injecting the organization into the civil rights struggle or the international, anticolonial movement was perhaps the farthest thing from Muhammad's mind.[21]

Despite the cumulative weight of the dilemmas facing the Nation, it was not state operations against the organization or Muhammad's infidelities or the succession issue that brought things to a head for the Muslim movement in the 1960s. Instead, it was insensitive remarks by Malcolm X in the wake of President John F. Kennedy's assassination in November 1963. Although counseled by Muhammad to refrain from commenting on the murder, Malcolm publicly characterized the killing as a case of "chickens coming home to roost," a bloody comeuppance for a country that had peddled and tolerated violence in Southeast Asia, the Congo, Central America, and the American South. Malcolm's criticism of the late president did not please Muhammad, who did not want the Nation to come under more government suspicion. As punishment, Malcolm was silenced for ninety days, then isolated – that is, cut off from the affairs of Muslims in good standing with the Nation. While some top Muslim officials exploited Malcolm's faux pas and the subsequent chastening by Muhammad for their own political ends, the entire episode laid bare many of the tensions that had been simmering in the Nation for some time.[22]

The paternal and intergenerational nature of the relationship between Muhammad and Malcolm, though under extreme stress, was poignantly illustrated by the events of late 1963 and early 1964. In a phone conversation with one confidante (and recorded by FBI eavesdroppers), Muhammad characterized Malcolm's silencing as analogous to an instance in which a "papa" was compelled to punish an errant child. He further asserted that more correction would be forthcoming if Malcolm "sticks out his lip and starts popping off." In a January 2 meeting with the humbled New York minister, Muhammad demanded that he "put out the fire" that had been started by rumors regarding the older man's marital indiscretions and reminded Malcolm that he remained Muhammad's "property." When Malcolm publicly announced his departure from the Nation in March 1964, Muhammad, still viewing him as a protégé and fictive kin, shed tears over the news during a press conference in his Phoenix home.[23]

To be sure, the relationship had evolved to be much more complicated and nuanced than a father-son paradigm would allow. Muhammad was genuinely insecure about Malcolm's prominence in the Nation and his capacity to affect its fortunes, such as insensitive statements about a dead president. During the winter of 1963–4, Muhammad gave into misgivings that he and others harbored regarding the New York minister's influence and used the silencing to limit Malcolm's ascendancy among African Americans and the media. Additionally, Muhammad was careful to warn Malcolm to stay out of "family matters," intimating that his extramarital exploits and his ire toward his son Wallace, who was openly flirting with a more orthodox brand of Islam, was no concern of the New York minister. This statement represented a rare articulation of familial and power boundaries between Malcolm and the "royal family" and could not be mistaken as being anything other than Muhammad considering the interests of his kinsmen and Chicago-based inner circle above all else in the Nation. In his efforts to outmaneuver organizational rivals who had Muhammad's ear and to bolster his own relevance, Malcolm, like Muhammad, carved out his own sphere of power based upon the tutelage of younger men. Some of these men – such as Boston minister Louis X – were attracted to the Nation by Malcolm and modeled their sermonic style and leadership approach after his. Others, most notably heavyweight boxer Cassius Clay (later known as Muhammad Ali), may have imagined Malcolm in paternal terms, perhaps a relational model patterned on Malcolm and Elijah Muhammad.

Despite the length of Malcolm's stay in the Nation, his departure was indeed a rupture. The break highlighted the ideological cleavages that had existed between Muhammad's core conservatism and Malcolm's burgeoning militancy and his desire for full engagement with the civil rights movement and the emerging postcolonial world. A hajj to Mecca during the spring of 1964 further provided the pretext for an even more decisive theological transformation of the old Malcolm X into a new "El-Hajj Malik El Shabazz," as he fully embraced Sunni Islam and repudiated the heterodox religious teachings of his erstwhile mentor. Further, the split was exacerbated by generational anxieties, Muhammad's precarious health condition, Malcolm's multifaceted talents as an organizer and speaker, and the matter of succession. Indicative of the high stakes that Muhammad associated with competing with Malcolm for followers, the Nation of Islam leader waged a propaganda war against his former pupil on the airwaves and in the pages of *Muhammad Speaks*. Clashes between supporters of the two men produced a number of injuries and even deaths by the end of 1964, with Malcolm's own home being firebombed early the following year. When Malcolm was assassinated before a gathering of supporters on February 21, 1965, Muhammad denied any involvement in the deed. His public assessment of Malcolm's significance, from then until his own passing a decade later in February 1975, was unkind and neglectful of the former New York minister's larger meaning to the struggle of African peoples for a dignified existence in the modern world.[24]

Endings and beginnings

The relationship between Elijah Muhammad and Malcolm X was a unique one in the history of African American leadership. At no other time before or since have two men performed the intertwined roles of fictive father and son, spiritual mentor and student, "divine messenger" and spokesman, and, ultimately, bitter rivals, so publicly and with such consequences for the evolution of black thought and struggles for civil rights. Subsequent relationships between Muhammad and other public figures in the Nation, whether Louis Farrakhan, Muhammad Ali, or his own son Wallace, can only be fully understood through the Muhammad–Malcolm X dynamic. The bureaucratic professionalization of the Nation following Malcolm's death – largely an outgrowth of both the group's increasing popularity during the Black Power period and the need to administer high-profile business ventures during the late 1960s and 1970s – somewhat untethered positions of power in the organization from individual personalities. Still, the continuing coexistence and distinct appeals of the Nation's brand of racialized Islam and more orthodox variants of the religion have origins in the spiritual divorce that characterized Malcolm's break with the Nation, which was further dramatized by Wallace Muhammad's reinvention of the organization as the Sunni-inspired World Community of Islam in the West, in 1976. Again, to read the relationship between Muhammad and Malcolm as static and consistent would be to misread the considerable elasticity and protean nature of their encounter over almost two decades. Depending upon the historical conditions and political exigencies of the moment, each man was – and is – constantly recast as progenitor, visionary teacher, gifted organizer, and self-made leader, as well as apostate, hypocrite, and flawed man of the people.[25]

NOTES

1. "Rare Interview with Messenger Muhammad!" (Part 1), *Muhammad Speaks*, January 28, 1972, p. 3; "Muhammad Meets the Press!" (part 2), *Muhammad Speaks*, February 4, 1972, p. 4; and "Muhammad Meets the Press!" (part 3), *Muhammad Speaks*, February 11, 1972, pp. 3–4.

2. John Ali, "Whiteman and the Hypocrites Love Malcolm," *Muhammad Speaks*, October 3, 1969, p. 20; Elijah Muhammad, "Lull Before the Storm," *Muhammad Speaks*, February 19, 1971, p. 16; Elijah Muhammad, *The Theology of Time*, transcribed by Abass Rassoull (Hampton, VA: U.B. & U.S. Communications Systems, 1992), p. 356; and Malcolm X and Alex Haley, *The Autobiography of Malcolm X* (1965; London: Penguin Books, 2001).

3. For the purposes of this essay, the use of the term *Muslim* will refer to the Nation of Islam, its membership, and its heterodox brand of Islam, unless otherwise noted. Malcolm X, *Autobiography*, pp. 349–50, 463.

4. For biographies of Elijah Muhammad and studies of the Nation of Islam, see Claude A. Clegg, *An Original Man: The Life and Times of Elijah Muhammad* (New York: St. Martin's Press, 1997); Karl Evanzz, *The Messenger: The Rise and Fall of Elijah Muhammad* (New York: Pantheon Books, 1999); E. U. Essien-Udom, *Black Nationalism: A Search for an Identity in America* (Chicago: University of Chicago Press, 1962); and C. Eric Lincoln, *The Black Muslims in America* (Boston: Beacon Press, 1961). For biographies of Malcolm X, see James H. Cone, *Martin & Malcolm & America: A Dream or a Nightmare* (Maryknoll, NY: Orbis Books, 1991); Peter Goldman, *The Death and Life of Malcolm X* (Urbana: University of Illinois Press, 1979); Bruce Perry, *Malcolm: The Life of a Man Who Changed Black America* (Barrytown, NY: Station Hill Press, 1991); and Eugene V. Wolfenstein, *The Victims of Democracy: Malcolm X and the Black Revolution* (London: Free Association Books, 1989). For studies on African Americans and Islam, see Michael A. Gomez, *Black Crescent: The Experience and Legacy of African Muslims in the Americas* (Cambridge: Cambridge University Press, 2005); and Richard B. Turner, *Islam in the African-American Experience*, 2nd edn. (Bloomington: Indiana University Press, 1997).

5. Walter Dean Myers, *Malcolm X: By Any Means Necessary* (New York: Scholastic, 1993), pp. 12, 14–15; Malcolm X, *Autobiography*, pp. 163, 220, 248–49, 251, 255, 266–7, 279–81, 295; and Clayborne Carson, and David Gallen (eds.), *Malcolm X: The FBI File* (New York: Carroll & Graf, 1991), pp. 58–60.

6. For the teachings of the Nation of Islam, see Elijah Muhammad, *The Supreme Wisdom* (1957; reprint, Newport News, VA: National Newport News and Commentator, n.d.); Elijah Muhammad, *Message to the Blackman in America* (Chicago: Muhammad Mosque of Islam Number 2, 1965); Elijah Muhammad, *The Fall of America* (1973; reprint, Newport News, VA: National Newport News and Commentator, n.d.); Elijah Muhammad, *Our Saviour Has Arrived* (1974; reprint, Newport News, VA: United Brothers Communications System, n.d.); Muhammad, *Theology of Time*; Erdmann D. Beynon, "The Voodoo Cult Among Negro Migrants in Detroit," *American Journal of Sociology*, 43.6 (May 1938), pp. 894–907; and Clegg, *An Original Man*, especially chapters 2 and 3.

7. Malcolm X, *Autobiography*, pp. 118, 253–4, 264–5, 278–9, 497; Clegg, *An Original Man*, pp. 3–106.

8. Carson and Gallen, *Malcolm X*, p. 60; Malcolm X, *Autobiography*, pp. 293–5.

9. Malcolm X, *Autobiography*, pp. 296–7, 299, 302.

10. Ibid., p. 314; Carson and Gallen, *Malcolm X*, p. 61.

11. Louis E. Lomax, *When the Word Is Given* (Cleveland: World Publishing, 1963), p. 24; Lincoln, *Black Muslims in America*, pp. 22–3; Benjamin Karim, *Remembering Malcolm* (New York: Carroll & Graf, 1992), pp. 103–4.

12. Ted Watson and Paul E. X. Brown, "Moslems Stage Goodwill Tour," *Pittsburgh Courier*, September 15, 1956, p. 19; Report on "Malcolm Little," Special Agent in Charge (SAC) New York, April 30, 1958, sec. 3 (Malcolm X FBI file), in Carson and Gallen, *Malcolm X*, pp. 141–4; *Messenger Magazine*, 1.1 (1959), in C. Eric Lincoln Papers, Special Collections, Clark Atlanta University, Atlanta, Georgia; Malcolm X, *Autobiography*, pp. 237–8; John Woodford, "Testing America's Promise of Free Speech: Muhammad Speaks in the 1960s, A Memoir," *Voices of the African Diaspora*, 7.3 (Fall 1991), p. 9; and Essien-Udom, *Black Nationalism*, p. 168.

13. Cone, *Malcolm & Martin*, p. 98; Taylor Branch, *Parting The Waters: America in the King Years, 1954–63* (New York: Simon & Schuster, 1988), p. 32. Malcolm and the New York Muslims would later sue the police department on Hinton's behalf: the result was a $70,000 award, the biggest settlement ever paid by the city of New York for police misconduct. Evelyn Cunningham, "Moslems, Cops Battle in Harlem," *Pittsburgh Courier*, May 4, 1957, p. 20; Malcolm X, *Autobiography*, pp. 335–6, 395, 420; "Moslem Announces $ Million NY Suit," *Pittsburgh Courier*, November 9, 1957, p. 7; Essien-Udom, *Black Nationalism*, p. 172; and Report on "Malcolm Little," SAC New York, April 30, 1958 and Report on "Malcolm K. Little," SAC New York, November 17, 1960, sec. 6 (Malcolm X FBI file), in Carson and Gallen, *Malcolm X*, pp. 139, 197–8.

14. "Black Muslim Debates James Baldwin, C. Eric Lincoln, Eric Goldman," (1962?), Undergraduate Library, University of North Carolina, Chapel Hill; Malcolm X, *Autobiography*, pp. 339, 350, 401.

15. Malcolm X, *Autobiography*, pp. 295, 397.

16. When Muhammad visited Mecca in 1959, he did not perform his pilgrimage at the time designated by the Islamic calendar; therefore, he was able to complete only the *umrah*, or "lesser pilgrimage." He changed the name of Nation of Islam meeting places from *temple* to *mosque* following his minor hajj.

17. Malcolm X, *Autobiography*, pp. 334, 338–9, 400, 402; Goldman, *Death and Life*, p. 110.

18. Malcolm X, *Autobiography*, pp. 352, 369, 406–7, 368–9, 453; Memo on "Nation of Islam," August 3, 1961, sec. 6, and Report on "Elijah Poole," SAC Chicago to FBI Director, October 9, 1964, sec. 8, p. 21; Elijah Muhammad file, 105–24822, Federal Bureau of Investigation, Washington, DC; Lincoln, *Black Muslims*, pp. 196–9; Essien-Udom, *Black Nationalism*, pp. 80–2; Clifton Marsh, *From Black Muslims to Muslims: The Transition from Separatism to Islam, 1930–1980* (Metuchen, NJ: Scarecrow Press, Inc., 1984), p. 109; "The Black Separatists: Elijah Muhammad on the Philosophy of the Black Muslims," interview by Ben Anderson, Phoenix, Arizona, (audio tape, 1964), Undergraduate Library, University of North Carolina; "Negro Cultist's Son Convicted," *New York Times*, March 24, 1960, p. 14; "Plea Denied in Draft Case," *New York Times*, November 1, 1961, p. 79; Herbert Muhammad, "An Interview with Elijah Muhammad's Successor," *Amsterdam News*, April 9, 1975, p. A16; Zafar

I. Ansari, "W. D. Muhammad: The Making of a 'Black Muslim' Leader (1933–1961)," *American Journal of Islamic Social Sciences*, 2.2 (December 1985), pp. 258, 260; Bruce M. Gans and Walter L. Lowe, "The Islam Connection," *Playboy*, May 1980, pp. 200, 256; Wallace D. Muhammad, *Religion On The Line* (Chicago: W. D. Muhammad Publications, 1983), pp. 43–4; and Steven Barboza, *American Jihad: Islam After Malcolm X* (New York: Doubleday, 1993), p. 110.

19. Hakim A. Jamal, *From the Dead Level: Malcolm X and Me* (New York: Random House, 1972), pp. 220–4; Karim, *Remembering Malcolm*, pp. 135–8; Clegg, *An Original Man*, pp. 163–75; Claude Clegg, "Nation under Siege: Elijah Muhammad, the FBI, and Police-State Culture in Chicago," in *Police Brutality: An Anthology*, ed. Jill Nelson (New York: W. W. Norton, 2000), pp. 102–31; and Louis E. Lomax, *To Kill a Black Man: The Shocking Parallel in the Lives of Malcolm X and Martin Luther King, Jr.* (Los Angeles: Holloway House, 1968), p. 97.

20. Clayborne Carson and David Gallen, eds. *Malcolm X: The FBI File* (New York: Carroll and Graf, 1991), pp. 15–54; "A Visit from the FBI," in John H. Clarke, *Malcolm X: The Man and His Times* (Trenton, NJ: Africa World Press, 1990), pp. 182–204; Elijah Muhammad file (#105–24822), FBI, Washington, DC; Kenneth O'Reilly, *"Racial Matters": The FBI's Secret File on Black America, 1960–1972* (New York: Free Press, 1989), pp. 1–47, 261–92; and Frank Donner, *Protectors of Privilege: Red Squads and Police Repression in Urban America* (Berkeley: University of California Press, 1992), pp. 44–196.

21. Perry, *Malcolm*, pp. 218–25; Clegg, *An Original Man*, pp. 98–100, 112–14, 160–3, and 184–9.

22. Muhammad, *Fall of America*, pp. 33–4, 117–18; Malcolm X, *Autobiography*, pp. 410–12; Perry, *Malcolm*, pp. 240–1; "Mr. Muhammad's Statement on the President's Death," *Muhammad Speaks*, December 20, 1963, p. 3; and "Malcolm X Scores US and Kennedy," *New York Times*, December 2, 1963, p. 21.

23. Malcolm X, *Autobiography*, p. 302; "Telegram to Muhammad," *Amsterdam News*, March 14, 1964, 1; Report on "Nation of Islam," SAC Phoenix to FBI director, December 6, 1963, sec. 8, pp. 4, 7; Report on "Nation of Islam," SAC Phoenix to FBI director, December 13, 1963, sec. 8, pp. 6–7; and Report on "Nation of Islam," SAC Phoenix to FBI director, January 23, 1964, sec. 8, pp. 1–5, Elijah Muhammad file (#105–24822), FBI, Washington, DC.

24. Malcolm X, *Autobiography*, p. 52; Karim, *Remembering Malcolm*, pp. 158–9; "Telegram to Muhammad," *Amsterdam News*, March 14, 1964, p. 1; James Booker, "Malcolm X: 'Why I Quit and What I Plan Next,'" *Amsterdam News*, March 14, 1964, p. 51; Clegg, *An Original Man, passim*; Report on "Nation of Islam," SAC Phoenix to FBI Director, December 6, 1963, sec. 8, pp. 4, 7; Report on "Nation of Islam," SAC Phoenix to FBI Director, December 13, 1963, sec. 8, pp. 6–7; Report on "Nation of Islam," SAC Phoenix to FBI Director, January 27, 1964, sec. 8, pp. 1–3; and Report on "Nation of Islam," SAC Phoenix to FBI Director, January 23, 1964, sec. 8, pp. 1–5, Elijah Muhammad file (#105–24822), FBI, Washington, DC.

25. Clegg, *An Original Man*, pp. 228–84. For biographical information on Louis Farrakhan, see Mattias Gardell, *In the Name of Elijah Muhammad: Louis Farrakhan and the Nation of Islam* (Durham, NC: Duke University Press, 1996); Amy Alexander (ed.), *The Farrakhan Factor* (New York: Grove Press, 1998); and Arthur J. Magida, *Prophet of Rage: A Life of Louis Farrakhan and His Nation* (New York: BasicBooks, 1996).

2

ALEX GILLESPIE

Autobiography and identity: Malcolm X as author and hero

Malcolm X's autobiography, written in conjunction with Alex Haley, is a gripping narrative of identity transformation. It is the extraordinary story of a young black child, Malcolm Little, adopted into a white household, who then becomes the ghetto hustler, Detroit Red, who in turn converts to the Nation of Islam and becomes Minister Malcolm X, and who finally breaks with the Nation of Islam to become El-Hajj Malik El-Shabazz, an international human-rights activist. The overall metamorphosis has a clear positive direction: each transformation seems to transcend the former, each brings with it new lessons, and the emergent Malcolm X could be likened to a butterfly escaping a cocoon.

From the point of view of studying the identity and development of Malcolm X, the *Autobiography* is as seductive as it is gripping. It seduces the reader into conflating the *Autobiography* with the actual life and identity of Malcolm X in three ways. First, autobiographies have inherent rhetorical power because they are first-person accounts. For example, autobiographies have historically been used as a mode of truth telling by people who have experienced a psychotic episode, a spiritual conversion, or slavery.[1] In the case of Malcolm's *Autobiography* this power is greatly heightened by the vivid writing style, which convinces the reader of the authenticity of the first-person account.

Second, it seduces us because it conforms to popular notions of personality transformation and to a range of post-Marxian theories concerning varieties of false consciousness and the "liberation" of the individual from "internalized oppression."[2] When finding confirmation of our own theories in the text, we tend to forget that both Alex Haley and Malcolm X were producing the *Autobiography* within a culture where these ideas were current and popular.

Third, there is what Paul Eakin calls the power of the "autobiographical dream."[3] This is the collusion between reader and writer in which both assume that the story being told is finished and has unity. The autobiographical genre encourages the writer to speak about her or his own life as if it were over, as if the autobiography itself were not part of the life described and as if the author were "outside the realm of lapsing time."[4] And being complicit in the assumptions of the genre, the readers rarely question this stance. The problem, of course, is that the life of the author is not finished and that narrating any life from a point outside of time is impossible.

Given these considerations, it is unsurprising that authors past and present have been tempted to read Malcolm X's identity straight from the pages of the *Autobiography*.[5] I want to suggest, however, that if one is to draw conclusions about his identity from the autobiography, one needs to take a more critical stance towards the text. Accordingly, the first section of this essay will examine how the *Autobiography* has been constructed, and in particular, the way in which Malcolm X and Haley make use of narrative resources. The second section shifts from conceiving of the *Autobiography* as a reflection of the life of Malcolm X to conceiving of it as an important part of the last years of his life. The concluding suggestion is that one can see in the *Autobiography* the actual process of Malcolm X's last transformation, namely his break with the Nation of Islam.

Metamorphosis: a narrative template

Narratives are not simply constructed out of the events to be reported. People use "narrative templates" to aid in the creation and communication of narratives.[6] These templates do not contain specific facts or events; rather they are abstract plot structures which shape many specific stories – just like one baking tray gives shape to many loaves of bread. The template that Malcolm X uses to construct his autobiography has variously been called a conversion narrative and a metamorphosis narrative.[7] It is a classic format: a story of someone who has fallen, in a moral sense, and who "sees the light." This narrative trope is set up in the moral degradation exemplified by Malcolm X conking his hair, and its culmination is in his conversion to the Nation of Islam. Consider first, Malcolm X's description about his hair:

> This was my first really big step toward self-degradation: when I endured all of that pain, literally burning my flesh with lye, in order to cook my natural hair until it was limp, to have it look like a white man's hair. I had joined that multitude of Negro men and women in America who are brainwashed into believing that the black people are "inferior."[8]

Malcolm X narrates his early self, Detroit Red, as "brainwashed" – a word that appears frequently in the *Autobiography*. The "self-degradation" refers to the lack of self-respect that is evident in trying to make one's hair, and in a larger sense oneself, into the image of the oppressor – the white man.

The problem, however, is that if we read between the lines of the *Autobiography*, the extent to which Malcolm X was actually "brainwashed" during this period becomes questionable. He tells us that he moved to a black ghetto in Boston, where he conks his hair, because he began to feel a "restlessness with being around white people." He states: "Where 'nigger' had slipped off my back before, wherever I heard it now, I stopped and looked at whoever said it." In Boston he thrived on black culture and food and "couldn't stand" the middle class black people who were trying to be white.[9] Arguably, conking, although it "relaxes" hair, is a distinctive black, not white, tradition. Was Detroit Red attempting to imitate white people, or was he being socialized into a hybrid, but nonetheless distinctively black, culture? While answering this question may be difficult, it is noteworthy that Malcolm X does not let it arise. Or rather, such questioning does not suit the narrative template, which needs Malcolm X's "self-degradation" in order to make more shining his subsequent salvation.

The salvation comes when Malcolm X is in prison. After conceding to an urge to get down upon his knees and pray, Malcolm X is rewarded with a "vision" of "Master W. D. Fard, the Messiah" and founder of the Nation of Islam. The narrative genre at this point is that of a spiritual conversion: Malcolm X is "saved." Malcolm writes:

> I remember how, some time later, reading the Bible in the Norfolk Prison Colony library, I came upon, then I read, over and over, how Paul on the road to Damascus, upon hearing the voice of Christ, was so smitten that he was knocked off his horse, in a daze. I do not now, and I did not then, liken myself to Paul. But I do understand his experience.[10]

This utterance is complex and contradictory. Malcolm X on the one hand likens his own experience to the divine conversion of Paul, while also stating that he does not "liken" himself to Paul. He borrows upon the story as a narrative template. Malcolm X authors himself, like Paul, as a complete unbeliever, as a man so vile the other prisoners called him "Satan" (Chapter ten), who has a conversion experience, through divine intervention. The point is that the Bible provides Malcolm X with the narrative resources, or symbolic resources, with which to author himself.[11]

When Malcolm X began narrating his autobiography, his original intention was to tell a story of his conversion to the Nation of Islam, and specifically how Elijah Muhammad had "saved" him. Indeed, the original dedication to the autobiography, as reported by Haley, was going to be: "This book I dedicate to The Honorable Elijah Muhammad, who found me here in America in the muck and mire of the filthiest civilization and society on this earth, and pulled me out, cleaned me up, and stood me on my feet, and made me the man that I am today."[12] Again in this one can perceive the narrative template of conversion: Malcolm X is liberated from his existence as Detroit Red and transformed into Minister Malcolm X. But the most interesting thing about this dedication is that Malcolm X chose not to use it. During the course of writing the autobiography, he broke with the Nation of Islam, and with Elijah Muhammad. The result was that Malcolm X had a new story to tell, namely, one which did not lionize Elijah Muhammad.

Another metamorphosis, the same story

There is a second conversion experience in the *Autobiography*, narrated and enacted through a pilgrimage narrative. Shortly after splitting with the Nation of Islam, Malcolm X went to Mecca to perform hajj. He authors himself as experiencing genuine brotherhood in Mecca: he gives up the idea that white people are the devil incarnate and states that there can be brotherhood between whites and blacks. He reports: "My pilgrimage broadened my scope. It blessed me with a new insight." That insight is most clearly expressed in his public letter from Mecca:

> You may be shocked by these words coming from me. But on this pilgrimage, what I have seen, and experienced, has forced me to *re-arrange* much of my thought-patterns previously held ... Each hour here in the Holy Land enables me to have greater spiritual insights into what is happening in America between black and white.[13]

Again we can see Malcolm X using a narrative template of conversion in the form of a pilgrimage: it brought "spiritual insights." Pilgrimage, as a narrative trope, is a socially accepted mode of personal transformation.[14] Indeed, if one goes on such a journey but is not transformed in some manner, then one has failed. Louis Lomax suggests that Malcolm X used the pilgrimage as a means to legitimate and narrate and ultimately give voice to views which had been suppressed while he had been serving as a Minister in the Nation of Islam.[15] If so, then both in the act itself and in the narration of that act, we can see Malcolm X once again using narrative resources.

It is interesting to examine how Malcolm X speaks about Elijah Muhammad after his second conversion. He began to "think for himself" "after twelve years of never thinking for as much as five minutes about myself."[16] Notice again the theme of liberation. This narrative is, perhaps, most clear in the final interview Malcolm X gave before he was assassinated. He says:

> I did many things as a Black Muslim that I'm sorry for now. I was a zombie then – like all Muslims – I was hypnotized, pointed in a certain direction and told to march. Well, I guess a man's entitled to make a fool of himself if he is ready to pay the cost. It cost me twelve years.[17]

This interview excerpt does not simply mark another transformation in the identity of Malcolm X. Rather, it reveals continuity of narrative form. Malcolm X is using the same template that he used to narrate his transformation into Minister Malcolm X to narrate his transformation out of being a Nation of Islam Minister. Indeed, the language is even similar. Previously he had explained his move into the Nation of Islam as one from being "brainwashed" to seeing "the greatest light." Now, that greatest light is characterized as a "zombie" or "hypnotized" state, and the movement is toward thinking for himself and "greater spiritual insights."

How can Malcolm X's movement into the Nation of Islam be a moment of divine enlightenment and also a hypnotization? If we try to read these self-understandings at face value we end up in contradictions. However, if we focus upon the narrative template that Malcolm X is using to author himself, then the contradiction is resolved and a remarkable continuity in Malcolm X's mode of self-narration becomes evident.

Autobiography as a rhetorical resource

So far we have examined Malcolm X's use of a conversion or metamorphosis narrative template. The *Autobiography* is a story that is told. But who is it being told to? And why is it being told? Stories, just like any utterance, should be situated in a communicative context and analyzed not only in terms of who is speaking and what is said, but who is being spoken to and for what purpose.[18] What then is Malcolm X doing with his *Autobiography*?

By narrating himself as someone who has been "brainwashed" and who has since seen "the greatest light," Malcolm X is able to claim a certain position and authority within his community. For example, in his *Autobiography*, as in many of his speeches, he uses his own narrative as a means to gain authority and thus convince others of his position.

> I believe that it would be almost impossible to find anywhere in America a black man who has lived further down in the mud of human society than I have; or a black man who has been any more ignorant than I have been; or a black man who has suffered more anguish during his life than I have. But it is only after the deepest darkness that the greatest light can come.[19]

Here the metaphor is of moving from darkness to light, while at other times he uses that of awakening from sleep to narrate his life. But in both cases, one can see how his theory of development, as a movement from being "brainwashed" to one who has seen "the greatest light," functions as a rhetorical tool that positions him to be a leader. Because Malcolm X himself has been ignorant and unaware, he is able to talk about black communities as "brainwashed" without insulting them, and he is also able to position himself as one who can lead these communities into the "light."

The autobiographical dream, of the autobiographical author standing outside of their own life, is shattered. The *Autobiography* is not an unproblematic description of Malcolm X's life; rather it is one of the actions that comprise Malcolm X's life. The *Autobiography* does not stand apart from the life it describes. In the pages of the *Autobiography* we can see Malcolm X as he was in 1963–5 attempting to justify his actions and position himself as a suitable leader. Rather than being a transparent window on his life it is better to conceive of it as a slice of the last years of Malcolm's life. However, this does not mean that the *Autobiography* cannot help to reveal Malcolm X's identity. The following section analyzes the identities at play in the *Autobiography*.

Accumulating discourses and identities

Although the narrative of the *Autobiography* is of one identity metamorphosing into another in sequence culminating with El-Hajj Malik El-Shabazz, the international human-rights activist, close analysis of the text and other sources suggests that Malcolm X's identity within the *Autobiography* is actually an accumulation of identities. That is to say, rather than completely transcending each previous identity, each new one is layered upon the previous identity.

Consider, for example, the early Malcolm X identity described in a chapter of the *Autobiography* titled "Mascot," which concerns Malcolm Little's early teenage years that he spent living with a white family and attending a predominantly white school. Here, Malcolm Little engaged white society on its own criteria and excelled: he was one of the best students in the class and became class president. It was at this school that he reports the interaction with Mr. Ostrowski, who discourages him from becoming a lawyer because of his skin color. Reflecting upon this event, Malcolm X states:

> I've often thought that if Mr. Ostrowski had encouraged me to become a lawyer, I would today probably be among some city's professional black bourgeoisie, sipping cocktails and palming myself off as a community spokesman for and leader of the suffering black masses … I'd probably still be a brainwashed black Christian.

Here again we find Malcolm X using the "brainwashed" metaphor to reject one of his previous identities, and implicitly to announce his current liberation.

But has Malcolm X really transcended this rejected identity? Reading the *Autobiography* closely we can find traces of the desires and interests of Malcolm Little in the later Malcolm X. For example, at the end, when reflecting upon his life as a whole, Malcolm X states: "My greatest lack has been, I believe, that I don't have the kind of academic education I wish I had been able to get – to have been a lawyer, perhaps. I do believe that I might have made a good lawyer."[20] The young scholarly Malcolm Little manifests in the *Autobiography* in a more fundamental sense than this wish.[21] Malcolm X, although he never went to university, remained a diligent and hardworking student. His eruditeness and familiarity with history shows that in his later life he also read, studied, and learned. Thus although Malcolm X ostensibly rejected the image of the bourgeoisie, in actuality he held several of its values, and if he had not, it is unlikely that he would have been as effective in debates and interviews as he was. The bookish Malcolm Little is thus integral to the world-renowned Malcolm X, who passionately argued against integration and the "black bourgeoisie."

A similar case for accumulating identities can be made with regard to Detroit Red's years in the ghetto as a hustler, pimp, drug dealer, and gangster. In his autobiography, Malcolm X presents this streetwise Detroit Red, with conked hair, as an exemplar of "self-degradation." It is Detroit Red who was "in the mud of human society" and who is used by Malcolm X to narrate his own transformation. However, reading between Malcolm X's lines, it is clear that, although he explicitly rejects Detroit Red he has not left him behind. Rather, Detroit Red remains an integral aspect of Malcolm's self. In the Epilogue, Alex Haley recalls Malcolm X telling him about his former life as Detroit Red. In Malcolm X's retelling, Detroit Red clearly returns to life:

> "Why, I'm telling you things I haven't thought about since then!" he would exclaim. Then it was during recalling the early Harlem days that Malcolm X really got carried away. One night, suddenly, wildly, he jumped up from his chair and, incredibly, the fearsome black demagogue was scat-singing and popping his fingers, "re-bop-de-bop-blap-blam –" and then grabbing a vertical pipe with one hand (as the girl partner) he went jubilantly lindy-hopping around, his coattail and the long legs and the big feet flying as they had in those Harlem days. And then almost as suddenly, Malcolm X caught himself and sat back down, and for the rest of that session he was decidedly grumpy.

Recalling the escapades of Detroit Red invokes in Malcolm X the embodied jiving personality of Detroit Red. He exists also in the discourse of Malcolm X. When the *Autobiography* describes someone as "really heavy on his religion," Minister Malcolm X says "My man!" But perhaps most importantly, the voice of Detroit Red comes to the foreground when Malcolm X gets angry. For example, talking about the "Uncle Tom" blacks, or "bourgeoisie blacks," who rejected his antiwhite stance, Malcolm X says:

> Why you should hear those Negroes attack me, trying to justify, or forgive the white man's crimes! These Negroes are people who bring me nearest to breaking one of my principal rules, which is never to let myself become over-emotional and angry. Why, sometimes I've felt I ought to jump down off that stand and get *physical* with some of those brainwashed white man's tools, parrots, puppets.[22]

The principal rule, "never to let myself become over-emotional and angry," presumably belongs to Malcolm X's identity as a religious minister. However, the tendency to "jump down" and "get *physical* with some of those brainwashed white man's tools, parrots, puppets," I would argue, is an impulse belonging to Detroit Red. This is not to suggest that the later Malcolm X was, in any way, false. Rather, I would claim that the coexistence of Malcolm Little, Detroit Red, and Minister Malcolm X within the same person at the same time is what characterizes, in part, the uniqueness and significance of Malcolm X. More specifically, in order to understand who he "really" was, I suggest that, instead of asking which identity is the "real" Malcolm X, we should be focusing upon the tensions between these different facets of his complex personality.

Dialogical tensions and the "real" Malcolm X

Although the autobiographical genre led Malcolm X to narrate a sequence of transitions, the evidence above suggests that the author of the *Autobiography* was in fact a composite of his former selves. What is interesting is how each earlier identity feeds into a new dialogical position within Malcolm X's dialogical self. Each social group has its own language and interests. In his trajectory through a complex social structure, Malcolm X appropriated a diversity of languages, which through him, entered into a creative and radical dialogue. In particular there was a tension between the tough-talking and militant side of Malcolm X and another more religious side. Arguably, the former aspect came from his life as a hustler while the latter came from his life as a minister. And although the *Autobiography* describes Malcolm X as transcending the former, one could argue that the hustler identity is essential to each of the later incarnations of Malcolm X.

One of the defining features of Malcolm X, compared to many other African American leaders of the time, was that he talked tough and had an air of militancy. Considering his past as Detroit Red, it is no surprise that Malcolm X and not Martin Luther King (who grew up in a middle-class family) preached against nonviolence. Had Malcolm X never been Detroit

Red, it is likely that his stance would not have been so militant. It is just this stance that whites found so unsettling, which earned him media coverage, and which energized him, fueling his motivation to rectify the injustices he perceived. This proactive and somewhat aggressive side to Malcolm X is evident in his early letters with Elijah Muhammad and can also be seen as partly constitutive of the later split with the Nation of Islam. Malcolm X was keen on action and tired of Elijah's patience.[23] After the split, and after much of the writing of the *Autobiography*, Malcolm X went on to set up two institutions. Arguably each addressed a different side of this tension. The Muslim Mosque, Inc. had a clearly religious mission, while the Organization of Afro-American Unity was political and focused upon radical change.

While one could argue that the Muslim Mosque, Inc. answered to the interests of Minister Malcolm X and the Organization of Afro-American Unity answered to Detroit Red, to do so would be an oversimplification. The Organization of Afro-American Unity related to concerns that Malcolm X had been cultivating as a Minister for the Nation of Islam and which had been denied expression by Elijah Muhammad. My point is not to make such simplifying equivalences, but instead to point out that the uniqueness of Malcolm X was not in a final unified identity but rather in the tensions between identities and discourses that he had accumulated during his trajectory.

Malcolm X recognized that his own identity development was not complete and that there were unresolved tensions. "I am man enough to tell you," Malcolm X said in one of his last interviews, "that I can't put my finger on exactly what my philosophy is now, but I am flexible."[24] He was not taken in by the autobiographical dream. As Paul John Eakin has pointed out, although the majority of the *Autobiography* conforms to the illusion of the complete and unified personality, Malcolm X himself is reported, by Haley, to have written: "I hope the book is proceeding rapidly, for events concerning my life happen so swiftly, much of what has already been written can easily be outdated from month to month."[25] Eakin, with considerable insight, has written:

> Malcolm X's final knowledge of the incompleteness of the self is what gives the last pages of the Autobiography together with the "Epilogue" their remarkable power: the vision of a man whose swiftly unfolding career has outstripped the possibilities of the traditional autobiography he had meant to write.[26]

Autobiography: reconstituting the self

To argue that Malcolm X's identity was larger and more complex than the available genre of autobiography would allow is to say that the *Autobiography* is in some sense inadequate or partial. But such an assessment fails to transcend the deep-seated idea that autobiographies are "mirrors" of an individual's life which can reflect that life with more or less veracity. In this concluding section, I want to point toward a reconceptualization of autobiography which situates the autobiography within the life of the individual, not as a reflection of that life, but as a reconstitutive moment in that life.

Selves are not essential forms carried within. Rather, they are constituted in dynamic performances which occur between people.[27] According to classic theorists of the self, such as William James and George Herbert Mead, the self arises when the individual becomes aware of herself or himself from the standpoint of others. This occurs because the perspectives of others are internalized, and as such social interaction itself becomes internalized.[28] James, in 1890, wrote that the self is duplex, that it is both subject and object.[29] Selves are constituted in social interaction because it is in this interaction that we become aware of ourselves from the standpoint of others, that is to say, we become an object to ourselves by taking the perspective of others upon ourselves. And this, I suggest, is exactly what occurs in the act of autobiography. In self-narration the author must orient to their real or imagined audience, and in so doing, narrate herself or himself from a third-person perspective. As such one could argue that the actual act of self-narration is self-constitutive. The transformative effects of self-narration can be seen in certain forms of letter writing, diaries, and autobiographies.

Consider first Michel Foucault's analysis of a letter from Marcus Aurelius to his master.[30] It details the activities of the day, and through the letter, Marcus Aurelius judges the minutiae of his life through the eyes of his master. He presents his sore throat, and what he has done about it. He describes what he ate, how he worked, how he talked, and how he helped his parents. This genre of letter, Foucault suggests, prefigures the Christian confession. Both are "technologies of the self." They are a means of self-transformation through giving an account of oneself to a respected other.

Consider also Wendy Wiener and George Rosenwald's analysis of diary writing.[31] They argue that, rather than reading through diaries to uncover some hidden facts, we must read them to see the diarist at work, to see the psychological process of diary writing, of self-examination, and of giving an account of oneself to oneself. Writing a diary puts the writer in a new relation to themselves. It entails stepping out of themselves, and attempting to narrate themselves from a position outside of ongoing life. Of course, such externality is impossible, but the effort is productive, and, as Wiener and Rosenwald argue, self-constitutive.

Autobiography can be conceptualized as another technology of the self. Autobiography as a genre is characterized by what Bashir El-Beshti calls a "double focus."[32] The author is split into the person being narrated and the narrator. Such an analysis chimes with what has been said above about the nature of the self. Paraphrasing James we might say that in autobiography the author is both author and hero. In this sense the autobiographical mode of writing encourages the author to become an object to herself or himself, and thus the act of creating an autobiography is self-constitutional.

In the case of the *Autobiography*, the social interaction is between Malcolm X, Alex Haley, and the actual or imagined audience. Within interaction people are held to account, and especially in the act of self-narration, one justifies past, present, and future action. In the *Autobiography* we encounter, in a very real sense, Malcolm X telling us his story – telling us who he is, what he has done, and what he feels he must do. In telling this story, he orients to us, and in orienting to us, he must try to reflect upon himself from our point of view. The act of self-narration thus draws the author out of themselves, encouraging them to imagine themselves from the standpoint of the imagined audience. Actions which may have seemed unproblematic before suddenly need justification, and the story told takes on quite a different frame in comparison to the story lived.

That the externality provided by the act of self-narration feeds into the developing identity is evident in relation to the *Autobiography*. For example, Malcolm X reveals that after narrating his relationship with his mother, for the *Autobiography*, he was preoccupied with thoughts about her.[33] She had been in a mental hospital for years and, realizing (through the narration) that he was unable to justify his neglect of her, he went to visit her there. When considering the *Autobiography* in the context of Malcolm X's life, it is possible that the process of self-narration of the *Autobiography* had a significant impact on his developing personality. In the years during which Malcolm X produced his autobiography (1963–5), he himself went through tremendous changes: he broke with the teachings of Elijah Muhammad, he left the Nation of Islam, he founded new organizations, he became an internationalist, he changed his views about white people and women, and he made overtures to more mainstream movements. Even for Malcolm X, this is a lot of change in a relatively short period of time. My speculation is that some of this change can be traced back to the autobiographical act of self-narration.

Of course it is difficult to make the argument that producing the *Autobiography* reconstituted the object (i.e. Malcolm X) that it was meant to describe. My aim here is not to make the argument conclusive, but merely to open upon the possibility and in so doing to present a novel perspective on how we might read the *Autobiography*. Rather than reading it as a mirror of Malcolm X's life, I am suggesting that it be read as an actual part of his life, and more than that, as a potentially transformative part. In other words, while reading the narrative we should be careful to avoid being completely seduced by it, taking it to be an account of transformations past; rather we should remain open to the possibility that the narrative itself is a constitutive part of Malcolm X's ongoing transformation. In such a reading the description of the autobiographer begins to feed back into the actual personality of the autobiographer, thus shattering the "autobiographical dream" and the illusion of the finished and unified personality.

NOTES

1. See William L. Andrews, *To Tell a Free Story: The First Century of Afro-American Autobiography, 1760–1865* (Urbana: University of Illinois Press, 1986).
2. These ideas were popularized by Paulo Freire, *Pedagogy of the Oppressed* (New York: Continuum, 1970), pp. 43–69.
3. Paul John Eakin, "Malcolm X and the Limits of Autobiography," in *African American Autobiography: A Collection of Critical Essays*, ed. William L. Andrews (Upper Saddle River, NJ: Prentice Hall, 1993), p. 161.
4. Ibid., p. 153.
5. Barrett John Mandel, "The Didactic Achievement of Malcolm X's Autobiography," *Afro-American Studies*, 2 (1972), pp. 269–74; Mark B. Tappan, "Domination, Subordination, and the Dialogical Self: Identity Development and the Politics of 'Ideological Becoming,'" *Culture & Psychology*, 11 (2005), pp. 47–75.
6. For a discussion of the concept of narrative templates, see James V. Wertsch, *Voices of Collective Remembering* (Cambridge: Cambridge University Press, 2002).
7. Eakin, "Malcolm X and the Limits of Autobiography," p. 151; Alex Gillespie, "Malcolm X and His Autobiography: Identity Development and Self-Narration," *Culture & Psychology* 11 (2005), pp. 77–88.
8. Malcolm X and Alex Haley, *The Autobiography of Malcolm X* (1965; London: Penguin Books, 2001), p. 138. All subsequent references to the *Autobiography* in a given paragraph will be collected into a single note.
9. Malcolm X, *Autobiography*, p. 143.
10. Ibid., p. 316.
11. The concept of symbolic resources has been developed in Tania Zittoun, Gerard Duveen, Alex Gillespie, Gabrielle Ivinson, and Charis Psaltis, "The Use of Symbolic Resources in Developmental Transitions." *Culture & Psychology*, 9 (2003): 415–48.
12. Malcolm X, *Autobiography*, p. 14.
13. Ibid., pp. 478, 454.
14. For a rich discussion of pilgrimage as a transformative process, see Victor Turner and Edith Turner, *Image and Pilgrimage in Christian Culture* (Oxford: Oxford University Press, 1978).
15. Louis E. Lomax, *To Kill a Black Man: The Shocking Parallel in the Lives of Malcolm X and Martin Luther King, Jr.* (Los Angeles: Holloway House, 1968).
16. Malcolm X, *Autobiography*, p. 416.
17. Quoted in Lomax, *To Kill a Black Man*, p. 242.
18. The idea that every story and utterance is oriented to someone is taken from Mikhail Bakhtin, *The Dialogic Imagination: Four Essays* (Austin: University of Texas Press, 1981).

19. Malcolm X, *Autobiography*, p. 498.

20. Ibid., pp. 120, 498–9.

21. It is not my intent to do as psychobiographers have done, namely, to trace the roots of the latter Malcolm X into his childhood. See Bruce Perry, *Malcolm: The Life of a Man Who Changed Black America* (New York: Station Hill Press, 1991); and Eugene V. Wolfenstein, *The Victims of Democracy: Malcolm X and the Black Revolution* (London: Free Association Books, 1989). Rather my intent here is to analyze the identity that manifests within the pages of the *Autobiography*, and related textual sources, in order to analyze the identities being performed – and then to explicate those performed identities in terms of the narrative contained within the *Autobiography* itself. As such, the present analysis does not make claims about either Malcolm X's actual past or his identity beyond the textual sources drawn upon.

22. Malcolm X, *Autobiography*, pp. 18, 286–7, 391. In the Penguin edition, Haley's Epilogue is placed at the beginning and entitled the Introduction.

23. Lomax, *To Kill a Black Man*, pp. 104–5.

24. Quoted in ibid., p. 230.

25. Malcolm X, *Autobiography*, p. 39.

26. Eakin, "Malcolm X and the Limits of Autobiography," p. 160.

27. See John Shotter, "Social Accountability and the Social Construction of 'You,'" in *Texts of Identity*, ed. John Shotter and Kenneth J. Gergen (London: Sage, 1989), pp. 133–51; Emma-Louise Aveling and Alex Gillespie, "Negotiating Multiplicity: Adaptive Asymmetries Within Second-Generation Turks 'Society Of Mind,'" *Journal of Constructivist Psychology*, 21 (2008), pp. 200–2.

28. I have made this argument in *Becoming Other: From Social Interaction to Self-Reflection* (Greenwich, CT: Information Age Publishing, 2006).

29. William James, *Principles of Psychology* (Cambridge: Harvard University Press, 1890).

30. Michel Foucault, "Technologies of the Self," in *Technologies of the Self: A Seminar with Michel Foucault*, ed. Luther H. Martin, Huck Gutman, and Patrick H. Hutton (London: Tavistock, 1988), pp. 16–49.

31. Wendy J. Wiener and George C. Rosenwald, "A Moment's Monument: The Psychology of Keeping a Diary," in *The Narrative Study of Lives*, ed. Ruthellen Josselson and Amia Lieblich (London: Sage, 1993), pp. 30–58.

32. Bashir M. El-Beshti, "The Semiotics of Salvation: Malcolm X and the Autobiographical Self," *Journal of Negro History*, 82.4 (1997), p. 359.

33. Malcolm X, *Autobiography*, p. 20.

3

BRIAN NORMAN

Bringing Malcolm X to Hollywood

Malcolm X's story hit cineplexes in 1992 as a biopic with a documentary-inflected style. Framed in neon marquee lights, the Hollywood film prompted many to return to, or first encounter, the iconic racial spokesperson, both infamous and celebrated. The film was the latest installment of what scholars describe as the mythmaking enterprise of Malcolm X.[1] It also provided a large-scale, familiar forum to consider the legacy of the American civil rights movement and its core debates between integration and racial autonomy. Indeed, the prospect of bringing Malcolm X to Hollywood ignited longstanding tensions between black nationalism and mainstream America, radicalism and respectability, and prophets and profitability. These tensions reflect problems of genre and visual culture, as much as biography and politics, because as Thomas Doherty avers, "For the young Malcolm Little, as for black Americans everywhere, the classical Hollywood screen was an inventory of negative stereotypes and a 35 mm projection of white power."[2] The film, with its surrounding hype, became a platform for high-stakes scholarly and political discussions.[3]

The effort to bring Malcolm X to Hollywood had begun in 1968 when Columbia Pictures asked famed writer and civil rights spokesman James Baldwin to adapt *The Autobiography of Malcolm X*. Film producer Marvin Worth bought the story rights in 1967 from Alex Haley, the collaborator on the 1965 autobiography, and Betty Shabazz, Malcolm's widow. Studio executives at Columbia Pictures rejected Baldwin's 250-page manuscript on the basis that it was not viable and "read more like a novel than a screenplay."[4] In order to preempt Hollywood's use of his work, Baldwin published his "scenario" in 1972 as what I describe as the curious genre of the "closet screenplay," a print version of a film never realized in the visual medium.[5] Eventually Spike Lee came aboard as director and script cowriter and leveraged his Hollywood clout gained from earlier successes, especially *Do the Right Thing* (1989). The resulting 1992 film was a mainstream success, gilded with award nominations and net profit. In its path to mainstream success and global distribution, the film prompted debates about competing versions of Malcolm X's story, especially around matters of genre and authorship, politics, and historical fidelity.[6] The screenplay, and its wending path from 1968 to 1992, gauges the shifting legacy of Malcolm X in the American cultural imagination. In fact, when Denzel Washington was nominated for an Oscar for his lead performance, many ticked off another entry in progress narratives of post-civil rights American race relations. When Clint Eastwood won instead, some lamented a lack of progress. Projecting such political hopes onto the Oscar stage is noteworthy, for inclusion into the film industry is not usually among the chief goals of integration-minded civil rights groups, and certainly far removed from the economic and political self-determination ideologies associated with Malcolm X. Indeed, street preachers in Harlem and studio executives in Hollywood high-rises make strange bedfellows.

Be it 1968, 1992, or today, bringing Malcolm X to Hollywood begs a question: Does a blockbuster film inherently fall short of Malcolm's radical vision? Jacqueline Stewart notes the potentially empowering narrative of African Americans achieving full entrance into Hollywood within ongoing struggles for first-class citizenship. Still, she reminds us: "The false promise of freedom and opportunity in the urban North is echoed in the persistently discriminatory practices of the cinema as the flagship medium of modernity."[7] Other film scholars, such as Mark Reid, agree that "resourceful and committed filmmakers can find honest work" in Hollywood, while decrying those who "mak[e] a fast buck" with "Molotov cocktails" that confirm negative black stereotypes.[8] Gerald Horne also notes, "the Malcolm X myth is as subject to that most traditional force of commodification as any other 'alternative' phenomenon."[9] Lee's film is one entry, albeit a weighty one, among other versions of Malcolm X circulating in print, film, oral history, cultural memory, and store shelves.

This essay discusses the two most important film-script versions of Malcolm X and their illustrative fates – Baldwin's and then Lee's – in order to explore the promises and pitfalls of bringing a relatively radical figure such as Malcolm X to a major mainstream American venue. By attending to multiple and competing versions, including especially Baldwin's aborted attempt, we see that in adapting Malcolm X's empowering separatism the Hollywood version raises unanswered questions about the limits of separatist visions in multicultural markets, citizenries, or global publics. Specifically, I compare the ordered, developmental versions of Malcolm X in popular circulation in the *Autobiography* and Lee's 1992 Hollywood film to Baldwin's more experimental script, whose chronological dysphoria and protofeminist and queer elements refuse a roadmap to a singular, inevitable version of Malcolm and racial progress. Ultimately I argue that the success of Lee's film and rejection of Baldwin's "scenario" by its Hollywood commissioners ultimately lie along the same lines: Malcolm's story is widely digestible once the immediacy of his protest recedes and he emerges as a past American hero the current mainstream can celebrate.

James Baldwin's Malcolms

The fate of Baldwin's script illustrates the price of bringing Malcolm X from the streets of Harlem and Mecca to mainstream American visual and market culture. In 1967, Baldwin discussed with Haley and Elia Kazan a possible stage play based on the *Autobiography*.[10] After Columbia approached him as scriptwriter, Baldwin reluctantly agreed and moved to the Beverly Hills Hotel. While there, he also first interacted with Black Panther Party members, including Bobby Seale and Eldridge Cleaver. After the studio disliked Baldwin's early drafts and forced Arnold Perl upon him as cowriter, he surmised that his script would be pared down to crude action scenes and would be a product that would bribe consumers with token inclusion in the Hollywood pantheon and a rather palliative story of overcoming racism. In fact, David Leeming notes that familiar actor-heroes were rumored for the lead, including Sidney Poitier, James Earl Jones, and even Charlton Heston, "darkened up a bit."[11] Baldwin ultimately concluded, "I didn't want to be a part of a second assassination."[12] No longer believing a Hollywood film could resurrect Malcolm's vision, Baldwin recused himself from Hollywood and hastily published his original script in 1972 as *One Day, When I was Lost*.[13] Worth and Perl produced a documentary instead, titled *Malcolm X*.[14] Baldwin reflected on the experience in *No Name in the Street* (1972) and on Hollywood's cultural pull in *The Devil Finds Work* (1976), but he was increasingly dismissed as a relic. By 1972, among black Americans, Black Power and self-determination ideologies had largely eclipsed civil rights integration ideals in a generational divide with Baldwin on the losing side. His screenplay fell into near-obscurity until it was reprinted in 1992 to capitalize on Lee's film and the posthumous near-deification of Malcolm.

The main reasons for the script's fate are threefold, at least. First, and most obviously, Warner Brothers and Lee de-emphasize and sometimes erase Baldwin's hand. For instance, DVD packaging attributes the screenplay solely to Perl and Lee, though Baldwin appears in the end credits.[15] Lee occasionally references Baldwin's script in *By Any Means Necessary: The Trials and Tribulations of Making Malcolm* and succinctly concludes, "But for one reason or another, they had gone through four or five scripts and the film never got made."[16] The second and third reasons for Baldwin's low profile are more interesting: the script's aesthetic vision and Baldwin's status as a gay, black, civil rights writer.

Baldwin's aesthetic vision is complex, especially his experimentation with narrative, historical, and biographical time, what together he calls "remembered time."[17] Baldwin overlaps multiple stages of the *Autobiography* so that speeches, statements, incidents, ideologies, and stances from different eras coexist. In the *Autobiography* and Lee's film, Malcolm is portrayed as discarding earlier ideologies and experiences at each developmental stage. On the contrary, while Baldwin's "scenario" contains familiar plot components of Haley's text, he convenes into single scenes seemingly incompatible moments of Malcolm's life and ideology without necessarily positioning one as newer, better, or truer. For instance, in Haley's and Lee's versions, the full name "Malcolm Little" only appears halfway through – the moment it is cast off – a move that frames Malcolm's younger days with the knowledge that he will eventually cast off his given identity in favor of the famous "X." But in Baldwin's "scenario" Malcolm states, "I have had so many names"[18] on page three while four names coexist simultaneously, each from a different era: the audio track follows the replacement of Malcolm's X by the ceremonial name Omowale (son who has returned), while visually two more images of nominal inscriptions appear, "El-Hajj Malik El Shabazz" in the Book of the Holy Register of True Muslims and "Malcolm Little" in a family Bible in 1925. Baldwin thus disrupts distinct stages of personal development. Malcolm's conflicting naming ceremonies navigate, not terminate, chapters in black history. The script is ultimately kaleidoscopic: familiar fragments of Malcolm's story appear in varying combinations through recursive flashbacks, audio-visual overlaps, time loops, overdubs, and long parenthetical directorial commands. Unlike the *Autobiography*, no post-saved Malcolm calmly narrates the picaresque journey to the familiar ending of slain prophet.

Baldwin's temporal experimentation troubled many, including eventually Spike Lee, prompting one scholar in 1977 to excoriate Baldwin for not sticking to the *Autobiography* and therefore Haley's dictum to "keep [Malcolm's] story safe from 'interpreters.'"[19] I suggest, however, that Baldwin's narrative structure continues to keep alive past eras and struggles to avoid historical teleology and closure embedded in autobiographical development narratives or religious conversion narratives.[20] Baldwin eschews a single road to enlightenment in favor of convening seemingly incommensurate moments of the *Autobiography*. Baldwin thus provokes anxiety that history is not settled and Malcolm's messages matter today. The curious "closet screenplay" genre further contributes to this temporal disorientation because it contains components of a narrative without the visual product (i.e. the film itself) to band them together into a seamless life story. Perhaps it is Malcolm X's work, not Baldwin's script, that is unfinished.

If Baldwin's aesthetic vision unsettles Malcolm's familiar narrative and certainty about one true version of Malcolm, a black gay writer committed to integration (while open to radicalism) also unsettles masculinist and homophobic postures dominant in Black Power circles. This is especially apparent when Baldwin inserts protofeminist and queer stances in unlikely places. Baldwin's protofeminism emerges in his depictions of two of Malcolm's former girlfriends, Laura and Sophia, one black and one white. Laura, from young Malcolm's life, eventually becomes a Harlem prostitute servicing white men. To Minister Malcolm's offer of his church as pathway off the streets, she rejoins: "You could have done something for me once … The only way for you to marry me now would be for you to have a boyfriend on the side. I don't go that way no more, except for bread. – You're funny. You're shocked. Why are ministers always shocked? You're supposed to know more about life than other people, not less."[21] Beyond the gay-baiting, we see that for Baldwin, Malcolm's rhetoric does not fully address black female experience. For Laura, Malcolm's brotherhood looks a bit queer. Laura's failed salvation and cynical self-awareness directly juxtapose crowd-pleasing scenes of Malcolm's successes and rousing speeches. As for Sophia, hustler Malcolm's rich white lover, in the *Autobiography* and Lee's film she recapitulates myths of black male hypersexuality and must be discarded when Malcolm converts to black nationalism. But Baldwin's Sophia exhibits double-consciousness regarding racial and gender roles. She schools Malcolm, "If I have to live a certain kind of life in Boston, well, maybe that helps to protect us – look: the world sees a girl like me in a certain way. And if you give the world what it wants to see, then it stops looking. It doesn't look any further. And then you're – free."[22] Whereas Baldwin's Sophia acutely understands the gender and racial roles into which she and Malcolm are thrust and offers a sophisticated psychological liberation, Lee's version restores Sophia's rather one-dimensional role as portrayed by Malcolm and Haley in the *Autobiography*: object of pathological black male desire for the white man's woman.

Baldwin also inserts some queer stances into the screenplay that Lee also expunges in favor of an unambiguously masculine hero well-suited to both Hollywood norms and black nationalist ideals. Alongside protofeminist depictions of female characters, Baldwin's screenplay highlights the masculinist nature of Malcolm's story. This is especially apparent when Baldwin juxtaposes the heteronormative brotherhood of the Nation of Islam in the United States with Malcolm's encounter with a more inclusive global Islam in Mecca, rife with earnest yet clumsy attempts at cross-cultural brotherhood. For instance, Muslims from across the world dress in uniform pilgrimage outfits. "We call this the Isar," the Egyptian instructs. "(Malcolm drapes his towel in the same way. The Egyptian throws another towel over his neck and shoulders.) … So – my brother.

Now we are ready for our pilgrimage."[23] In Mecca, Malcolm discovers neither Haley's long-lost African/African American kinship nor the Nation of Islam's fabled dynasty, though Baldwin still romanticizes otherness (orientalism). Instead, Malcolm finds a vision of racial understanding that attempts (even if it fails) to cross cultural and identity lines without erasing them. More than homosocial but not openly sexual, Baldwin's "brotherhood" is forged through eroticism and difference, a brotherhood that might include someone like Baldwin, and perhaps even Laura and Sophia.

For Baldwin, the screenplay's un-filmed fate evidences America's failure to invest in black history and politics, as well as resistance to informed criticism of Black Power's place in multicultural societies. Baldwin positions Malcolm's story not as autobiographical analog to discrete eras of black history but as unfinished project which accrues new meanings and possibilities when its familiar parts enter new territories, identities, and ideologies. The title bespeaks an inability to fit Malcolm into one narrative location: *One Day, When I Was Lost: A Scenario Based on Alex Haley's "The Autobiography of Malcolm X"*. The clunkiness and multiple voices (Haley, Malcolm X, Baldwin, "I") are an asset. Ironically, Baldwin's closet screenplay, while rejected by Hollywood, may successfully perform the biopic genre's function. Glenn Man explains, "A biopic then is not so much a film about a life as it is a film about competing and intersecting discourses, with the life itself being simply one of those discourses that is transformed by the work of the others."[24] Baldwin was right to call his script a "scenario": one version of Malcolm aware of other extant versions – and versions yet to come.

Spike Lee's Malcolm

In 1992, two decades after Baldwin left Hollywood, *Malcolm X* was successfully realized by Warner Brothers through director Spike Lee's production company, Forty Acres and a Mule. Boasting an all-star cast (including Washington as Malcolm X and Angela Bassett as his wife) and big budget (about $34 million),[25] the film opened in 1,124 theaters, ultimately grossing over $48 million (domestic), joined by cross-marketing campaigns for paraphernalia such as "X" ball caps, followed by strong international returns and video rentals and sales, and honored with Oscar nominations and other accolades. Painting himself as underdog, Lee repeatedly frames budget talks with Warner Brothers through plantation metaphors. Lee avows, "We had to fight tooth and nail, fight like hell to get what we wanted on the screen ... We had to win this one."[26] So, when Malcolm X adorns the silver screen, Lee positions himself, the film, and big Hollywood budgets as testament to, and metonymic stand-in for, Black Power's success in America.

Though Lee revised the Baldwin–Perl script, the film ultimately removes Baldwin's chronological experimentation and follows quite faithfully the *Autobiography*. Thus, the film is a conversion narrative with three distinct stages: childhood and hustler days, prison and self-education, then religious and political leadership, both in the Nation of Islam and after – ending with the assassination. Still, within this rather conventional biopic, Lee inserts footage from later periods in the opening and ending scenes. The opening credits feature media footage of contemporary racism, such as the 1991 Rodney King beating. The final scene is also new: a teacher declares "You are Malcolm X" and black school children across the globe reply, "I am Malcolm X." This is capped by an appearance by Nelson Mandela, a black-and-white photo montage of Malcolm X, then famous African Americans wearing "X" caps in the end credits. For Melvin Donalson, these moves "suggest that the contemporary status of black men in 1992 was not so far removed from the earlier decades of the 1940s–1960s covered within the film."[27] Throughout, spliced-in or recreated footage of actual speeches bolsters feelings of historical fidelity while the bookends of contemporary scenes reinforce a clear sense of historical chronology and continuity. Lee's other main innovation is that key scenes linger in visual delight, such as an extended dance hall scene, the stand off between Harlem residents and the NYPD, and a Nation of Islam worship service starkly segregated by gender among uniformly-clad parishioners while a stark horizontal plane separates these faithful from non-Muslims in the balcony.

In the end, Lee declares, "*Malcolm X* is my artistic vision. The film is my interpretation of the man. It's nobody else's."[28] Lee acknowledges Baldwin's original script as his main source, along with alternates by David Mamet, David Bradley, and others. But he charges, "At the time [Baldwin] was drinking really heavily, and eventually another writer named Arnold Perl helped him finish it."[29] Notwithstanding Lee's unfamiliarity with Baldwin (surprise at heavy drinking, avoiding the informal "Jimmy"), Lee paints Baldwin's script as wanting because "it fell down in the third act" and could not address the still-raw split between Malcolm and the Nation of Islam. Lee also later objected, "Baldwin had stuff out of order. He had Malcolm giving speeches at the beginning of the movie that didn't really come until 1963 or 1964, so we had to get rid of those."[30] So Lee excised Baldwin's temporal innovations to restore Haley's chronological tale. Historian Nell Irvin Painter faults Lee heavily for mistaking the *Autobiography* for biographical fact,[31] though Lee did also interview many direct acquaintances of Malcolm, including family members and, perhaps most crucially, Minister Louis Farrakhan, current Nation of Islam head. Lee's documentary techniques exacerbate Painter's concern, such as splicing in footage of Martin Luther King and manufacturing black-and-white shots with present-day actors. In the end, Painter suggests that the film is more a reflection of 1992 than a historical document. That explains why Lee inserts Black Panther Bobby Seale and Reverend Al Sharpton as street preachers, which "establish[es] a continuity of black nationalist leadership" since the 1960s, thereby making Malcolm a singular icon well-suited to mythography in racialized drama, a continuity Baldwin rejects because it leaves out so many possibilities.[32] Horne asserts that Lee avoided nuance to prevent backlash by black nationalists. Still, Horne reports, much of the black-oriented press such as the *New York Amsterdam News* and Black Power figures such as Stokely Carmichael condemned the film and Lee, often with vitriol.[33]

Horne's and Painter's historian concerns reflect only one major objection to Lee's film. Other key complaints include matters of aesthetic conservatism, political conservatism, market friendliness, feminist unfriendliness, and over- or under-simplified contexts. I suggest that in Baldwin's more experimental script, scholars might find the more radical and nonnormative aspects of Malcolm X for which they have sought largely in vain in Lee's film. Indeed, Donald Bogle praises the film but notes a central irony that it is Lee's "most conventional film" yet, despite the fiery subject matter and Lee's reputation for innovation and independence. "The casting of Washington," Bogle opines, "also helped to make [Malcolm] acceptable to the mainstream audience" due to Washington's sheer likeability.[34] Preemptively rejecting Lee and Hollywood whole cloth, Black Arts writer Amiri Baraka spearheaded the group United Front to Preserve the Memory of Malcolm X and the Cultural Revolution before filming even began. He painted Lee as the "quintessential buppie" and objected to his previous films' "caricature of Black people's lives, their dismissal of our struggle and the implication of their description of the Black nation as a few besieged Buppies surrounded by irresponsible repressive lumpen."[35] Along these lines, in his symposium in *Cinéaste*, Gary Crowdus deems the film "remarkably subdued" by "placing stress on themes of personal redemption in a cinematic style thought most appropriate for younger people and a crossover audience."[36] These political and aesthetic critiques lead to concerns about market culture more generally. William Lyne suggests the box office is no place for transformational politics, but rather the commodification of them, so that Lee and Haley, whom he deems "political conservatives," appear as radicals even when the story of Malcolm X is read "not as a fulcrum for mass activism but rather as a bible for personal improvement."[37] To wit, John Locke notes that in Lee's film Malcolm X only uses the divisive term "white devils" twice: in a narrated letter and an interview in the past tense.[38] Many critics single out the "X" ball caps as commodification at the price of politics because, as Dan Georgakas writes, "Withheld is how

Malcolm X was defining El-Hajj Malik El-Shabass [sic]. That new identity does not fit neatly on a baseball cap, and it does not play well in Peoria."[39]

These marketability concerns join longstanding feminist critiques of Lee's women, who have lost all the feminist possibilities Baldwin inserted. Black feminist bell hooks, for instance, castigates the film because "In Lee's cinematic world, every relationship between a black man and a woman, whether white or black, is mediated by his constant sexualization of a female."[40] Feminist critiques fit well into sundry objections about contexts left out of Lee's film, including the role of Malcolm's family, especially the women,[41] the international setting for Malcolm's politics, for which Horne detects a "pervasive narrow nationalism," and the disputed role of the Nation of Islam in Malcolm's assassination, which Horne suggests "reflects a conflict that some would prefer to erase from the pages of history."[42]

These concerns about market pressures and normativity ultimately drove Baldwin out of Hollywood, whereas Lee persisted a generation later. Indeed, many eventually praise Lee's film, despite strong objections, by recognizing the high-wire act of bringing an important, contested, and radical figure into mainstream venues. Kalim Aftab suggests that Lee tames the Hollywood beast because "He displayed celebrity power usually reserved for those on Hollywood's A-list."[43] Bogle and Reid likewise suggest that the emergence of black film in mainstream Hollywood signals progress. Some of Lee's harsher critics cede this point, too, such as Jonathan Scott Lee who laments the lack of transformational politics but still detects in *Malcolm X* an evolution away from romantic street stories and toward an emergent "counter-aesthetic."[44] Hollywood often escapes censure by critics invested in radical politics because many now agree with Jacquie Jones's contention that "The charge of Hollywood has never been to produce functional political documents."[45] But, as Crowdus notes, "Malcolm X is not the sort of person Hollywood biopics normally celebrate."[46] So, by virtue of its high-profile venue, Lee's film, more than any other version of Malcolm save for Haley's autobiography, courts heated scholarly and public discussions about Malcolm's politics and legacy, both on political and aesthetic terms. Bringing Baldwin's script into that discussion retrieves alternative versions of Malcolm, especially for feminist, queer, and radical readers, while underscoring the price and payoff of bringing Malcolm to Hollywood.

Conclusion: "I am Malcolm," black Hollywood and Malcolm X's legacy

In the end, Lee's high-profile product joins the ongoing saga of staking claims on Malcolm's story and status. As Michael Eric Dyson put it in 1992, "Who speaks for Malcolm X? The writings of just about everybody."[47] But not all claims are equal, especially when they vary on whether they acknowledge other competing versions, past, present, and possible. Lee's departing "I am Malcolm" and "X" cap montages represent one resilient version of Malcolm that aspires to unity, be it black or global, especially through anticipation of Malcolm's imminent adoption of more inclusive visions of global justice or impending reconciliation with the Nation of Islam just before his assassination. Horne counters, "This story of reconciliation is part of a myth that promotes a form of contemporary black unity. But it happens to be inaccurate," which explains Lee's decision to avoid including Farrakhan.[48] Painter identifies strain between the reality of intraracial conflict, dissent, and difference on the one hand, and black nationalist goals of racial unity on the other. She concludes, "If Malcolm X is to work as a racial symbol, it is best not to look at him too closely."[49] When that story achieves iconic status, especially in the biopic genre, the distinction between man and myth is particularly unclear.

What competing version is most valuable, accurate, or useful, and by what measuring tape? Who is heir to Malcolm, who isn't, and who can fill the void he left? These questions dog Malcolm X's legacy, but Lee has a trump card given the cache of a big-budget Hollywood film in a visual- and popular-culture-driven world. By 1992, black film was well ensconced in mainstream cinema, thanks in part to Lee's earlier work, so there is little, if any, oppositional politics intrinsic to including Malcolm in Hollywood's pantheon. As Dyson points out, Lee's film capped a spike in renewed interest in Malcolm X as "a response to the current need, deeply felt by many, for a confrontational stance toward this country's continuing racism and the seductive mythology of the perfect black man."[50] That is, Lee's film feeds nostalgia for Malcolm X and the radicalism he came to represent. In Baldwin's time, debates between integration and black nationalism were still fresh and pressing, even in mainstream politics. Perhaps a major studio biopic could have been more in harmony with Malcolm's calls for radical changes to American economic and democratic structures back when Baldwin was first involved in 1968.

NOTES

1. See Michael Eric Dyson, *Making Malcolm: The Myth and Meaning of Malcolm X* (New York: Oxford University Press, 1995); and Gerald Horne, "'Myth' and the Making of 'Malcolm X,'" *American Historical Review*, 98.2 (1993), pp. 440–50.
2. Thomas Doherty, "Malcolm X: In Print, On Screen," *Biography*, 23.1 (2000), p. 29.
3. See Gary Crowdus (ed.), "By Any Reviews Necessary: *Malcolm X* Symposium," *Cinéaste* 19.4 (1993), pp. 4–24, among many others.
4. David Leeming, *James Baldwin: A Biography* (New York: Penguin, 1994), p. 300.
5. See my "Reading a 'Closet Screenplay': Hollywood, James Baldwin's Malcolms, and the Threat of Historical Irrelevance," *African American Review*, 39.1–2 (2005), pp. 103–18.

6. Doherty, "Malcolm X", and Norman, "Reading a 'Closet Screenplay'"; Crowdus, "By Any Reviews"; Horne, "'Myth'"; Nell Irvin Painter, "Malcolm X Across the Genres," *American Historical Review*, 98.2 (1993), pp. 432–9.

7. Jacqueline Stewart, *Migrating to the Movies: Cinema and Black Urban Modernity* (Berkeley: University of California Press, 2005), p. xiii.

8. Mark Reid, *Black Lenses, Black Voices: African American Film Now* (Lanham, MD: Rowman and Littlefield, 2005), pp. 14–15.

9. Horne, "'Myth'", p. 449.

10. Leeming, *James Baldwin*, p. 284.

11. Ibid., p. 297. Heston portrayed Moses in *The Ten Commandments* (1956) and participated in the 1963 March on Washington for Jobs and Justice.

12. James Baldwin, *No Name in the Street* (New York: Dial, 1972), p. 11.

13. Ibid., *One Day, When I Was Lost* (1972; reprint, New York: Dell, 1992).

14. *Malcolm X*, directed by Arnold Perl (1972 Burbank, CA: Warner Brothers, 1995). Warner Brothers bought the rights from Columbia Pictures after Baldwin left the project.

15. *Malcolm X*, DVD, directed by Spike Lee (1992; Burbank, CA: Warner Brothers, 2000).

16. Spike Lee with Ralph Wiley, *By Any Means Necessary: The Trials and Tribulations of the Making of "Malcolm X"* (New York: Hyperion, 1992), p. 9.

17. Baldwin, *One Day*, p. 6.

18. Ibid., p. 3.

19. Patsy Brewington Perry, "Baldwin's Unfulfilled Obligation," in *James Baldwin: A Critical Evaluation*, ed. Therman O'Daniel (Washington, DC: Howard University Press, 1977), p. 213.

20. I call this "the problem of historical irrelevance," in Norman, "Reading a 'Closet Screenplay,'" p. 104.

21. Baldwin, *One Day*, pp. 182–3.

22. Ibid., pp. 85–6. See also John Locke, "Adapting the Autobiography: The Transformation of *Malcolm X*," *Cinéaste*, 19.4 (1993), p. 6.

23. Baldwin, *One Day*, pp. 229–30.

24. Glenn Man, "Editor's Note," *Biography*, 23.1 (2000), p. vi.

25. About $28 million from Warner Brothers, the rest from private sources, including leading black celebrities. Lee with Wiley, *By Any Means*, pp. 71, 165.

26. Lee with Wiley, *By Any Means*, pp. 30, xiiv.

27. Melvin Donalson, *Black Directors in Hollywood* (Austin: University of Texas Press, 2003), p. 111.

28. Ibid., p. xiv.

29. Ibid., p. 24.

30. Gary Crowdus and Dan Georgakas, "Our Film Is Only a Starting Point: An Interview with Spike Lee," *Cinéaste*, 19.4 (1993), p. 20.

31. Painter, "Malcolm X Across the Genres," p. 432.

32. Ibid., p. 433.

33. Horne, "'Myth'", p. 445.

34. Donald Bogle, *Toms, Coons, Mulattoes, Mammies, and Bucks: An Interpretive History of Blacks in American Films*, 4th edn. (New York: Continuum, 2001), p. 355.

35. Amiri Baraka, "Spike Lee at the Movies," in *Black American Cinema*, ed. Manthia Diawara (New York: Routledge, 1992), p. 146. Lee retorts,

"Malcolm X belongs to everybody, and there were going to be people who felt the film we were going to make was not going to be the authentic story." He adds, "I don't know what is more middle class than being a college professor" (Spike Lee, as told to Kaleem Aftab, *That's My Story and I'm Sticking To It* [New York: Norton, 2005], p. 143).

36. Crowdus, "By Any Reviews," p. 4.
37. William Lyne, "No Accident: From Black Power to Black Box Office," *African American Review*, 34.1 (2000), p. 55.
38. Locke, "Adapting the Autobiography," p. 5.
39. See Dan Georgakas, "Black Supremacy and Anti-Semitism: Religion in *Malcolm X*," *Cinéaste*, 19.4 (1993), p. 16. See also Mark Reid, "The Brand X of PostNegritude Frontier," *Film Criticism*, 20.1–2 (1995), pp. 17–25.
40. bell hooks, "Male Heroes and Female Sex Objects: Sexism in Spike Lee's *Malcolm X*," *Cinéaste*, 19.4 (1993), p. 14. For another feminist critique, see Maurice Stevens, "Subject to Countermemory: Disavowal and Black Manhood in Spike Lee's *Malcolm X*," *Signs*, 28.1 (2002), pp. 277–301.
41. See Painter, "Malcolm X Across the Genres," p. 434.
42. Horne, "'Myth,'" pp. 446, 447.
43. Lee and Aftab, *That's My Story*, p. 146.
44. Johnathan Scott Lee, "Spike Lee's *Malcolm X* as Transformational Object," *American Imago*, 52.2 (1995), pp. 157–8. He cites rips in the otherwise seamless chronology, though I suggest such moments are remnants of Baldwin's script.
45. Jacquie Jones, "Spike Lee Presents *Malcolm X*: The New Black Nationalism," *Cinéaste*, 19.4 (1993), p. 10.
46. Crowdus, "By Any Reviews," p. 4.
47. Michael Eric Dyson, "Who Speaks for Malcolm? The Writings of Just About Everybody," *New York Times Book Review*, November 29, 1992, p. 3.
48. Horne, "'Myth,'" p. 444.
49. Painter, "Malcolm X Across the Genres," p. 433.
50. Dyson, "Who Speaks," p. 3.

4

JEFFREY B. LEAK

Malcolm X and black masculinity in process

Now that we have entered what some pundits have called a post-racial America – one in which race should matter less but often matters even more – the best-selling memoirs of James McBride (*Color of Water*) and Barack Obama (*Dreams from My Father*) may eclipse the *Autobiography of Malcolm X* in college courses and in bookstore sales.[1] One of the reasons for this possibility is that white American mothers figure prominently in the lives of these black men, thus it could be argued that their autobiographical selves make the case for their Americanness in a way unavailable to Malcolm X. Framed another way, McBride's and Obama's direct connection and lineage to the white world may render them more sympathetic, more appealing, to white Americans than black male autobiographers whose backgrounds do not embody such perceived symbolic cache. Moreover, when he was the Democratic presidential candidate in 2008, President Obama's biracial story cultivated even more interest among white Americans. But if we were to jettison Malcolm's *Autobiography* from our collective memory, we would remove a foundational and innovative text in an ever-evolving African American autobiographical tradition. A most powerful voice that spoke honestly and, yes, erringly, about the role of black men in American society, Malcolm offered intriguing and at times controversial notions of what constituted appropriate black male behavior. The *Autobiography* is a bridge between Richard Wright's *Black Boy* and the perils of life under Southern and Northern Jim Crow and the forerunner to literary contemporaries like McBride, Obama, and Nathan McCall (*Makes Me Wanna Holler*).[2]

As actor and humanitarian Ossie Davis made clear in his eulogy at Faith Temple in Harlem, Malcolm X "was our manhood, our living black manhood."[3] When Davis spoke about manhood, he was referring to the physical, social, and material conditions that conspired against the very notion of black manhood in America. One of the most poignant placards that emerged during the black freedom struggle in the 1960s (especially during the black sanitation workers' strike in Memphis, Tennessee) said it all: "I am a Man." In a culture that empowered only white men to achieve the traditional criteria for manhood – wealth, property, political and economic privilege, and sexual power – to the exclusion and mistreatment of many other Americans, black men, no matter their age, were considered nothing more than boys in the social imagination of white America; except, that is, in the case of potential sexual encounters with white women. One of the most heinous and widely publicized examples of this was the murder of Emmett Till in Mississippi in 1955.

Ed Guerrero, who has written extensively about issues of race and manhood in American and African American film, explains the problem of black manhood in this way:

> One must also consider the social contradiction and hoax inflicted on black men, which originates in the very definitions of self-worth and manhood in our society. It has come to be a cruel joke that in a culture driven by media fantasies of sex, violence, and power; a culture where material wealth is the highest measure of self-worth; a culture that defines "manhood" by the ability to provide economic survival for one's self and family – in this culture, the very means of achieving "manhood" are systemically and institutionally kept out of the grasp of all too many black men.[4]

It is this fundamental understanding of manhood that Malcolm focused on with unceasing intensity, given his own father's struggle to support his family and his premature death under mysterious circumstances. The Malcolm of Davis's memory argued for the right of black men to insist upon their self-worth, even if this was realized through violent means. What Malcolm, though flawed in his reductive ideological assertions, understood was that black male identity would ultimately be determined by the degree to which black men could exercise the traditional forms of American manhood. Of course both he and Martin Luther King, Jr. erred in failing to critique the sexism, homophobia, and exploitative aspects of this model. But despite these serious analytical miscues, both understood that black manhood in America had to embody (at least to a degree) the rudimentary expectations of providing for family and accessing political and economic power, as well as the social acknowledgment of their roles as men.

Although the true authorship of the *Autobiography* is a complex blending of Malcolm and Haley, the final creation provides a bridge between the concepts of black manhood (having the material resources to be a man) and black masculinity (using these resources to challenge more narrow, retrograde notions of black male identity). Some critics may argue that the narrative is more Haley's construction than Malcolm's, but the latter had to approve every word. In my view, this complex collaborative text has assumed a life of its own, probably far from the expectations or imaginings of either man. Whatever Malcolm omitted or embellished, however Haley chose to frame Malcolm's recollections, the narrative addresses the core issues related to black manhood and masculinity in twentieth-century America. What is undeniable is that the story of the man who began as Malcolm Little, morphing into Detroit Red, Malcolm X, and ultimately El-Hajj Malik El-Shabazz (his final Muslim name), is probably the most popular black autobiography of the twentieth century, comparable to Frederick Douglass's accomplishment in the nineteenth century. As such, we should be mindful of a fundamental truth regarding memoir (which covers a portion of a life) and autobiography (which covers the full life): that reconstructions of a life, whether told by one person or collaboratively, are inherently fictional; that people and events are not always remembered or introduced exactly as they were. In Malcolm's case, many of the people in his story are composites (a standard feature in auto-biography for legal and organizational purposes). Also, the *Autobiography* is doubly reconstructed, with Malcolm's recollections then framed by Haley's interpretive decisions. Given this configuration, along with the fictional dimensions of reconstructing a life for presentation in book form, I am not invested in proving the accuracy of every aspect of the narrative, but in pointing out how the *Autobiography* reveals in both form and content potential paths to a more socially enlightened and viable black masculinity, a way of being conscious of one's identity as a black man without accepting the social pathologies often associated with black men.

Rewriting tradition

To begin with, the *Autobiography* is the result of years of collaboration between Haley and Malcolm. During this process both men spent concentrated periods of time preparing Malcolm's story for publication. No other text in Malcolm's oratorical or written repository went through such rigorous and repeated examination. This narrative, in the words of Arnold Rampersad, "remains the central text about Malcolm's life, the rock on which the edifice of his reputation is supposed to rest."[5]

The *Autobiography* is also informed by many of the slave narrators of the nineteenth century. They, and the rhetorical limitations of the slave narrative as a literary form, are crucial to understanding the relationship between Malcolm and Haley. Most of the first subjects in eighteenth- and nineteenth-century slave narratives and autobiographies were not the sole or primary author of their texts. Because they were often illiterate, they told their stories to an amanuensis or editor (usually, if not always, white), and even as African Americans began to pen their own stories in the mid-nineteenth century, in almost every instance, the story was prefaced with a claim of legitimacy and racial authenticity by a white authority figure. For Phillis Wheatley, the nominally enslaved but educated poet (*Poems*) in the eighteenth century, she received her stamp of intellectual legitimacy from the prominent white men of Boston.[6] For Douglass (*Narrative of the Life of Frederick Douglass*), William Lloyd Garrison and Wendell Phillips made the case for his first and most popular narrative. For Harriet Jacobs (*Incidents in the Life of a Slave Girl*), Lydia Maria Child served as both editor and authenticator.[7] In the twentieth century, Dorothy Canfield Fisher vetted the autobiography (*Black Boy*) of Richard Wright.

Even for Malcolm X, a journalist named M. S. Handler, with whom he had established a meaningful relationship, introduced him as author. The challenge for a slave, former slave, or a free black person in the eighteenth or nineteenth century was to tell their story on their terms, even if they were illiterate. For black writers, this phenomenon of securing the imprimatur of a white authority figure lasted well into the 1960s. In Malcolm's case he overturned the model of dictated autobiography – one in which African Americans told their stories to white writers – and created a new, collaborative model with a black man. But this negotiation has not been fully appreciated for the way in which it presents a form of black masculinity predicated on understanding and respecting the intellectual concerns of another black man. There are certainly problematic dimensions of the *Autobiography* (which I will address shortly), but the circumstances in which it was created reflect the concept of black masculinity in process. Neither man, in the end, insisted on absolute control; both understood that the book project took precedence over their egos. Haley outlines the terms of their agreement in the Epilogue:

> Another letter was dictated, this one an agreement between him [Malcolm] and me: "Nothing can be in this book's manuscript that I didn't say, and nothing can be left out that I want in it."
>
> In turn, I asked Malcolm X to sign for me a personal pledge that however busy he was, he would give me a priority quota of his time for the planned 100,000-word "as told to" book which would detail his entire life. And months later, in a time of strain between us, I asked for – and he gave – his permission that elsewhere in this book I could write comments of my own about him which would not be subject to his review. (14–15)

What makes this agreement so instructive is the example of two black men, rather than, in the case of a slave narrative, a white person and a black person, working together to produce a narrative rendering of Malcolm's life. In unambiguous terms he said to Haley what their predecessors in bondage could never have said explicitly: that he controlled the content. For Frederick Douglass, such an assertion had to be subtly crafted and strategically incorporated, lest he offend the largely white readership. In this example, he framed the reminder around the physical injuries for which the institution of slavery was responsible: "My feet have been so cracked with the frost that the pen with which I am writing might be laid in the gashes."[8] In language that awakened the senses, Douglass achieved two goals: revealing the impact of slavery on the black body and reminding the reader, with his "pen," of who was guiding the narrative.

Malcolm was not inclined toward such rhetorical maneuvers, but in response to his condition of controlling content, Haley requested substantial time with Malcolm along with the right to publish the Epilogue, which would be outside Malcolm's right to review. In other words, Malcolm had to enter an agreement whereby Haley could criticize or contradict anything he said. He had to accept the fact that his view or perception of a particular event or moment was just that – his, and that his collaborator could offer a contrary perspective. Moreover, from the start of their union, Malcolm never trusted the promises of the publisher to meet its contractual guarantees, but he learned to trust Haley. What better example than for two black men to reach across the social and class divide, as both felt compelled to do, to engage black identity in America on their own terms. For Malcolm's family, this collaboration provided them with financial security they never had while he was alive, as he decided to channel profits to them, rather than to the Nation of Islam leadership, as he routinely had done with all of his speaking fees and honoraria.

Can a woman get some credit?

The progressive engagement that characterized Malcolm's relationship with Haley is much more difficult to locate when examining his opinions about and interactions with women. But to understand the construction of black masculinity in the *Autobiography*, an exploration of Malcolm's relationship with women is paramount. His relationships with his mother and with Ella, his half-sister, illustrate Malcolm's struggle with paternalism and sexism with all the women in his life. In the opening chapter, he describes his parents' marriage and his mother's role as a woman, revealing the difference between his knowledge of racial inequality and of gender inequality. Violence, perpetrated by his father, Earl, against Louise Little and all the children was prevalent:

> They seemed to be nearly always at odds. Sometimes my father would beat her. It might have had something to do with the fact that my mother had a pretty good education. Where she got it I don't know. But an educated woman, I suppose, can't resist the temptation to correct an uneducated man. Every now and then, when she put those smooth words on him, he would grab her. (82)

Malcolm's explanation for his father's violence against his mother speaks more about the self-doubt of Earl Little or his own. In fact, as Malcolm looks back on the early days of his life, he seems morally oblivious to the violence launched against his mother, a light-skinned woman from the tiny island nation of Granada. Because she found a way to become "educated" – which may have meant that she read and spoke English in standard fashion – the dark-skinned family patriarch took offense at her showing off her learning. Malcolm seems to feel that Earl believed this was her way of ridiculing him, her "uneducated" husband. Following the symbolic logic of racial complexion, this man, of a dark hue, could not allow his wife, a woman with obvious bloodlines to the white world of education and privilege, to have any verbal power in their marriage. It was bad enough he had to deal with the white man, so he would say to himself; surely, he would be above reproach in *his* house. With such feelings of inadequacy men often revert to what they know best: physical conquest.

In one of the most critical readings of Malcolm, Hilton Als offers a searing critique of this early moment in the narrative, pointing out the absurdity of how Malcolm renders his own mother invisible. At turns, Als, whose mother also hailed from what had been the British West Indies, poses questions that he imagines Louise Little would have about her son's reconstruction of her role in his life:

> Is this not mad? Being smart – it made Mrs. Little feel so different. It made my mother silent so as not to feel different. Did Mrs. Little ask, by speaking, to be punished? Is that how she lost her mind, really? The famous photograph of Malcolm standing at the window in his house with a gun looking out the window – I believe he is on the lookout for his mother. What did he see, looking out that window? Did he see his mother's quite appropriate anger? Based on the fact that in the *Autobiography* he refers to her as Louise and in *Malcolm: The Life of a Man Who Changed Black America*, Bruce Perry refers to her as Louisa. What was her name? Her date of birth? What parish was she born in in Granada? When Malcolm looked out that window, did he see his mother holding a diary? What was written in it? Mrs. Little (as I call her) did not write: He did not know my name. He could not bear my presence.[9]

For Als, Louise Little only serves two purposes for Malcolm: to give birth to him and to symbolize the stain of white blood on the Negro race. Malcolm objectifies her, rendering her as nothing more than an extension of white supremacy and colonialism. He is able to explain why his father would strike her, but he fails to explain or consider the notion that his mother had a right to offer an opinion (and even a criticism) when necessary. Employing a loose, creative form of psychoanalysis, Als delineates how this particular black man's sense of self (and that of his father) is bound to the unmitigated subjugation of the woman who ushered him into life.

With such a troubling depiction of his mother, Malcolm certainly began his ruminations about his life with, at best, a deep indifference toward women. Within the *Autobiography* there is one relationship that depicts Malcolm's struggle with patriarchy and his willingness to reveal his rather narrow-minded views about women, perspectives that by the end of the *Autobiography* are in the process of reformulation but far from complete revisions. Nonetheless, the role Ella played in his life is nothing short of transforming. When he moves to Boston as a young "hick," Ella is the one who provides guidance and support, although he ignores her advice. In describing her, he continues a pattern set forth in the first chapter in discussing the physical characteristics of his parents:

> Ella had fixed up a nice little upstairs room for me … Ella still seemed to be as big, black, outspoken and impressive a woman as she had been in Mason and Lansing. Only about two weeks before I arrived, she had split up with her second husband – the soldier, Frank, whom I had met there the previous summer; but she was taking it right in stride. I could see, though I didn't say, how any average man would find it almost impossible to live for very long with a woman whose every instinct was to run everything and everybody she had anything to do with – including me. (121)

As he articulates his sympathy with men who have fled from Ella, Malcolm never questions their behavior or the degree to which her assertiveness and independence, while clearly part of her personal makeup, could also be attributable to the lack of black men who could support her in meaningful ways. Put another way, part of Malcolm's masculine dilemma is his inability to imagine beyond his conservative views regarding the roles of men and women. Aside from assisting men, women rarely emerge as independent, complex figures. Throughout the *Autobiography*, Malcolm offers commentary on the roles of black women. Certainly through his childhood as Malcolm Little and his later incarnations, women are primarily depicted in relation to serving the needs of men. Recall Malcolm's experience living with prostitutes:

> Domineering, complaining, demanding wives who had just about psychologically castrated their husbands were responsible for the early rush. These wives were so disagreeable and had made their men so tense that they were robbed of the satisfaction of being men. To escape this tension and the chance of being ridiculed by his own wife, each of these men had gotten up early and come to a prostitute … No matter how little virility a man has to offer, prostitutes make him feel for a time that he is the greatest man in the world. That's why these

prostitutes had that morning rush of business. More wives could keep their husbands if they realized their greatest urge is *to be men*.   (180)

In Malcolm's view these prostitutes could teach the wives of these morning "clients" a lesson or two on how to keep their men at home. Of course his reading of sexual relations between men and women is somewhat skewed, absent of any understanding of what might be the experience of these wives. Did he and Haley discuss the fundamental assertion – that women are mostly responsible for their philandering husbands – offered in the above selection? With Malcolm's intellectual acuity, surely he knew that some would receive his comments as sexist, even misogynist. A progressive treatise on feminism the *Autobiography* is not, but Malcolm's level of revelation – conscious or not – regarding his views about and relationships with women is refreshing in its honesty, if not its accuracy. Regarding Ella, she undoubtedly was one of the pillars in his life, but in her strength, he saw emasculation.

Ironically, the initiative and drive that dominate Ella's personality were partly the reason for Malcolm's unusual prison experience and his eventual transfer to Norfolk Prison Colony, which "represented the most enlightened form of prison that I have ever heard of. In place of the atmosphere of malicious gossip, perversion, grafting, hateful guards, there was more relative 'culture,' as culture is interpreted in prisons." The prison's library, willed to the institution by a "millionaire named Parkhurst," provided inmates with access to thousands of books. "At Norfolk, we could actually go into the library, with permission – walk up and down the shelves, pick books. There were hundreds of old volumes, some of them probably quite rare. I read aimlessly, until I learned to read selectively, with a purpose" (251). Malcolm writes extensively about the impact of this prison, that this was the equivalent of a college education. Again, one of the main facilitators behind his move to Norfolk was his "castrating" sister:

> [M]y sister Ella had been steadily working to get me transferred to the Norfolk, Massachusetts, Prison Colony, which was an experimental rehabilitation jail … The Colony was, comparatively, a heaven, in many respects. It had flushing toilets; there were no bars, only walls – and within the walls, you had far more freedom. There was plenty of fresh air to breathe; it was not in a city.   (250)

More than any other single person in his life up to his incarceration, Ella operated with an understanding of Malcolm's potential, of his possibilities rather than his limitations. She is the ever fearless and faithful black mother who persevered through slavery to keep the family unit together. But in so doing, following the one-sided logic of race and gender set forth in the narrative, she is, for Malcolm, a source of frustration.

At every major stage of his life, as it is reconstructed in the text, Malcolm points to Ella as a prime mover in his life. The same holds true for his journey to Mecca, a sacred pilgrimage that every orthodox Muslim should take at least once in their life, if at all possible. For his journey in 1964, Malcolm turned yet again to this "*strong* big, black, Georgia-born woman":

> Her domineering ways had gotten her put out of the Nation of Islam's Boston Mosque Eleven; they took her back, then she left on her own. Ella had started studying under Boston orthodox Muslims, then she founded a school where Arabic was taught! *She* couldn't speak it, she hired teachers who did. That's Ella! ... She told me there was no question about it; it was more important that I go. I thought about Ella the whole flight back to New York. A *strong* woman. She had broken the spirits of three husbands, more driving and dynamic than all of them combined. She had played a very significant role in my life. No other woman ever was strong enough to point me in directions; I pointed women in directions. I had brought Ella into Islam, and now she was financing me to Mecca.
>
> (431)

In these remarks, Malcolm offers his best attempt at acknowledging the efforts of the sole person responsible for financing his trip to Mecca. Even as he points out how she founded a school, hired teachers, and made shrewd entrepreneurial decisions, the word he italicizes twice is telling: *strong*. Indeed, Ella's strength is the source of his pilgrimage, but Malcolm views it, along with her dark complexion, as signs of some kind of disorder, one from which he benefits of course, but nonetheless not to be replicated, say, in the lives of his daughters. In his discussion of his relationship with and respect for Ella, we see Malcolm at his best and worst in terms of masculinity. He is not so foolhardy to decline his sister's support, but he accepts it with a major caveat: pointing out her debilitating impact on men. In Malcolm's view, she is not the woman to marry, but the woman to go to when you need help.

In a significant way, Ella occupies a role similar to two black women in Douglass's 1845 *Narrative*: his mother, Harriet Bailey, and his wife, Anna Murray. In describing his mother, who was of a "darker complexion," and who as a slave worked on another plantation, only able to see her son off to sleep at night, Douglass comments on his response to her death: "She made her journeys to see me in the night, travelling the whole distance on foot, after the performance of her day's work. Never having enjoyed, to any consider-able extent, her soothing presence, her tender and watchful care, I received the tidings of her death with much the same emotions I should have probably felt at the death of a stranger."[10] It is certainly understandable that Douglass felt cheated out of having a traditional relationship with his mother, where the creature comforts of the mother-child bond would have been present, but in looking back, even as an adult, Douglass finds little comfort in the effort his mother made, after a day of labor, to return to the plantation to make sure he was safe and that his basic needs were met.

In the final chapter, as Douglass reveals some of the aspects of his escape, he makes a comment that is rooted in understatement: "At this time, Anna, my intended wife, came on; for I wrote to her immediately after my arrival at New York, (notwithstanding my homeless, houseless, and helpless condition,) informing her of my successful flight, and wishing her to come on forthwith."[11] Similar to the way in which he takes for granted the sacrifices of his mother, Douglass fails to acknowledge to any degree Anna's role in securing his freedom, and a major role did she play: first, she financed his journey; and secondly, she suggested that he don the clothes of a sailor and proceeded to assemble the necessary apparel. This woman, also of a "darker complexion," was clearly a major player in Douglass's escape, but her role was never explored in any of his three autobiographies. From offering a rhetorical slight of his mother in the first chapter to speaking about his wife in the last, Douglass demonstrates that Malcolm's struggle with black women is one that dates back at least to the early years of the American republic. Malcolm does acknowledge Ella's role in his life, more so than Douglass does Anna's, but neither narrator appears comfortable in the knowledge that black women are major sources of power and freedom in their lives. From 1845 to 1965, one of the primary challenges of black masculinity involved acknowledging and affirming the presence of black women, not simply as helpmates for black men, but as primary conduits for African American emancipation.

Conclusion

As the iconic black male autobiography of the twentieth century, Malcolm's narrative situates black masculinity at the crossroads of progress and reversion. In one sense Malcolm's movement – having left the Nation of Islam for orthodox Islam and having reformulated his thinking regarding the validity of black nationalism – offers a model of black masculinity that is not static but in process. Put another way, the Malcolm who cannot see beyond calcified notions of race and gender, even when discussing his mother, is a troubling figure. On the other hand, the autodidactic Malcolm, the one who acknowledges (while at the same time lamenting) the role of his sister in his growth, represents a potentially brighter day for black male consciousness. It is clear, from the *Autobiography* and the contemporary struggles of African American men, that black women, like Ella, are essential to imagining and creating a more substantive, truly emancipated, form of black masculinity. If Malcolm, to return to Ossie Davis's eulogy, stands as the embodiment of our "living black manhood," black communities especially should be the first to insist that this manhood, in its finest form, develops not at the social expense of black women, but in concert with them.

Black feminist scholar Patricia Hill Collins offers some important observations regarding Malcolm's contribution to the African American struggle and the necessity of analyzing his life in full. "Malcolm X's extraordinary ability to think for himself leaves us a complicated legacy. While the ideas he expressed during the three major periods of his life remain controversial and contradictory, they simultaneously indicate the magnitude of growth he achieved through sustained intellectual struggle with complex, important questions." Turning to gender, Collins reminds us that this analysis will situate Malcolm with most men, black and white, of his era:

> It would be nice to think that Malcolm X simply left women out of his analysis. But he didn't. His comments about women, especially those contained in his *Autobiography*, offer one avenue to his underlying views on gender. Taking his cues from the dominant gender ideology of his times, Malcolm X's view on women reflected dominant views of white manhood and womanhood applied uncritically to the situation of African Americans.[12]

Collins rightfully steers us away from romanticizing or demonizing Malcolm. He was the product of a racist and sexist patriarchal world. His movement forward on questions of race and nationalism, and his more restrained progress on questions of gender equality, speak to his "controversial and contradictory" life. Following the trajectory of his development at the end of his life, I think it safe to surmise that given more time he would have become more attuned to the lives of women in his life, for ultimately forward-thinking African American men must not stand in front of black women, but alongside them.

NOTES

1. James McBride, *The Color of Water: A Black Man's Tribute to his White Mother* (New York: Riverhead Books, 1996); Barack Obama, *Dreams from My Father: A Story of Race and Inheritance* (New York: Three Rivers Press, 1995); Malcolm X and Alex Haley, *The Autobiography of Malcolm X* (1965; London: Penguin Books, 2001). (Subsequent references to the *Autobiography* are given in the text. In the Penguin edition, Haley's original Epilogue is placed at the beginning and entitled the Introduction.)

2. Richard Wright, *Black Boy: A Record of Childhood and Youth* (1945; New York: Harper & Row, 1966); Nathan McCall, *Makes Me Wanna Holler: A Young Black Man in America* (New York: Vintage, 1995).

3. Ossie Davis, "Eulogy of Malcolm X," in *For Malcolm: Poems on the Life and the Death of Malcolm X*, ed. Dudley Randall and Margaret G. Burroughs (Detroit: Broadside Press, 1969), p. 121.

4. Ed Guerrero, "The Black Man On Our Screens and the Empty Space in Representation," *Callaloo*, 18.2 (1995), p. 397.

5. Arnold Rampersad, "The Color of His Eyes: Bruce Perry's Malcolm and Malcolm's Malcolm," in *Malcolm X: In Our Own Image*, ed. Joe Wood (New York: St. Martin's Press, 1992), p. 118.

6. Phillis Wheatley, *Poems on Various Subjects, Religious and Moral* (1773; New York: AMS Press, 1976).

7. Harriet A. Jacobs, *Incidents in the Life of a Slave Girl, Written By Herself* (1861; Cambridge: Harvard University Press, 1987).

8. Frederick Douglass, *Narrative of the Life of Frederick Douglass* (1845; New Haven: Yale University Press, 2001), p. 28.

9. Hilton Als, "Philosopher or Dog?," in Wood, *Malcolm X: In Our Own Image*, pp. 93–4. Als suggests that Malcolm misspells his mother's name in the *Autobiography*, but actually it is Bruce Perry who refers to her both as "Louise" and as "Louisa." Perry, *Malcolm X: The Life of a Man who Changed Black America* (Barrytown, NY: Station Hill Press, 1991), pp. 2–5, 30.

10. Douglass, *Narrative*, p. 14.

11. Ibid., p. 76.

12. Patricia Hill Collins, "Learning to Think for Ourselves: Malcolm X's Black Nationalism Reconsidered," in Wood, *Malcolm X: In Our Own Image*, pp. 60, 74.

5

SHEILA RADFORD-HILL

Womanizing Malcolm X

In the early stages of this project, I told a colleague that I had been asked to write an article about women and Malcolm X. She didn't directly respond to this news but her expression was a talking book which seemed to ask: *Is there really anything more for a black feminist to say about Malcolm X?* I understand the premise of the question. After all, black feminists and womanists have already sculpted the dominant theoretical narrative on Malcolm X. For example, in the 1980s and 90s, black feminists wrote a series of essays generally praising his political insight and excoriating his misogyny. Michelle Wallace, Audre Lorde, bell hooks, Angela Davis, Patricia Hill Collins, and Barbara Ransby, among others, depicted Malcolm X as a race leader who was either the precursor to the core of misogyny at the center of Black Power politics, a warrior among the various leaders of the civil rights and black nationalist organizations of the 1960s, or a religious figure whose ministerial vocation and penchant for truth-seeking may well have enabled him, had he lived, to become a champion for women's empowerment.[1] Women writers in the Black Arts movement such as Maya Angelou, Alice Walker, and Sonia Sanchez saw Malcolm X as a black hero and praised his love for his people as well as his strength, courage, and intellectual integrity.[2] More recently, scholars such as Tracye Williams and Farah Jasmine Griffin have argued that black women can love what Malcolm X stood for but they must still challenge the sexism reflected in his teachings and in the movements he inspired.[3]

Black feminists and womanist scholars have theorized Malcolm X differently from men; yet, men have largely shaped his public legacy. With few exceptions, women have generally not produced significant scholarship about his life, his work, or his impact on contemporary political thought and social action. Since Malcolm X's assassination in 1965, male scholars from many different disciplines, backgrounds, and perspectives have consistently written about him and worked to maintain his legacy. From Alex Haley's *Autobiography of Malcolm X* to Manning Marable's forthcoming biography titled *Malcolm X: A Life of Reinvention*, males have rigorously studied his life and writings; for example, in the 1990s alone, there were at least eighteen Ph.D. dissertations on Malcolm X, several of which were published.[4] Other studies, many of which were written by men, analyze Malcolm X's political and religious beliefs in relation to other civil rights and black nationalist leaders.[5] Men also maintain Malcolm X's online presence in several websites and in digital archives containing thousands of pages of audio, visual, and written documents.[6] Male rap artists introduced images of Malcolm X and black nationalism to the hip-hop generation while Spike Lee's controversial 1992 film about Malcolm X spawned dozens of commentaries and critiques.

Yet despite this impressive body of work, few men have focused their research on the gender controversies and dilemmas that are evident in Malcolm X's life and work.[7] Few have theorized about the cultural implications of Malcolm's embrace of a dogmatic religion that simultaneously honored and suppressed black women. Male scholars criticize Malcolm's misogynist views including his statements about how women wanted to be mistreated and about how women, because they are naturally weak and willfully deceitful, need strong male guidance, but few men have theorized about the *cultural dynamics that produced these views* and fewer still have explored the reasons why many of Malcolm's experiences with black women confute his statements. Black women should explore the contradiction between Malcolm X's misogynist statements *about women* and his actual relationships *with black women*, most of whom were thoughtful, politically astute, educated, and as resourceful and committed as he was to the liberation of black people. With respect to black women, the differences between Malcolm's rhetoric and his reality raise interesting questions about the politics of black masculinity. From this standpoint, the dearth of women's research on Malcolm's life and work reinforces outmoded and dangerous gender politics. Malcolm X's story is mesmerizing, instructive, inspiring, and tragic, but the interpretations of his life and work are too often framed and analyzed in ways that obscure the important role that women played in helping him become the man he was. While Malcolm X and his representations may remain indelibly associated with black manhood, neither his life nor his legacy should be treated as a male preserve.

This essay challenges scholars to womanize Malcolm X. First, I define womanizing as a form of gender theorizing that places Malcolm's life and work within the web of female relationships that ensured his survival and supported his development as a political and religious figure. From this perspective, womanizing Malcolm X means shifting the scholarly focus from Malcolm X as an iconic figure to the impact of women's agency on his life and work. Secondly, womanizing Malcolm X involves an interpretive analysis of Malcolm's life, work, and legacy that is gendered, i.e. focused on both an explicit understanding of the role that gender played in the Black Power and civil rights movements and on gender as a unit of analysis in the politics of black radicalism. Thirdly, womanizing Malcolm X explores the black cultural values and emancipatory gender norms promoted by the intellectual descendents and heirs to Malcolm's legacy. Finally, womanizing Malcolm X involves applying the lessons learned from these analyses to contemporary social conditions and political movements.

Black women and Malcolm X

Women significantly influenced the history of Malcolm Little and later that of Malcolm X and El-Hajj Malik El-Shabazz. In contrast to the patriarchal rhetoric of the Nation of Islam, Malcolm's life reveals his willingness to relate to and rely on self-determined black women. Their willingness to nurture him lifted him out of a rebellious and self-destructive life. Their guidance helped him to educate himself and to gain the sense of purpose and direction that he needed to become a transformational black leader.

Malcolm first learned self-reliance and race consciousness from his family; he learned the urban codes of black manhood in cities including Boston, Detroit, Baltimore, and New York, but it was from women such as his mother and his sisters that he learned the importance of race pride and self-identity.[8] From women, Malcolm learned how to be proud of his heritage; he learned to be resourceful and strategic. Women taught him to have a plan. They guided his maturation and impressed him with the importance of spirituality. He learned to filter his faith through his intellect and to always think, examine, question, seek God's truth, and take action. There is a long list of women who had an impact on Malcolm. They include: Louise Helen Norton Little, his mother, Hilda Little, his older sister, Ella Collins, his older half-sister, and Betty Shabazz, his wife. In his autobiography, Minister Malcolm acknowledged the influence of Sister Clara Muhammad, the wife of Elijah Muhammad and of Mother Marie, Elijah Muhammad's mother, on his relationship with Elijah Muhammad.[9]

To develop his political program in the aftermath of his break with the Nation of Islam, El-Hajj Malik El-Shabazz reached out to women including Maya Angelou, Shirley Graham DuBois, Fannie Lou Hamer, and Coretta Scott King. He was also recruiting women such as Lynne Shifflett, Muriel Feelings, and Alice Mitchell to play key roles in the early development of the Organization of Afro-American Unity.[10] Finally, after his death, a number of women including Ruby Dee, Abbey Lincoln, Florynce Kennedy, worked to raise the money Betty would need for her family to survive.[11]

Malcolm's mother Louise Little was a woman whose life had a profound impact on her son. Despite her eventual mental breakdown – after years of marital discord, domestic abuse, poverty, humiliating welfare dependency, and long-term institutionalization in a mental hospital – Louise Little was a proud and resourceful woman. Like her husband, Earl Little, she espoused the beliefs of Marcus Garvey, who in 1914 founded the Universal Negro Improvement Association based on race pride, Pan-Africanism, and black economic independence.[12] According to Philbert, Malcolm's older brother, Yvonne Woodward, his youngest sister, and Ilyasah Shabazz, the third of his six daughters, Louise Little provided education, race consciousness, and spiritual direction for her children.[13] After her husband died under mysterious circumstances in 1931, Louise struggled to keep the family together but as her mental stability began to deteriorate under the strain of raising her children alone in abject poverty, Malcolm's older sister Hilda cared for the family. In fact, Malcolm credits Hilda and Wilfred with trying to hold the family together and years later, he remembered that it was Hilda's suggestion that he take academic courses while in prison.[14]

In 1946, Malcolm was sentenced to the Massachusetts State Prison in Charlestown. During his incarceration, Malcolm's family continued to show their support and to give him sound advice. His love and respect for his family helped lead him to the Nation of Islam, which they told him was the one true religion for the black man. Three of his brothers, Wilfred, Philbert, and Reginald, and his sister Hilda had joined the Nation prior to convincing Malcolm to do the same.

It was an effort led by Malcolm's half-sister Ella Collins that got him transferred to better prison facilities in Norfolk, Massachusetts, and that ultimately helped secure his parole in 1952. Malcolm describes her in his autobiography as a truly proud black woman, the first he had ever known. In *The Seventh Child*, Rodnell Collins, Ella's son, describes Malcolm's respect for her, and depicts her as an enterprising woman who helped her family and fought Boston's white power structure to protect them. She gained a reputation for her tenacity and resourcefulness as well as for her community work.[15] Ella was the last member of the family to join the Nation of Islam but she became disenchanted with its practices and left the organization. Yet she remained committed to educating people about Islam. For example, she founded a Muslim school in Boston and, in 1964, she financed Malcolm's travels to Africa encouraging his desire to study Islam. After Malcolm's death, Ella was determined to continue his work. She became the self-appointed leader of the newly formed and short-lived Organization for Afro-American Unity.

In Malcolm's days as a hipster and hustler turned criminal, he learned from his relationships with wayward women. In *Autobiography*, Malcolm writes about women, including Sophia, Laura, and others, from whom he learned how to get what he wanted by being as persistent, aggressive, and abusive as he needed to be to peddle drugs and women. He was cunning, charismatic, and reckless enough to have an interracial affair knowing that racial purity was perceived to be at the core of American racism and that violating the apparent American taboo against interracial sex could result in his death.[16] In fact, in his *Autobiography*, Malcolm claimed that his tryst with the white woman he called Sophia, but whose real name was Bea Caragulian, resulted in a longer prison sentence than he would otherwise have received.[17]

Malcolm X dedicates his autobiography to his wife Betty Shabazz and their children, which notes the sacrifices made by his family and how essential these were to his work. Betty Shabazz was a well-educated black woman who was willing to conform to the Black Muslim feminine ideal. This ideal involved submissiveness and single-minded attention to the care and nurture of black children, the fruit of the black nation.[18] Betty was one of the many Muslim women who did not outwardly defy their husbands as their behavior was intimately connected to their religious conviction.

Women like Betty Shabazz respected the Nation's masculine ideal as it offered provision, protection, honor, and respect for black women who had an important, though subordinate, role in building the black nation. Within the model of a Muslim woman, Betty worked to promote the teachings of the Honorable Elijah Muhammad. For instance, after joining the Nation, she became an instructor for the Muslim Girls Training camp, the woman's branch of the religious organization, which taught the proper behavior for girls, stressing nutrition, modesty, and submissiveness. Mylie Evers-Williams, a long-time friend of Betty Shabazz describes her as a "highly unusual woman of strength and courage."[19]

Minister Malcolm preached the conservative values of the Nation of Islam. These included moral respectability, hard work, and black unity. The Nation believed that these values and race respectability would accomplish more for blacks than nonviolent resistance and political demands for integration. Women were expected to be nurturers practicing virtue, modesty, and humility. But in contrast to the Nation's feminine ideal, Malcolm X admired women who were committed agents of social change. His visits to Africa introduced him to women whose leadership skills gave them professional opportunities and influence in African affairs of state. For example, Malcolm reported on a meeting with Shirley Graham Du Bois, the writer and widow of W. E. B. Du Bois, then living in Ghana, and later observed how black women should be proud of influential women leaders like her.[20]

Through his travels, Malcolm X learned that not all revolutionaries were black, even in Africa. He learned about the power of organizing and mass mobilization from studying the anticolonialist struggles and independence movements sweeping the African continent in the 1960s; that not all white people hated black people; that women as a group were oppressed around the world economically, socially, politically, and culturally; and that the nations that were advancing most rapidly were those where women were allowed freedom and self-determination.

After Malcolm left the Nation of Islam, his views about the role of women in the struggle for Pan-African liberation seemed to change. Arguably, his experiences with powerful and committed women activists had an impact on his emerging religious, social, and political beliefs. For instance, since Malcolm did not want black men to remain passive in the face of white aggression and disrespect, he often preached that black men should protect black women. He expressed this male protectionist view about Fannie Lou Hamer who was invited to speak at a rally in support of the Mississippi Freedom Democratic Party, but he also connected Hamer's leadership with international freedom movements and the need for black mass mobilization in the United States. At an evening rally on December 20, 1964, Malcolm introduced Hamer to the crowd, calling her "one of the world's greatest freedom fighters."[21]

Malcolm X, masculine regimes, and the politics of gender

Black feminist and womanist scholars have long recognized that black nationalism promoted a pernicious machismo. Some associate the rise of the politics of black manhood with Malcolm X. Others have blamed the gender calamities of Black Power politics on the "myth of the matriarchy" and the backlash against American radicalism. Some black feminists and womanists have been less critical of Malcolm's misogyny, preferring instead to blame it on the influence of the chauvinistic Nation of Islam. Still others have cautioned us not to excuse or ignore Malcolm's views on women but to realize that, much like the man himself, his views about women cannot be easily categorized.

Black feminist and womanist critics have produced insightful analyses about female sex-role expectations as well as the cultural norms invoked to control women's sexuality. Feminists and womanists have also exposed how patriarchal dominance manipulates female expectations of men to enforce gender codes favorable to male interests. But another aspect of gender research involves how black manhood is constructed and performed. The short history of Malcolm's manhood suggests that his family provided examples of determined black women and that as he developed politically, he remade his masculine subjectivity in ways that allowed him to see women as agents of social change. Although this evolution in Malcolm's perception was neither perfect nor complete, the fact that it occurred as he developed an international perspective on the struggle for human rights has profound political and cultural implications for black radicalism.

Malcolm X internalized masculine regimes or attitudes, values, and beliefs about manhood based on cultural norms, race consciousness, religious identity, and the social norms of the urban working class. The masculine performances appropriate to a street hustler and petty criminal converged in the personas of Malcolm Little, Detroit Red, and Satan but as Malcolm transformed himself from Little to X, a new masculine regime was formed. Like thousands of other men before and since Malcolm's conversion his behavior changed to conform to the Nation of Islam masculine ideal. The masculine attitude of the street thug was replaced by a more disciplined yet hegemonic manhood.[22] Malcolm Little accepted the dominant gender norms of urban and working-class black America. As a Black Muslim, Minister Malcolm espoused rigid gender roles for men and women and advocated a conservative sexuality consistent with Nation dogma. Yet even though Malcolm X preached what amounted to male supremacy, he experienced his maleness in ways that allowed him to maintain relationships with women as confidantes and collaborators.

El-Hajj Malik El-Shabazz saw the limits of the Nation of Islam's depiction of women and the presence of committed female freedom fighters. As a result of his movement away from the Nation, his development as a Pan-Africanist, and his desire to practice the Sunni Islamic faith, he was compelled to restructure his thinking about the role of both men and women in the struggle for human dignity. Because of his faith, his political evolution, and his longstanding relationships with black women committed to ending racism, El-Hajj Malik El-Shabazz was beginning to shape, mold, and transform his manhood into a model for black resistance.

El-Hajj Malik El-Shabazz changed his views about women because he had experiences with women activists who were outside the Nation feminine ideal and because his faith gave him the moral clarity he needed to discern the transnational nature of black cultural and political movements. The political philosophy of black nationalism as articulated by Malcolm X shifted from black separatism to a radical transformation of the global economy and political solidarity with oppressed people around the world. How did the new regimes for black manhood endorsed by El-Hajj Malik El-Shabazz differ from the masculine norms that gained ascendancy after 1966 when Black Power burst onto the cultural scene?

When Black Power became the organizing paradigm for black nationalism, black liberation slowly came to be defined simply as freedom for black manhood. Although Adam Clayton Powell first used the term "Black

Power," Stokely Carmichael shouted the phrase in Greenville, Mississippi, on the March Against Fear from Memphis to Jackson in 1966. The phrase caught fire. Later that year, the first Black Power Planning Conference was held in Washington DC. In 1967, the first National Conference on Black Power was held in Newark, New Jersey, and in Oakland, California, Huey P. Newton and Bobby Seale released the ten-point program for the Black Panther Party for Self-Defense.

As a phrase, Black Power had many meanings. To some people it meant political power, to others it meant economic opportunity; still others defined black power as self-determination and race pride. Many defined it as pride in black heritage and black culture. When it served their interests, black activists and white reactionaries defined Black Power as violent social change.[23] Although the term lacked a consistent definition, Black Power became a masculine regime that sought to institutionalize all forms of male privilege. In the years following Malcolm X's death, black rage was conflated with Black Power and Black Power with black nationalism. As a political expression of black rage, Black Power had a profound effect on the black masculine psyche and its regimes. Extreme expressions of black anger led to the insurrections and urban riots of the late 1960s. In the aftermath of these violent configurations, local, state, and federal governments began treating black communities as though they were enemies of the state. The government response to the pent-up anger of black people, antiwar protesters, and other radical activists was surveillance, infiltration, and assassinations designed to cripple progressive movements for social change.[24]

Under increasing political attack, the nationalist impulse of the late 1960s and 1970s became more patriarchal, more self-absorbed, and more focused on a definition of black liberation that glorified men by denigrating women. The masculine regimes associated with the rhetoric of liberation became depoliticized, non-introspective, impulsive, self-involved, violent, and antithetical to community.[25]

During the 1970s, black women pushed back against a corrupt nationalist ideology. Black women refused to become invisible and irrelevant to social movements that they had helped to build. Black women's activist connections and their commitment to black liberation were often characterized as examples of matriarchal domination. But black feminists, such as Toni Cade Bambera, Kathleen Clever, and others, refused to accept male leadership that was increasingly insensitive to black women's concerns. Sectarian divisions within mainstream feminism and the political warfare within black nationalism subverted black unity and denied black women the cultural and psychic space they needed to articulate and mobilize around their concerns. Black feminist organizations were founded to create these spaces. Women in organizations like the

Third World Women's Alliance and the National Black Feminist Organization created forums for critical analysis and crafted the political discourse on race, class, and gender in ways that reshaped both movements.[26]

Brothers and sisters: The descendents of Malcolm X

Although Malcolm X will, no doubt, continue to be represented as the quintessential revolutionary black man, he should be studied and remembered as a political philosopher who defined late twentieth-century black radicalism. While he did not live to fulfill his activist aspirations, his critique of American culture is enduring and profound. The heirs to Malcolm X's intellectual legacy are committed to a Pan-Africanist struggle, one that educates black people about their social condition and organizes their ongoing political struggle for social change. For more than forty years, male descendents of Malcolm X have fostered an intellectual insurgency that stands in opposition to the corporate conservatism of the post–civil rights movement, the commodification of black culture, and the misrepresentation of black life. Contemporary black nationalists including Haki Madhubuti, Robin D. G. Kelley, Tavis Smiley, and others, continue to build institutions, educate young people, and advocate fairness and equity. They promote the values of black manhood that inspire men to protect their children, care for their families, support and uplift black women, and strengthen black communities.

Beyond being responsible for their own communities, contemporary black nationalists continue to remind black people in America that their heritage is African as well as American and that their demands for justice are part of a transnational struggle for human dignity and human rights. The intellectual descendents of Malcolm X realize that global capitalism intensifies the struggle for justice. The worldwide movement of capital and labor as well as goods and services means that the gap between rich and poor will continue to increase. Human suffering based on differences in race, religion, ethnicity, and poverty will accelerate while militarism, tyranny, damage to the environment, and crushing national debt will continue to limit the life chances of millions of people in countries around the world.

From a social perspective, black nationalists promote masculinities that value critical thinking over sexual prowess. For instance, in a section of *Black Men: Obsolete, Single, Dangerous?*, entitled "Black Manhood: Toward a Definition," Haki Madhubuti, an intellectual descendent of Malcolm X, offers a definition of manhood that is both poetic and political. Madhubuti's normative characteristics of black manhood include: (1) considering the needs of your people first, (2) making your life accessible to children, (3) respecting elders and being a protector of blacks who are weak, (4) giving direction and being sensitive to black women's needs and aspirations, and (5) building a vision, seeking truth, and loving life and all that is beautiful. He ends his definition of black manhood with advice: "believe that our values and traditions are not negotiable."[27]

On the cultural front, contemporary womanists and black nationalists have analyzed how popular images of black anger and rage are sexualized, packaged, and sold by elites to young people worldwide. Corporate media promote destructive masculine regimes claiming that they are simply marketing "black entertainment" to voracious consumers. The intellectual heritage of Malcolm X is reflected in the work of contemporary nationalists who promote oppositional masculine regimes focused on teaching young black men to maintain their integrity, support black women as companions and partners, and resist imperialism, militarism, and xenophobia.

Just as early black feminists invoked Malcolm's legacy to critique mainstream feminism and black nationalism, contemporary black feminists and womanists have refined his method of critical analysis and have maintained his uncompromising commitment to social justice. Their radical critiques of American political culture and social practice continue to mobilize black women around coalition-based political agendas that challenge black and brown, men and women to engage the radical praxis that oppressed people need now.[28]

For black women in general, and poor black women in particular, the struggle is immense. For instance, there is a worldwide epidemic of violence against women that disproportionately threatens women of color. Domestic abuse, limited access to health care, lack of education, and poverty as well as displacement due to war, famine, political violence, and environmental degradation terrorize women and children in the United States and in many countries around the world. Despite deteriorating social conditions, black women are struggling to raise black boys to equate manhood with strength rather than domination and with leadership rather than exploitation. Similarly, black women continue to struggle against their representation as sexual commodities rather than as human beings. The challenges faced by black women amply illustrate the need for women's voices to extend Malcolm's prodigious legacy. This enterprise requires black women to understand his life and the lives of the women who supported him. It also requires that we understand Malcolm's gender contradictions in light of the manifold complications of racism and the complexities of black culture that have evolved in opposition to race supremacy and patriarchal dominance. Without getting stuck in the political miseries and misadventures of the past, black activists can adapt the insights of Malcolm X and his descendents to help black women affirm standards of black womanhood that are sensual, full of potential, and open to loving relationships.

Conclusion: lighting the fire, right now

Black nationalism is one important aspect of an African American epistemology. The nationalist analysis of social divisions that threaten national security, undermine world economies, and deny prospects for peace continues to be relevant in today's globalizing world. Yet, just as in Malcolm X's time, the dominant political culture in America is likely to ignore, dismiss, subjugate, or misrepresent black radical thought. The controversy over the relationship between Barack Obama, the first African American President, and the Reverend Dr. Jeremiah A. Wright, his former pastor, is a case in point.

Wright, the pastor emeritus of Trinity United Church of Christ in Chicago, became a very controversial figure in presidential election politics when video clips of some of his sermons that were critical of United States race relations and foreign policy were posted on *YouTube*. Senator Obama's political opposition tried to use his twenty-year membership at Trinity Church to discredit him during the primary campaign. At the height of the controversy, news outlets repeatedly aired sound bites from one of Wright's sermons that seemed to indict America for contributing to the international climate of violence that resulted in the terrorist attack on September 11, 2001. Members of the religious establishment rushed to either defend or condemn Wright while some media pundits branded his remarks as racially divisive and anti-American. After weeks of speculation, intrigue, and folderol over Wright, his sermons, his church, and the black church in general, Obama denounced Wright's comments and eventually resigned his membership at Trinity Church. His decision quelled the controversy and Obama made history by winning the Democratic nomination for President of the United States and going on to become the nation's forty-fourth president.[29]

As I watched the media frenzy surrounding the Reverend Dr. Wright and Senator Obama I was struck not so much by Obama's connection to Wright but rather by Wright's connection to Malcolm X. To explore Wright's work as a contemporary example of Malcolm X's political philosophy, I reread his collection of sermons in *What Makes You so Strong?* The sermons may be understood to show that Jeremiah Wright is an intellectual descendent of Malcolm X, a man who was himself politically descended from historical figures including David Walker, Marcus Garvey, Franz Fanon, Amilcar Cabral, and other black nationalist thinkers.[30] For the most part, the media coverage of the national debate over Wright's sermons did not suggest a significant link between Malcolm X's legacy and Reverend Wright's ministry, and did not emphasize that the work of black theologians and religious historians could have informed the discussions about black theology and the black church.[31] Unfortunately, the media's mantra about Wright's anti-Americanism allowed the public to dismiss his perspective without serious consideration. Most Americans were unwilling and unprepared to examine Wright's claims or to use them as the basis for an ongoing and much needed dialogue about race in America. Meanwhile, Obama needed to end the flap that could have derailed his candidacy, so he delivered an important speech that challenged us to look beyond our racial differences and come together as Americans for the common good.[32] The speech and his resignation from the church reassured some Americans about electing Obama.

People can disagree with Wright's sermons or with his comments in response to the criticism he received, or with the tone or timing of his explanations about his remarks, or with a host of other issues raised by the controversy. Nonetheless, when reading Wright one encounters a faith-based nationalist critique of American culture that invites serious discussion about race and black radicalism. From this standpoint, the Wright controversy was a missed opportunity. Arguably, American democracy needs Wright's radicalism, just as the country needed the nationalist critiques of Malcolm X. Only when all Americans are willing to examine their perspectives on race and to engage in discourse that challenges their values, assumptions, and biases can the nation even hope to genuinely move beyond its divisions.[33]

Black women can draw on the power of radical thought to actively oppose social and economic conditions that threaten us or our families and communities. In a sermon titled 'When You Forget Who You Are', Wright gives an activist interpretation of the biblical story of Esther to make a similar point. Recounting Esther's background as Hadassah, a refugee from Jerusalem who became a Babylonian queen, Wright compares her situation with black people who fully assimilate into the dominant culture. As queen, Esther was part of Babylonian society and had such high status that she almost failed to act after her husband was manipulated into approving an order to annihilate her people. Wright's sermon explains that Mordecai, Esther's adopted father, had to remind Esther of her real heritage because she was the only person uniquely positioned to intervene. Wright emphasizes that Esther had to execute a radical plan and risk her position to succeed. Although a womanist interpretation of Esther's story would critique the gender inequality at the core of Esther's position in Babylonian society, he uses her story to caution black people to remember their racial heritage and not to be afraid of taking radical action on behalf of the masses of black people who remain oppressed.[34] Like the biblical Esther, black women, despite their varied personal experiences, can claim a shared historical legacy, one that positions them to champion the cause of oppressed people.

As a new generation of black women political activists develops new strategies and tactics for political action, the hope is that they will continue to be inspired by Malcolm's life, by the evolution of his thinking, and by the women who supported his efforts as well as by those activists, intellectuals, pastors, and theologians who continue to advance his legacy.

NOTES

1. For examples see Michelle Wallace, *Black Macho and the Myth of the Superwoman* (New York: Dial Press, 1978); Audre Lorde, *Sister Outsider: Essays and Speeches* (Berkeley: Crossing Press, 1984); bell hooks, *Ain't I a Woman: Black Women and Feminism* (Boston: South End Press, 1981); bell hooks, *Yearning: Race, Gender, and Cultural Politics* (Boston: South End Press, 1990); Angela Y. Davis, "Meditations on the Legacy of Malcolm X," in *Malcolm X: In Our Own Image*, ed. Joe Wood (New York: St. Martin's Press, 1992), pp. 36–47; Patricia Hill Collins, "Learning to Think for Ourselves: Malcolm X's Black Nationalism Reconsidered," in Wood, *Malcolm X: In Our Own Image*, pp. 59–86; and Barbara Ransby, *Ella Baker and the Black Freedom Movement: A Radical Democratic Vision* (Durham: North Carolina University Press, 1993).

2. Maya Angelou, *Heart of a Woman* (New York: Random House, 1981), pp. 196–200; Maya Angelou, *All God's Children Need Traveling Shoes* (New York: Random House, 1986), pp. 180–1; Alice Walker, *Good Night, Willie Lee, I'll see You in the Morning* (New York: Dial Press, 1975); Sonia Sanchez, *Homegirls and Handgrenades* (New York: Thunder Mouth Press, 1997); and Amanda Davis, "To Build a Nation: Black Women Writers, Black Nationalism, and Violent Reduction of Wholeness," *Frontiers: A Journal of Women Studies*, 25.3 (2004), pp. 24–53.

3. Tracye A. Mathews, "No One Ever Asks What a Man's Role in the Revolution Is: Gender Politics and Leadership in the Black Panther Party 1966–71," in *Sisters in the Struggle*, ed. Bettye Collier Thomas and V. P. Franklin (New York: New York University Press, 2004), pp. 230–56; and Farah Jasmine Griffin, "Ironies of the Saint: Malcolm X, Black Women and the Price of Protection," in ibid., pp. 214–29.

4. Robert E. Terrill, *Malcolm X: Inventing Radical Judgment* (East Lansing: Michigan State University Press, 2004); Louis A. DeCaro, Jr., *On the Side of My People: A Religious Life of Malcolm X* (New York: New York University Press, 1996); and Michael Eric Dyson, *Making Malcolm: The Myth and Meaning of Malcolm X* (New York: Oxford University Press, 1995). See dissertation titles listed at www.brothermalcolm.net/research/dissertations.html. For 2000–7, ten dissertations where Malcolm X is one of the subjects of the research are listed in US dissertations abstracts.

5. James H. Cone, *Martin & Malcolm & America: A Dream or a Nightmare* (Maryknoll, NY: Orbis Books, 1991); Celeste Michelle Condit and John Louis Lucaites, "Malcolm X and the Limits of Rhetoric of Revolutionary Dissent," *Journal of Black Studies*, 33.2 (1993), pp. 291–313; Reiland Rabaka, "Malcolm X and/as Critical Theory: Philosophy, Radical Politics, and the African American Search for Social Justice," *Journal of Black Studies*, 33.1 (2002), pp. 145–65; Kerry P. Owens, "The Dual Voices of the Civil Rights Movement: The Heroic Narration of Martin Luther King, Jr. and Malcolm X" (Ph.D. diss. Louisiana State University/ Agricultural and Mechanical College, Baton Rouge, LA, 1995); and Regina Jennings, "Cheikh Anta Diop, Malcolm X, and Haki Madhubuti: Claiming and Containing Continuity in Black Language and Institutions," *Journal of Black Studies*, 33.1 (2002), pp. 126–44.

6. There are dozens of Malcolm X websites. For examples that provide research quality information, see Abdul Alkalimat (ed.), *Malcolm X: A Research Site*, www.brothermalcolm.net. See also the estate of Malcolm X, *The Official Website of Malcolm X*, ww.cmgww.com/historic/malcolm/home.php; and the official website of The Nation of Islam, www.noi.org. Other interesting sites include: *The Smoking Gun: The Malcolm X Files*, www.thesmokinggun.com/malcolmX/malcolmX.html; and *Malcolm-X.it*, www.malcolm-x.it/en/directory.htm.

7. A notable exception is Jeffrey B. Leak's essay in this volume.

8. Rodnell P. Collins and A. Peter Bailey, *The Seventh Child: A Family Memoir of Malcolm X* (New York: Kensington Publishing, 1998), pp. 48–69.

9. Malcolm X and Alex Haley, *The Autobiography of Malcolm X* (1965; London: Penguin Books, 2001), p. 302. For a discussion of the life and work of Mother Clara Muhammad, see Roberta Ross, *Witnessing and Testifying: Black women, Religion, and Civil Rights* (Minneapolis: Fortress Press, 2003).

10. Russell J. Rickford, *Betty Shabazz: Surviving Malcolm X* (Naperville, IL: Sourcebooks, 2003), pp. 48, 203.

11. Ibid., p. 263.

12. Malcolm X, *Autobiography*, pp. 80–1.

13. William Strickland and Cheryll Y. Greene, *Malcolm X: Make It Plain* (New York: Viking Press, 1994), p. 16, 26; Judy Richardson and James Turner, "Malcolm X: Make It Plain: The Documentary and Book as Educational Materials," in *Teaching Malcolm X*, ed. Theresa Perry (New York: Routledge, 1996); and Ilyasah Shabazz with Kim McLarin, *Growing Up X: A Memoir by the Daughter of Malcolm X* (New York: Ballantine Books, 2002), p. 53.

14. DeCaro, *On the Side*, p. 79.

15. Malcolm X, *Autobiography*, p. 114; Collins and Bailey, *Seventh Child*, p. 64.

16. Ronald Takaki, *Iron Cages: Race and Culture in Nineteenth-Century America* (Oxford: Oxford University Press, 1990), pp. 114–17.

17. Malcolm X, *Autobiography*, pp. 242–3.

18. Ibid., pp. 326–7, 328; Rickford, *Betty Shabazz*, p. 48.

19. Myrlie Evers-Williams, "Foreward," in Rickford, *Betty Shabazz*, p. ix.

20. To understand Shirley Graham Du Bois and her contributions to race and gender equality, see Gerald Home, *Race Woman: The Lives of Shirley Graham DuBois* (New York: New York University Press, 2000).

21. Malcolm X, *Malcolm X Speaks*, ed. George Breitman (New York: Pathfinder Press, 1965), pp. 133–5.

22. Raewyn W. Connell, *Masculinities* (Berkeley: University of California Press, 1995), pp. 204–5; and Jay C. Wade, "African American Men's Gender Role Conflict: The Significance of Racial Identity," *Sex Roles*, 34.1–2 (1996), pp. 17–33.

23. For a didactic definition of black power, see Kwame Ture (Stokely Carmichael) and Charles V. Hamilton, *Black Power: The Politics of Liberation* (1962; reprint, New York: Vintage Press, 1992).

24. Ward Churchill and Jim Vander Wall, *The COINTELPRO Papers: Documents from the FBI's Secret Wars Against Dissent in the United States* (Boston: South End Press, 1990), pp. 91–165; Joy James, *Transcending the Talented Tenth: Black Leaders and American Intellectuals* (London: Routledge, 1997) pp. 101–14; and

Manning Marable, *Race, Reform and Rebellion: The Second Reconstruction of Black America, 1945–1982* (New York: Palgrave Macmillan, 1984).

25. Ruth-Marion Baruch and Pirkle Jones, *Black Panthers 1968* (Los Angeles: Greybull Press, 2002), p. 18; Philip Foner (ed.), *The Black Panthers Speak* (Philadelphia: Lippincott Company, 1970), pp. 146–50.

26. Kimberly Springer, *Living for the Revolution: Black Feminist Organizations 1968–1980* (Durham, NC: Duke University Press, 2005), pp. 2–43.

27. Haki R. Madhubuti, *Black Men: Obsolete, Single, Dangerous?* (Chicago: Third World Press, 1990), p. 16.

28. Rebecca Walker, "Foreword: We Are Using This Power to Resist," in *The Fire This Time: Young Activists and the New Feminism*, ed. Vivien Labaton and Dawn Lundy Martin (New York: Anchor Books, 2004), pp. xi–xx. This book contains a list of feminist organizations that the authors want to promote.

29. A video of Wright's sermon is available here: www.youtube.com/watch? v=9yq055NAsrQ. On March 14, the day after Wright's sermons were featured on ABC's *Good Morning America*, Obama posted a response at the widely read "Huffington Post" blog, in which he stated, in part, that he "vehemently" disagreed with, "strongly" condemned, and in sum "rejected outright the statements by Rev. Wright that are at issue." Barack Obama, "On My Faith and My Church," www.huffingtonpost.com/barack-obama/on-my-faith-and-my-church_b_91623. html. Ronald Kessler, a NewsMax.com political writer, represented the views of many of Obama's critics when he referred to Obama as "a candidate who claims to be a unifier and yet he belongs to a church where they specialize in denouncing whites." "Under Pressure, Obama Prepares for Race and Unity Speech," March 17, 2008, elections.foxnews.com/2008/03/17/under-pressure-obama-prepares-for-race-and-unity-speech.

30. Jeremiah A. Wright, Jr., *What Makes You So Strong?: Sermons of Joy and Strength*, ed. Jini Kilgore Ross (Valley Forge, PA: Judson Press, 1993). See also Franz Fanon, *The Wretched of the Earth* (New York: Grove Press, 1968); Amilcar Cabral, *Return to the Source: Selected Speeches of Amilcar Cabral* (New York: Monthly Review Press, 1973) and Anna Hartnell, "Between Exodus and Egypt: Malcolm X, Islam, and The 'Natural' Religion of the Oppressed," European Journal of American Culture, 27.3 (2008): 207–225.

31. Notables such as C. Eric Lincoln, James Cone, and Delores Williams, among others were barely referenced and the sound-bite discussions of black theology could hardly be described as a nuanced interpretation of black nationalism and faith. See C. Eric Lincoln, *Race, Religion and the Continuing America Dilemma* (New York: Hill and Wang, 1984); James H. Cone, *Black Theology and Black Power* (New York: Harper and Row, 1969); and Delores S. Williams, *Sisters in the Wilderness: The Challenge of Womanist God-Talk* (Maryknoll, NY: Orbis Books, 1993).

32. Barack Obama, "A More Perfect Union," www.americanrhetoric.com/speeches/barackobamaperfectunion.htm.

33. Terrill, *Malcolm X*, pp. 154–6.

34. Wright, *What Makes You So Strong?*, pp. 61–75.

6

JAMES SMETHURST

Malcolm X and the Black Arts Movement

Malcolm X exerted a profound and complex influence on the Black Arts Movement, the network of politically engaged African American artists and arts institutions during the 1960s and 1970s that poet, playwright, critic and activist Larry Neal termed the "aesthetic and spiritual sister of the Black Power concept."[1] Malcolm X served as inspiration, icon, model, polemicist, theorist, and adviser to the movement, especially in its formative years in the early and middle 1960s, despite the fact that he rarely discussed the arts in any great specificity in his public speeches – at least until his break from Elijah Muhammad and the Nation of Islam and the formation of the Organization of Afro-American Unity. For some Black Arts and Black Power activists, Malcolm X was a relatively distant, though commanding figure, often coming to them through the mass media, especially television and radio. However, for many others, especially in such early Black Arts Movement centers as New York, Philadelphia, Detroit, Boston, Chicago, and Oakland, he was a much more personal presence, a leader who always seemed to have time to talk to and take an interest in grassroots people. This engagement with the grassroots in turn strengthened Malcolm X's longstanding interest in African American culture, making it a central part of the program of the Organization of Afro-American Unity – which in turn further influenced radical black arts activists, such as Amiri Baraka, Gwendolyn Brooks, Etheridge Knight, Larry Neal, Sonia Sanchez, and Askia Touré and promoted the rise of cultural nationalism as a powerful, organized tendency within the Black Power movement.

One aspect of the impact of Malcolm X on the Black Arts Movement that is sometimes underestimated is the frame and platform that the Nation of Islam provided him, however much he would come to feel constrained by the limits that it and its leader Elijah Muhammad placed on him. Revolutionaries are frequently attracted to countries and even organizations that embody some version of what a revolutionary society in the United States might resemble, even if they find that those countries and organizations fall short of their dreams in important aspects. Over the years, black Marxists of various stripes, for example, saw in the Soviet Union, the People's Republic of China, socialist Cuba, and Nkrumah's Ghana manifest confirmation that, despite their short-comings, another world was possible. Similarly, not only did the theology of Elijah Muhammad and the Nation imagine an Afrocentric (or perhaps more accurately an Afro-Asiatic-centric) world order and cosmic destiny, the Nation of Islam's physical presence, its discipline, the visual impact of its members, its penchant for building spiritual and secular institutions (mosques, barber-shops, bakeries, grocery stores, the University of Islam, the newspaper *Muhammad Speaks*, and so on) had not been seen in a black nationalist organization since the heyday of the Garvey movement concretely demon-strated what a society run by black people in the United States might be, that it could be – even if, again, many did not find the relatively conservative social and cultural mores of the Nation uniformly attractive. As one observer noted, "The thing that would attract you right away with Malcolm and his group was the appearance and the discipline. They were the best-looking group you could find out there on the street."[2] This sort of politics of embodying visually and institutionally a political and cultural alternative society not only marked, as one might expect, the efforts of radical black artists, but also nationalist political organizations ranging from the revolutionary nationalist Black Panther Party for Self-Defense to the cultural nationalist US organization of Maulana Karenga. In short, as Larry Neal pointed out, the initial power of Malcolm X's words and individual image was closely related to his identity as the most prominent public spokesperson of what Neal called "the womb of the Nation of Islam" and the very visible leader of the organization in Harlem, where his ability to direct thousands of disciplined Nation members did much to establish his reputation in the larger community:

> Through Malcolm, the Nation of Islam effected a more open discussion of identity – a subject that had always been a part of our ideological continuum. But not since Garvey had anyone proposed organizing around identity on a mass scale. And most important, no one in our generation had proposed this identity to be distinct and *separate*.[3]

Of course, much of Malcolm X's effectiveness as a spokesperson and theorist-activist-leader in his own right had to do with his verbal style and his mastery of the sonic cadences and visual intricacies of generations of black popular culture as well as "mainstream" mass culture:

> Then we began to hear Malcolm, the black voice skating and bebopping like a righteous saxophone solo – mellow truths inspired by the Honorable Elijah Muhammad, but shaped out of Malcolm's own style, a style rooted in black folk memory, and the memory of his Garveyite father. We could dig Malcolm because the essential vectors of his style were more closely related to our own

urban experiences. He was the first black leader, in our generation, to resurrect all of the strains of black nationalism lurking within us.[4]

In other words, much of Malcolm X's appeal was his consummate ability to operate in and combine a dizzying array of black rhetorical styles. Though he had left his past as a criminal, hustler, hipster, prison inmate, and denizen of the urban demimonde far behind, he communicated enough of the feeling and style of the city as to make him particularly attractive to the young black artists and intellectuals who in the main came from the urban black working class that had come to increasingly dominate the African American community after 1940.

A particularly important part of the emergence of Malcolm X as a national figure was his adeptness in negotiating the mass media, especially television and radio – somewhat ironically, perhaps, he may have been the first major political spokesperson to fully realize the potential of talk radio long before the conservative surge in that medium. As Amiri Baraka noted, many Black Arts Movement activists first encountered Malcolm X through television programs and debates, especially the 1959 Mike Wallace documentary *The Hate That Hate Produced*:

> One night I saw Malcolm lay waste completely to Kenneth Clark, Constance Baker Motley, and some other assorted house Negroes, just as he had wasted David Susskind and Mike Wallace. (The Wallace program, "The Hate that Hate Produced," had shot Malcolm X and the Nation into the public eye.) This kind of thing would thrill me so completely because Malcolm said things that had gone through my mind but he was giving voice to. Or he'd say things and instantly it'd make sense or confirm something I'd not even thought but felt.[5]

Part of the thrill of these programs was watching Malcolm X demolish white liberal journalists and talk-show hosts who made the racist assumption that their experience in the television medium, their articulateness, and their reasoned moderation would allow them to dominate a vitriolic black demagogue. Quite a few Black Arts Movement participants report their particular pleasure in the moment when Malcolm X's opponents in these debates came to realize that he was far more intelligent, prepared, and skilled in these situations than they – a realization that frequently showed in their faces and their demeanor to the delight of many black viewers. As Peter Goldman, a journalist who wrote extensively about Malcolm X and went on to become a senior editor at *Newsweek*, pointed out, "Malcolm was, I think, the first master of the sound byte."[6]

In short, Malcolm's intellectual sharpness, his ability to outmaneuver white (and black) antagonists on what was ostensibly their own ground, his artistry with language in a range of black modalities drew many of the young black artists to him because he provided a model of how one might be a black man and artist-intellectual and still be grounded in the African American community. Like many artists and intellectuals in the United States, many of these artists felt isolated from the people among whom they had grown up, often living in bohemian communities of similarly alienated white, Latina/o, and Asian American artists. They sensed that most people in the United States saw the pursuits of poetry, visual arts, avant-garde theater, free jazz, and so on, to be marginal at best and, in the case of male artists, essentially unmanly. As a result, Malcolm X's stance as a radical leader whose mass appeal and masculinity were uncompromised by his emphasis on the intellect and education and his deep interest in culture (and without macho posturing) was even more attractive to young people who would form the Black Arts Movement than to the general black population.

In addition to the powerful impact Malcolm X made through the mass media was the more personal influence he exerted in many of the early centers of the Black Arts Movement. He took an intense interest in the minutia of black life, particularly grassroots civil rights activity. Despite his fame, demands on his time, and threats to his life, particularly after his public break with Elijah Mohammad and the Nation of Islam in 1964, he took the time to talk with rank-and-file activists and community members, many of whom went on to participate in one or another aspect of the Black Arts Movement. For example, the poet and playwright Sonia Sanchez recalls going to hear Malcolm X at a street rally while she was working with the Congress of Racial Equality (CORE) in Harlem. She approached him after the rally and told him that she liked some of the things she heard and disagreed with others. He listened to her carefully (and over the objections of his bodyguards) and suggested she would come to agree with his positions (and those of the Nation) without dismissing her and her points.[7]

He spoke in an enormous variety of venues and events (such as the one at which Sonia Sanchez heard him) from the plain to the prominent, including the stretch of Harlem's 125th Street at Seventh Avenue (now Adam Clayton Powell Boulevard) in front of Lewis Micheaux's National Memorial African Bookstore, famed as a spot for street orators. As the Asian American radical and friend of Malcolm X, Yuri Kochiyama (who cradled him after he was shot down at the Audubon Ballroom in New York City in 1965) noted, he was likely to appear anywhere, at rallies, trials, and so on, involving black people. This ability and willingness to listen to, and even seek out grassroots people as well as his powers of personal persuasion not only moved these people toward nationalism, but also helped forge a network of ideologically diverse militants dedicated to black political self-determination.

Another facet of this individual appeal and Malcolm X's efforts at network-ing was his conscious efforts to reach out to more and less well-known political activists, especially socially engaged artists and intellectuals and popular cul-ture figures whose profiles and politics might make them unlikely friends of the Nation of Islam – at least if one were only familiar with the relatively-conservative black capitalist ideology of Elijah Muhammad. In part, this might be due to his longtime interest in popular music, dance, and the arts, which was most obvious during his pre-Nation hipster-criminal life in Boston and New York. While in most respects he left this life behind after he joined the Nation of Islam, he continued to seek out major black popular-culture figures. The most publicized of these was unquestionably Muhammad Ali, but he was also close to such pop stars as the singer Sam Cooke (whose "A Change Is Gonna to Come" was played at Malcolm X's funeral) and the football running back (and later film star) Jim Brown. Malcolm X as both personality and polemicist also struck a deep chord among jazz musicians, many of whom were attracted to Islam, especially Ahmadiyya Islam, even before the Nation of Islam was much in the public view.

Malcolm X also reached out to veterans of earlier waves of nonnationalist (or only semi-nationalist) black radicalism, especially the black intelligentsia of Harlem and Chicago that had come out of the African American cultural and political circles of the Communist Left, even though the Communist Party as an organization (unlike the Trotskyist Socialist Workers Party) remained largely hostile to his political stance. For example, he attended the funeral of Lorraine Hansberry, herself a longtime, if relatively young leftist, in 1965, at which Paul Robeson gave a eulogy. Later Malcolm X, an admirer of Robeson, approached Ossie Davis about arranging a meeting with the actor-singer-activist and most prominent black victim of McCarthyism. While this did not happen because of Malcolm X's assassination, it indicates not only his openness to links with such figures of largely secular radicalism, but also his initiative in seeking them out. Of course, his relationships with such stalwarts of the cultural world of the old Harlem Left as Davis (whose eulogy on Malcolm X, "Our Shining Prince," remains a classic commentary), Ruby Dee, Maya Angelou, writer, editor, and historian John Henrik Clarke, writer Julian Mayfield (one of Malcolm X's hosts during his visit to Ghana), and Shirley Graham DuBois, demonstrate his networking in this regard (as well as the openness of many black activists and intellectuals associated with the Communist Left to him) even more concretely. A number of these activists, particularly Clarke, played important roles in the formation of the Organization of Afro-American Unity after Malcolm X's return from Africa, following his break with Elijah Mohammad and the Nation of Islam in 1964.

This radical networking was aided by Malcolm X's willingness to speak under the auspices of left-wing groups, particularly the forums of the Socialist Workers Party, in a time when McCarthyism was still very much alive. While far fewer African Americans, especially artists and intellectuals, had been associated with the Socialist Workers Party than the Communist Party, for a variety of reasons, leading members of the Socialist Workers Party, especially George Breitman, were publicly much more supportive of Malcolm X. This did not lead many young African American artists and intellectuals to join the Socialist Workers Party – or engage much with Trotskyist ideology (except in Detroit). However, these forums not only circulated further Malcolm X's ideas and style in an interracial radical community (and facilitated interactions between the broader radical community and Malcolm X), but also served as a place where political and cultural activists still in the ghetto might meet and network with black bohemians living and working largely outside African American neighborhoods – especially in New York where such a combination of "uptown" and "downtown" militants formed the core of the Black Arts Repertory Theater and School in Harlem after Malcolm X's murder in 1965.

Of course, it was not just how Malcolm X presented himself, but what he said that made such an impact on young black artists and activists. Even here, as Sonia Sanchez recalls, the sense of his speaking widely shared truths to power, of articulating what many black people felt and would discuss in private, but that was rarely articulated so directly in such a variety of public venues, from network television to 125th Street, delighted young African Americans:

> He said it in a very strong, a very manly fashion, one that says, "I am not afraid to say what you've been thinking all these years." That's why we loved him so very much. He said it out loud. Not behind closed doors. He took on America for us.[8]

What was remarkable about Malcolm X's thought, as far as the young militants (and even older radicals such as Ossie Davis, Ruby Dee, Margaret Burroughs, and John Henrik Clarke) were concerned, was his ability to synthesize many strands of African American nationalism with the new internationalism of the anticolonialist movement and the Non-Aligned Movement that grew out of the 1955 Bandung African-Asian Conference organized by the newly independent nations of Africa and Asia. For many of the younger black radicals the Bandung Conference was a declaration of independence from white European and North American political, economic, and cultural domination. Their cry of a "Bandung World" named a moment in which the nationalist vision articulated by Malcolm X was part of an international movement toward liberation and self-determination on the part of the vast majority of the earth's population rather than an extreme position of a relative handful within a "minority" of the United States.

One of the distinctive aspects of Malcolm X's speeches and organizational work, especially in the Organization of Afro-American Unity, was his willingness to engage publicly with various sorts of leftist radicalism in ways that civil rights leaders (even those who like Martin Luther King, Jr. had a history of left sympathies) and many nationalists (especially Elijah Muhammad) avoided in the thin political atmosphere of the Cold War. It was not simply that he was willing to work with largely non-Islamic (and often nonreligious) veterans of the old left. After all, Muhammad did this, too – especially with the staff of *Muhammad Speaks*, which contained a considerable number of Communists and ex-Communists that he hired and long protected. Instead, it was the public interest in and defense of the strains of Marxism and socialism that marked the new nations (or in the case of China and Cuba, perhaps, renewed nations) of Asia, Africa, and Latin America with whom Malcolm felt sympathy and solidarity, recasting and internationalizing "civil rights" as "human rights" and linking those rights with a worldwide struggle against imperialism and for national liberation, perhaps most famously in "The Ballot or The Bullet" speech he gave before a black audience in Cleveland after leaving the Nation of Islam:

> When you expand the civil-rights struggle to the level of human rights, you can then take the case of the black man in this country before the nations in the UN. You can take it before the General Assembly. You can take Uncle Sam before a world court. But the only level you can do it on is the level of human rights … Expand the civil-rights struggle to the level of human rights, take it into the United Nations, where our African brothers can throw their weight on our side, where our Asian brothers can throw their weight on our side, where our Latin-American brothers can throw their weight on our side, and where 800 million Chinamen are sitting there waiting to throw their weight on our side.[9]

Of course, other black radicals had held such positions earlier – and no doubt influenced Malcolm X. Clearly, "The Bullet or the Ballot" owes something to the famous "We Charge Genocide" petition, an indictment of racist oppression, especially legal and extralegal violence against African Americans, presented by Paul Robeson and the Communist leader William Patterson to the United Nations in 1951. Indeed, one might find the antecedent to Malcolm X's willingness to speak publicly what he saw as the truth whatever the personal cost to Robeson's prominent defiance of Cold War pressures which resulted in the destruction of his career and great damage to his physical and mental health, primarily through the efforts of the United States government.

However, Malcolm was able to combine this radicalism with different aspects of black nationalism and an international spirit of independence in a manner that made it new and avoided the baggage that old left groups, including the Communist Party and the Socialist Workers Party, carried. Toward the end of his life he increasingly identified black nationalism with political activism and social revolution. His well-known address to the conference, "Message to the Grassroots," at the largely nationalist (and significantly left) Northern Negro Grass Roots Leadership Conference in Detroit in 1963, proclaimed, "All the revolutions going on in Asia and Africa are based on what? – black nationalism. A revolutionary is a black nationalist. He wants a nation … If you're afraid of black nationalism, you're afraid of revolution. And if you love revolution, you love black nationalism."[10]

Malcolm X also updated the old Communist notion of a "Black Belt nation" in the rural South that the Nation of Islam had adopted. He altered what might be thought of as a variant on the Bolshevik "Land to the Tiller" slogan to something like "Land to Those Who Live on It." In other words, his was a far more urban conception of nationhood than either that of the Communist Party in the 1930s or the Nation, encompassing black political, economic, cultural, and spiritual control of African American communities and suggesting a vision of liberated city-states that exerted an enormous influence on Black Arts activists, including (and especially) Amiri Baraka:

> Black people are a race, a culture, a Nation. The legacy of Malcolm X is that we know we can move from where we are. Our land is where we live. (Even the Muslims have made this statement about Harlem.) If we are a separate Nation, we must make that separateness where we are. There are Black cities all over this white nation. Nations within nations.[11]

As Baraka suggests here, one obvious conclusion drawn from the position that African Americans constitute a nation is that they have a distinct culture, one that needs to be strengthened and developed in ways that reinforces its independence from "white" culture. Again, late in his life, and perhaps influenced through his contact with younger nationalists, Malcolm X saw this culture as African at base and advocated a reclamation and renewal of this base through a migration back to Africa "culturally, philosophically, and psychologically, while remaining here physically, the spiritual bond that would develop between us and Africa through this cultural, philosophical and psychological migration would enhance our position here, because we would have our contacts with them acting as roots or foundations between us."[12] In keeping with Malcolm X's understanding and adroitness in negotiating the mass media, he also suggested that this migration would not simply entail the adoption of African aesthetics, attitudes, and mores, but also involve the recapturing and recasting of popular culture images and meanings of Africa:

> Having complete control over Africa, the colonial powers of Europe projected the image of Africa negatively. They always project Africa in a negative light: jungle savages, cannibals, nothing civilized. Why then naturally it was so negative that it was negative to you and me, and you and I began to hate it. We didn't want anyone calling us Africans. In hating Africa and in hating the Africans, we ended up hating ourselves, without even realizing it. You can't hate your origin and not end up hating yourself. You can't hate Africa and not hate yourself.[13]

It is worth noting that the vision of African culture projected here and elsewhere in Malcolm X's late speeches is not very specific. Even in the "Statement of Basic Aims and Objectives of the Organization of Afro-American Unity" and the "Basic Unity Program Organization of Afro-American Unity" there is not much concrete about what such a migration might entail other than language study. In short, Malcolm X set out a cultural project rather than a program – one that inspired and authorized a wide range of responses in the Black Arts Movement and the Black Power movement.

This sort of call to action, to begin a project rather than to impose a minutely defined program or ideology, characterized the later statements of Malcolm X and the Organization of Afro-American Unity on culture – again, reflecting, perhaps, a sense of the dynamic spectrum of African American cultural activity already under way in the United States in the early 1960s. For example, its "Statement of Basic Aims" proposed: "We must work toward the establishment of a cultural center in Harlem, which will include people of all ages, and will conduct workshops in all the arts, such as film, creative writing, painting, theater, music, Afro-American History, etc."[14] While there is some specificity about the general activities of this center, little is said about the method and content of these workshops. Still, it provided a call that Malcolm X was prevented from answering himself by his assassination.

However, his death prompted the founding of crucial early Black Arts Movement institutions, as his assassination took the name and image of Malcolm X as political and cultural icon to a much higher level. The murder motivated Amiri Baraka, Larry Neal, Sonia Sanchez, Askia Touré, and others to answer the Organization of Afro-American Unity call for a cultural center in Harlem with the establishment of the Black Arts Repertory Theater and School as a center of radical education and performance. The Black Power activist, leader of the Revolutionary Action Movement, and historian Muhammad Ahmad recalls that he and Baraka discussed what should be done in the aftermath of the assassination. He suggested to Baraka that he work to fulfill that call. Though internal conflicts and external pressures led to the theater group's short life – less than a year – Baraka, Neal, Sanchez, *et al.*, saw themselves and it as the vanguard of a national arts movement, and were taken as such by militant black cultural workers around the United States, inspiring the growth of groups such as Black Arts West in San Francisco, Black Arts West in Seattle, the Black House in San Francisco, and BLKARTSOUTH in New Orleans. While radical arts groups and institutions, and, increasingly, radical black nationalist arts groups and institutions, had been founded in the years immediately preceding the establishment of the Black Arts Repertory Theater and School, it was the sense of heralding a movement that grew out of the tighter networking of existing institutions and the creation of new ones that distinguished it from its predecessors, even those such as the journal *Liberator* and the Du Sable Museum which outlived it. Again, it was the energy released by Malcolm X's death, the sense that something had to be done, that impelled the Black Arts Movement forward as an identifiable, if not completely coherent, movement.

Malcolm X, especially after his death, also became one of the most frequently invoked figures in work by Black Arts Movement artists – as well as by older black artists on the periphery of the movement (e.g. the poets Margaret Walker and Margaret Danner) and even some who were at times hostile to it (e.g. the poet Robert Hayden). Only John Coltrane, for example, rivaled Malcolm X as the subject for Black Arts Movement poetry. The poetic response to the murder was so pronounced, in fact, that it led to the first book project of the premiere Black Arts Movement publishing house, Broadside Press of Detroit, *For Malcolm*, edited by its founder and publisher Dudley Randall and writer-artist, initiator of Chicago's Du Sable Museum, and longtime left activist Margaret Burroughs. It was conceived after discussion among Randall, Burroughs, and Margaret Walker at the 1966 Fisk Negro Writers Conference about the plethora of new poems about Malcolm X after his death. The writers contributing to the anthology are, for the most part, a mixture of older African American poets, including Walker, Hayden, Brooks, and Danner (many of whom, like Burroughs herself, came of age in the Popular Front in the Midwest), and younger black poets, such as Baraka, Sanchez, Haki Madhubuti, and Larry Neal who, though often with some past left connections, were closely linked to the emerging nationalist movements. It is a truly national anthology with a range of poets from the East and West Coasts and, to a lesser extent, the South. Far more than Amiri Baraka and Larry Neal's *Black Fire* (1968), an anthology that some scholars have taken to be a précis of early Black Arts, *For Malcolm* attempts to bridge the generations and eras of political activism while maintaining a militant, nationalist stance. In short, the earlier anthology represented a major step in the transformation of Broadside from an occasional publisher of poetry broadsides to the literary backbone of the Black Arts Movement, issuing dozens of titles (many times the number of books of black poetry issued by "mainstream" publishers in the decade before 1965) and putting hundreds of thousands of volumes into circulation.

In short, Malcolm X provided a model of how one might be an intellectual and an artist (especially an artist with language) and a political radical and still be rooted in the African American community. He presented a vision of black freedom that was linked to generations of black radicalism (especially, but not solely black nationalism) and to the new liberation movements and the new independent nations of Africa and Asia. While his adeptness in using various mass media, often in situations designed to demonize and discredit him, the Nation of Islam, and black nationalism generally, brought his words and image to millions of black (and white, Latina/o, and Asian American) people, much of his impact on the Black Arts Movement also derived from his personal interactions with grassroots artists and activists (and artist-activists), as he mentored and encouraged them. At the same time, these interactions also marked his political evolution as culture and the arts became a larger public concern for him in his post-Nation period and for the Organization of Afro-American Unity. While he did not outline what a new (or recovered) liberated black culture would look like in any detail, he issued a call for a movement to develop such a culture, one that at base was closely tied to African culture and modes of thought. Again, Malcolm X's death prevented him personally from pursuing this cultural revolution to any great extent. Still, that death catalyzed the creation of a host of Black Arts Movement institutions that engendered a much intensified sense of a national movement and a plethora of groups and ideological stances, from revolutionary nation-alists to cultural nationalists, who in their various (and sometimes conflicting) ways sought to answer Malcolm X's challenge.

NOTES

1. Larry Neal, *Visions of a Liberated Future: Black Arts Movement Writings* (New York: Thunder's Mouth Press, 1989), p. 62.
2. William Strickland and Cheryll Y. Greene, *Malcolm X: Make It Plain* (New York: Viking, 1994), p. 101.
3. Larry Neal, "New Space/The Growth of Black Consciousness in the Sixties," in *The Seventies*, ed. Floyd B. Barbour (Boston: Porter Sargent, 1970), pp. 19–20.
4. Ibid., p. 19.
5. Amiri Baraka (LeRoi Jones), *The Autobiography of LeRoi Jones* (Chicago: Lawrence Hill, 1997), p. 274.
6. Strickland and Greene, *Make It Plain*, p. 134.
7. Ibid., p. 74.

8. Ibid., p. 231.
9. Malcolm X, *Malcolm X Speaks*, ed. George Breitman (New York: Pathfinder Press, 1965), p. 35.
10. Ibid., p. 10.
11. Amiri Baraka (LeRoi Jones), *Home* (New York: Morrow, 1966), p. 248.
12. Malcolm X, *Malcolm X Speaks*, p. 210.
13. Ibid., p. 169.
14. George Breitman, *The Last Year of Malcolm X* (New York: Pathfinder Press, 1967), p. 111.

7

ANGELA D. DILLARD

Malcolm X and African American conservatism

As a child of the Civil Rights movement, I find it amazing to wake up and find that a black neoconservative Supreme Court justice named Clarence Thomas has suddenly become the symbolic guardian of racial justice in America. And as if that weren't amazing enough, it turns out that Clarence Thomas's erstwhile hero is, was, or has been none other than Malcolm X.
Patricia J. Williams, "Clarence X, Man of the People"

There are at least two ways of considering the relationship between Malcolm X and conservative traditions within African American political and intellectual culture. One involves assessing the ways in which contemporary black conservatives have attempted to write Malcolm X into their intellectual canon, claiming him as one of their own. This approach focuses largely on what might be called the politics of appropriation and draws us into debates – among liberals, leftists, conservatives, nationalists, and others – over who and what can be rightfully regarded as part of Malcolm X's historical legacy. Second only to Martin Luther King, Jr., he is one of the most appropriated figures in African American culture; in being made to stand for so much to so many, his image runs the risk of being reduced to an empty signifier. Yet, many continue to return to this particularly iconic figure for sustenance, insight, and, invariably, legitimation. That some contemporary black conservatives would also assert the right to drink from this replenishing well is hardly surprising.

This is not to suggest, however, that all present-day black conservatives see a positive engagement with Malcolm X's image as desirable. He is less useful to those who adhere to an ideology of color-blindness: the polar opposite, politically, of Malcolm X's black nationalism. Hence, for conservative critics such as Shelby Steele Malcolm X is part of the problem, not the solution. "Black nationalism is a tragedy of white racism," Steele has written, "and can sometimes be as ruinous as the racism itself."[1] The very idea that blackness might be invested with moral significance and used as a foundation for group identity and for group rights is, from this point of view, anathema. Rather, it might be argued that Steele and other "color-blind" conservatives seem to insist that African Americans must pursue the path of greater assimilation into mainstream American culture as individuals and citizens: they must reject a victim status and a victim politics; they must release and be released from an angry rhetorical stance of blame and recrimination against whites; they must, in short, turn their backs on the compensatory image of Malcolm X as a militant (and militaristic), black nationalist revolutionary and stand with their feet planted squarely on American soil.

And African Americans must do most of this work on their own. Many contemporary black conservatives believe in self-help strategies. Sometimes known as "bootstrap" conservatism (as in pulling oneself up by one's own bootstraps), in this version of racial uplift African Americans are urged to rely on private resources and not to depend on state interventions in either law or public policy. As with other variants of modern American conservatism, a large part of this self-help effort is tied to the logic of the free market, and black conservatism becomes coterminous with black capitalism. Given that conservatives tend to disagree over the efficacy of claiming a racial identity, with color-blind conservatives on the one end and conservative nationalists on the other, it is not surprising that they also tend to split over the question of what role race should play in framing self-help doctrines. Self-help might be construed as primarily an individualistic effort, involving oneself and one's family. Or, self-help can be configured as a racial and collective project in which the definition of private, nongovernmental resources is extended to encompass not only families but also neighborhoods and whole communities. Here, race can be seen as an effective and pragmatic tool for unification. In this latter context, Malcolm X's black nationalism, informed by his years as a prominent minister in the Nation of Islam and entrenched in the insistence on black unity and self-sufficiency, emerges as an important touchstone for contemporary conservatives seeking to justify their rendering of this seemingly radical ideology.

Another, and by far more difficult, means of considering the relationship between Malcolm X and African American conservatism involves an exploration of how his beliefs were informed by a distinctive brand of conservatism that resides within historical variants of black nationalism. Because black nationalism – and especially Black Power – is frequently regarded as inherently progressive it is easy to overlook its more conservative and even reactionary elements, particularly in terms of religious expression, moral conventions, and gender relations. Malcolm X was a convert to the black nationalist faith of the Nation of Islam, and as one of their ministers he used that faith to convert hundreds of others. The nature of that faith and the social and political program that it supported, therefore, is among the most important sources for understanding how such an uncompromising antiracist and human rights activist can also be regarded as an equally uncompromising conservative.

Even Shelby Steele has noted that Malcolm X "was a deeply conservative man," a "conservative through and through":

> As a black nationalist, he was a hard-line militarist who believed in the principle of self-mastery through force. His language and thinking in this regard were oddly in line with Henry Kissinger's description of the world as a brutal place in which safety and balance of power is maintained through realpolitik. He was Reaganesque in his insistence on negotiating with whites from a position of strength – meaning the threat of violence. And his commitment (until the last years of his life) to racial purity and separatism would have made him the natural ally of [ex-Klansman and Republican politician] David Duke.[2]

Malcolm X's stance on black self-help and black nationalism, along with his strict adherence to Islamic strictures against alcohol, tobacco and other drugs, adultery and premarital sex, as well as his authoritarian vision of leadership and his patriarchal attitude toward women can all be drawn on to write Malcolm X into the black conservative tradition in America. But we turn first to the question of appropriation.

Appropriating Malcolm X

As contemporary black conservatives aligned with the American right have become an increasingly visible fixture on the political landscape, they have faced intense challenges to their political, and especially racial, credibility. While some scholars point to figures such as Booker T. Washington, Zora Neale Hurston, and George S. Schuyler in acknowledgment that the promotion of conservative perspectives is nothing new in African American history, others tend to regard contemporary black conservatives as, in the harsh words of critic and poet Amiri Baraka, "pods growing in the cellar of our politics."[3] By invoking the pod people from the *Invasion of the Body Snatchers* film, Baraka's intention is to highlight the supposed inauthenticity of black conservatism and indeed of black conservatives themselves. In the face of such hostile assaults not only on their politics but also on their very identities, black conservatives have turned to history as a source of legitimation. In response to the charges that they have no coherent philosophy, no authenticity, and no relevance to African American political culture, black conservatives have sought to substantiate themselves by enlisting prominent historical icons. Some of these iconic figures have been such obvious choices as Booker T. Washington, in many ways the founding figure of black conservatism, and Schuyler, perhaps the preeminent black conservative of the mid-twentieth century, whose 1966 autobiography, *Black and Conservative*, has been regarded as a minor classic in African American letters. Other figures have been more dubious, at least at first glance.

Alan Keyes has been among the best known of the "new" black conservatives who came to prominence in conservative and Republican circles during the Reagan administration (1980–8). As a perennial candidate for high public office, including the presidency in 1996, 2000, and 2008, he has also become a notable presence in American politics. In his *Masters of the Dream: The Strength and Betrayal of Black America* (1995), Keyes draws on a history of values and character – especially the traditions associated with self-help and uplift – as expressed by African American leaders from Washington to Marcus Garvey to Martin Luther King to defend black conservatism and denounce black liberals for sacrificing this empowering past in favor of easy appeals to black anger and victimhood. "In many respects," Keyes writes, "[Booker T.] Washington's approach prefigured the ideas of black separatists, such as Elijah Muhammad." Washington's compromise with segregation arose not from "a willingness to acknowledge or accept black inferiority" but reflected "the traditionally strong black preference for self-sufficiency." Washington parts company with Muhammad, the Nation of Islam, and Malcolm X, however, in his rejection of permanent separation or the establishment of an independent black state believing instead "that economic integration would make it possible to develop self-reliant black communities."[4] Moreover, Keyes is uncompromisingly harsh toward those black leaders, including Louis Farrakhan, current head of the Nation of Islam, who refuse to hew closely to this tradition and who push an agenda premised, in his view, on black victimhood:

> When we talk about issues involving race or conditions among blacks, the old debunked stereotypes of blacks as dehumanized victims still prevail, even among black leaders who surely should know better by now. The problem is that the truth about black values, virtue and character doesn't fit the victim's role that black Americans have been forced to play in order to justify constant expansion of the bureaucratic welfare state. It doesn't fit the passion play of absolute annihilation and national redemption a leader like Farrakhan evokes to appeal to black anger. It doesn't fit the assumption of a white monopoly on traditional virtues that underlies the too-narrow national vision of some conservative thinkers and politicians.[5]

As in the case with most conservatives, regardless of where they fall along the spectrum of conservative ideology, Keyes embraces capitalism and the free market while shunning "dependency" on welfare, affirmative action, and other government handouts. While he does not deny the centrality of race (he is not, that is to say, an advocate of color-blindness), he tends to see the dynamics of racial inequality as the result less of white racism and systemic discrimination than of flaws in the character and culture of blacks, especially the black poor, themselves.

It is in this contentious light that contemporary appeals to the legacy of Malcolm X should be contextualized. Take, for instance, the minor controversy that erupted in the wake of Clarence Thomas's invocation of Malcolm X in the late 1980s and early 1990s. In an interview that formed the basis of journalist Juan Williams's *Atlantic Monthly* profile of Thomas, the future Supreme Court Justice praised Malcolm X for his rejection of integration. "I don't see how the civil rights people today can claim Malcolm X as one of their own," Thomas said. "Where does he say black people should go begging the Labor Department for jobs? He was hell on integrationists. Where does he say you should sacrifice your institutions to be next to white people?"[6] As these remarks resurfaced during the Senate hearings on Thomas's suitability as a de facto replacement for Justice Thurgood Marshall on the nation's highest court, Thomas's long standing regard for Malcolm X was depicted as a form of identity theft by his detractors. Columbia law professor and *Nation* columnist Patricia J. Williams memorably equated Thomas's gesture with a stylized marketing ploy: "Clarence Thomas is to Malcolm X what 'Unforgettable. The perfume. By Revlon' is to Nat King Cole."[7]

Few critics took seriously the idea that Thomas and Malcolm X may indeed possess certain similarities. Yet Thomas was just one of scores of young black men who found themselves reflected in the pages of *The Autobiography of Malcolm X*. As a student at Holy Cross in the late 1960s, Thomas hung a poster of Malcolm X on his dormitory wall and donned a black leather jacket and beret, Black Panther-style. During what he now refers to as his "radical years," he also joined the campus Black Student Union, worked in a Panther-inspired free breakfast program, and marched against the Vietnam War – all while immersing himself in Malcolm X's writings and speeches. This is not to suggest that he became a revolutionary black nationalist. Thomas rejected separatism and kept at least one foot firmly planted in "the white world." But he did find solace and inspiration in Malcolm X's assertion of black manhood and race pride as well as a reaffirmation of the stern lessons in self-reliance taught by the grandfather who raised Thomas in the segregated town of Savannah, Georgia. Thomas's old poster of Malcolm X has been replaced by the portrait of Booker T. Washington that now hangs in his Supreme Court chambers, but he was drawn to – he appropriates – both figures for some of the same underlying reasons.[8]

In a short but intriguing article published in the *Lincoln Review* – the organ of the Lincoln Institute for Education and Research, the nation's oldest black conservative think tank – Bill Kauffman attempts to draw a similar parallel between Thomas and Zora Neale Hurston. While acknowledging that

Thomas's intellectual lineage "threads through Malcolm X, Thomas Jefferson, Booker T. Washington, Richard Wright and Thomas Sowell," he goes on to assert that Thomas's "closest ancestor … is the current darling of multiculturalists and Dead White Male-bashers, the novelist and folklorist Zora Neale Hurston." Described as a "proud daughter of the South, a patriotic black nationalist and a believer in limited constitutional government," there are two additional aspects of Hurston's political identity that emerge as especially appealing for contextualizing contemporary black conservatives. The first is her view of race. She famously claimed not to be "tragically colored," no member of the "sobbing school of Negrohood who hold that nature somehow has given them a lowdown dirty deal and whose feelings are all hurt about it." Second, Hurston is admired for her scorn of the incipient welfare state, "The Little White Father," and for her insistence on individual drive and initiative.[9]

Both aspects of her political thought lead her to denounce the Supreme Court's 1954 *Brown v. Board of Education* ruling as an insult to African Americans for suggesting that blacks want or need closer physical proximity to whites for equality to be made real. "I can see no tragedy," she wrote, "in being too dark to be invited to a white school affair." And she was equally concerned about the court's ruling as government "by fiat." Instead of a sweeping desegregation order, the Court would have done better, she asserts, to concern themselves with improving the quality of black schools, enforcing compulsory education with truant officers, "and looking after conditions in the homes from which the children come." For, ultimately, Hurston holds it as a contradiction to advocate race pride and equality while at the same time "spurning Negro teachers and self-association."[10]

Reading the ideas of contemporary black conservatives such as Thomas through the lens of a historical tradition incorporating figures such as Hurston and Malcolm X is not a matter of simple misappropriation and can indeed help to illuminate the ways in which modern-day black conservatives can plausibly, or at least arguably, claim an organic connection to African American political culture. Clarence Thomas, Alan Keyes, and other black conservatives of a similar stripe are not necessarily illegitimate heirs to Malcolm X and Hurston, not to mention Garvey and other black nationalists. It might be argued that many black conservatives have tended to unite cultural affiliation with African American values with a critique of white racism. Many have supported self-help and individual initiative. Many have scorned an over-reliance, or dependency, on the federal government, and some have castigated blacks themselves for their social and moral failings. But is this enough to regard Malcolm X, in particular, as a black conservative? Is the appropriation of the man by African Americans aligned with the right enough to make him truly one of their own?

Malcolm X as black conservative

The relationship of Malcolm X and African American conservatism need not be exclusively seen as a passive appropriation. Rather, a case can be made for Malcolm X's active embrace of tenets and ideas associated with conservative traditions, particularly those rooted in the Islamic faith of the Nation of Islam as well as in social and economic doctrines of black nationalism stretching back to the nineteenth century. Malcolm X's engagement with black nationalism comes from two sources: first, from his father's identification with Marcus Garvey's Universal Negro Improvement Association,[11] and second, from the Nation of Islam.

Malcolm X was converted to the Nation of Islam in 1948 while still imprisoned and, from then until his final break with it in March 1964, his thinking was defined by his personal and spiritual relationship with the Honorable Elijah Muhammad, the Messenger of Allah, whose authority was unquestioned and divine. Minister Malcolm X viewed his relationship to the Messenger not only in familial terms of father and son but, more dramatically, in the performative language of a ventriloquist and his dummy. "It is my mouth working," he explained to black journalist Louis Lomax, "but the voice is his [Muhammad's]."[12] This substantial part of Minister Malcolm X's life, especially as presented in his *Autobiography*, is a verdant terrain on which black nationalism and black conservatism intersect.

The bulk of the narrative was dictated before Malcolm X's final break with the Nation of Islam and his pilgrimage to Mecca. At Alex Haley's insistence, he agreed not to revise these pre-Mecca sections and therefore they remain a distillation of Malcolm X's interpretation of the philosophy of the Nation and of Elijah Muhammad. They also serve as the main repository of Minister Malcolm X's religious and social thought. Among the more relevant topics to be found herein for building a case for Malcolm X as a conservative are his views on self-help and his concomitant rejection of integration; the stress on moral propriety and religious values; the patriarchal and heavily gendered dimensions of his thought; and the authoritarian nature of his understanding of leadership.

On the topic of integration, Malcolm X says:

> "No *sane* black man really wants integration! No *sane* white man really wants integration! No sane black man really believes that the white man will ever give the black man anything more than token integration. No! The Honorable Elijah Muhammad teaches that for the black man in America the only solution is complete *separation* from the white man!"[13]

It was not only that integration was not possible. It was also that integration was not desirable. Note the distinction he draws between separatism and segregation:

To *segregate* means to control. Segregation is that which is forced upon inferiors by superiors. But *separation* is that which is done voluntarily, by two equals – for the good of both! The Honorable Elijah Muhammad teaches us that as long as our people here in America are dependent upon the white man, we will always be begging him for jobs, food, clothing and housing. And he will always control our lives, regulate our lives, and have the power to segregate us.[14]

Separation, therefore, is a remedy for segregation. The only way to remain strong and independent is resist any form of dependency on the government and the emergent welfare state, which is what Clarence Thomas had in mind when he suggested that Malcolm X would have never gone begging for jobs to the Labor Department. Black pride and black self-sufficiency demanded this rejection of integration, and the Nation of Islam pushed instead the development of small business and other modes of petty-bourgeois black capitalism to maintain social and economic independence.

This call to separation also had a religious component. American society had been condemned not only by Elijah Muhammad but also by God. America, and the West in general, has become so "'overrun with immorality'" that "'God is going to judge it, and destroy it.'" Salvation, then, lies in avoiding contamination via integration and pursuing instead a separatist strategy "'to a land of our *own*, where we can reform ourselves, lift up our moral standards, and try to be godly.'"[15] This desire to be godly should not be underestimated. Malcolm X's conversion to the Nation of Islam was deeply intertwined with his conversion away from his former life as a criminal, a pimp, and a drug addict. And this conversion, moreover, is linked to his proselytizing for the Nation. As he explains in the *Autobiography*, one could not declare himself a follower of Elijah Muhammad "then continue the same old, sinful, immoral life," including a life of chemical treatments of the hair (i.e. "conking"), smoking, drug addiction, the consumption of alcohol, gambling, criminal behavior, and so forth. A Muslim "first had to change his physical and moral self" to meet a strict set of rules.[16]

The Nation of Islam maintained enormously successful faith-based prison and drug rehabilitation ministries. As Malcolm X tells us, Elijah Muhammad always instructed his ministers to "'Go after the black man in the mud,'" because such converts often made the best Muslims.[17] Indeed, the Black Muslim approach was so successful that Malcolm X openly wonders why the organization is attacked rather than subsidized by the state to save millions of dollars a year for the government. But, as is the case for some contemporary government-funded faith-based initiatives, their methods often blurred the lines between rehabilitation and religious indoctrination. The organization that saved you would readily punish or expel you for any moral lapses. And Minister Malcolm X himself was as strict and moralistic as any evangelical Christian who proclaims a similar vision of godliness and propriety. He was equally quick to blame black men and women – the main audience for his sermons at the Nation of Islam Mosques in cities across the country – for moral laxity and indulgence in sin. Above all, Minister Malcolm X preached the virtues of "family values," including a belief that God (or Allah) demands women to be submissive to men.

The Christian Right takes as one of its goals the restoration of the "proper" relationship between men and women, especially in the context of the traditional family. Minister Malcolm X was essentially no different. As he admits in the *Autobiography*, "In my twelve years as a Muslim minister, I had always taught so strongly on the moral issues that many Muslims accused me of being 'anti-woman.'"[18] Calls for moral uplift tend to fall most heavily on women, especially within black nationalist traditions. Women are both "Mothers of the Race," who insure racial purity and the proper education of the next generation, and they are the primal source of (sexual) sin and immorality. "Since the time of Adam and Eve in the garden," Malcolm X preached at a Temple in Philadelphia in 1956, "woman has led man into evil and the one she was created to serve became her slave. She rules him entirely with her sex appeal."[19]

According to these teachings, it is precisely because women have the disposition and the power to corrupt and emasculate men, that they need to be tightly controlled. They need to be submissive and obedient to men, to have the proper conservative dress and decorum, and to be good mothers able to pass on cultural traditions to children. They need, above all, to accept the authority of men. In conservative Christian traditions, women are admonished to submit to their husbands as the church submits to the authority of God. Something similar happened inside the Nation of Islam, where absolute submission to Allah and complete obedience to Elijah Muhammad were preconditions to membership and belonging. In this highly patriarchal system, the right relationship between men and women reflected the right relationship between leaders and followers. Minister Malcolm X accepted and taught these precepts wholeheartedly.

Conclusion

In his brilliant excavation of the "Golden Age" of black nationalism, historian Wilson J. Moses identifies the "authoritarian collectivist ideal" as one of the tradition's hallmarks and among its most conservative features.[20] It is, Moses asserts, not far removed from the organic collectivism that found expression in the work of Edmund Burke, the eighteenth-century "father" of modern conservatism. Minister Malcolm X's philosophy is heavily inundated by a similar vision of organic collectivism under strict authority, with its traditional emphasis on moral character, religious propriety, and sexism.

During his years as a Nation of Islam minister and Elijah Muhammad's chief spokesperson Malcolm X also accepted the classic black-nationalist belief that all black people could and should act in concert under the leadership of one powerful man or group of men. But that man, in this case Muhammad, had to retain his moral authority. Malcolm X held as fundamental that "we Muslims regarded ourselves as moral and mental and spiritual examples for other black Americans, *because* we followed the personal example of Mr. Muhammad."[21] Thus, it stands to reason that what shook his faith and led to his rejection of the Nation was a moral lapse, actually a series of them, on the part of Muhammad. Once Malcolm X discovered and verified Muhammad's acts of adultery, in some cases resulting in illegitimate children, the entire edifice of his conservative, authoritarian faith in Elijah Muhammad, and by extension, the Nation of Islam, was destroyed.

After his break with the Nation and his transformative trip to Mecca Malcolm X began to embrace a form of Sunni Islam and his social and political views began to change – all of which gave his lived autobiography and his political faith an even more protean quality. Envisioning Malcolm X as a black nationalist and as a conservative helps to contextualize and further understand these elements of his political, social, and religious thought. This is a dimension of his philosophy that is often not fully embraced and credited, in my view, except by a smattering of contemporary black conservatives in search of reputable icons. He need not be seen as *only* a conservative, however; in some ways he remains their antithesis, with his searing indictment of racism and white supremacy and his evocative expressions of black rage. He is also an internationalist, a socialist, and a revolutionary; a human rights activist and a man of God. Emphasizing just one aspect of this complex and contradictory figure, especially in the service of promoting a political ideology, is to do damage to a fuller and richer appreciation of his life, his search for meaning in a chaotic world, and his quest for justice.

And yet, as I have argued, the case for Malcolm X's conservatism cannot be dismissed as mere misappropriation and political opportunism. Rather, an open and critical approach to the study of Malcolm X's life, particularly during his tenure as a Nation of Islam minister, demands an appreciation of the deeply conservative elements of the beliefs that guided this dynamic figure whose legacy we continue to struggle to understand.

NOTES

1. Shelby Steele, "Malcolm Little," *New Republic*, December 21, 1992, p. 31.
2. Ibid., p. 30.
3. Amiri Baraka, "Malcolm as Ideology," in *Malcolm X: In Our Own Image*, ed. Joe Wood (New York: St. Martin's, 1992), p. 21.

4. Alan L. Keyes and Martin L. Gross, *Masters of the Dream: The Strength and Betrayal of Black America* (New York: William Morrow, 1995), p. 74.

5. Ibid., p. 5.

6. Jnan Williams, "A Question of Fairness," *Atlantic Monthly Online*, February 1987, www.theatlantic.com/politics/race/thomas.htm.

7. Patricia J. Williams, "Clarence X, Man of the People," in Wood, *Malcolm X: In Our Own Image*, p. 192.

8. On Thomas and Malcolm X, see Kevin Merida and M. Fletcher, *Supreme Discomfort: The Divided Soul of Clarence Thomas* (New York: Doubleday, 2007), especially chapter 11.

9. Zora Neale Hurston quoted in Bill Kauffman, "Zora Neale Hurston and Clarence Thomas," *Lincoln Review,* 10 (1991–2), pp. 11–12.

10. Zora Neale Hurston, "Letter to the *Orlando Sentinel*," August 11, 1955, teachingamericanhistory.org/library/index.asp?document=643.

11. Malcolm X and Alex Haley, *The Autobiography of Malcolm X* (1965; London: Penguin Books, 2001), pp. 79–81.

12. Louis E. Lomax, *When the Word Is Given* (Cleveland: World Publishing, 1963), p. 93.

13. Malcolm X, *Autobiography*, pp. 347–8.

14. Ibid., p. 348.

15. Ibid.

16. Ibid., pp. 362–3.

17. Ibid., p. 367.

18. Ibid., p. 403.

19. Malcolm X quoted in James H. Cone, *Martin & Malcolm & America: A Dream or a Nightmare* (Maryknoll, NY: Orbis, 1991), p. 275.

20. Wilson Jeremiah Moses, *The Golden Age of Black Nationalism, 1850–1925* (New York: Oxford University Press, 1978), p. 21.

21. Malcolm X, *Autobiography*, p. 396, emphasis mine.

8

RICHARD BRENT TURNER

Malcolm X and youth culture

This essay explores the legacy of Malcolm X as it is reinterpreted among contemporary young people with an emphasis on his influence on African American Muslim youth in university communities through rap music. Islam has been the iconic religion of hip-hop (rapping, dejaying, breakdancing, and graffiti art) since the beginning of this complex youth-music culture in New York City in the 1970s.[1] Previous studies of Malcolm's influence on hip-hop have focused on his early years as a hustler and later as a member of the Nation of Islam with an interpretation that resonates with the urban street–reporting themes of drug dealing and incarceration in gangsta rap.[2] However, analysis of the aspects of Malcolm X's Pan-African internationalist insights and programs in the Muslim Mosque, Inc. and the Organization of Afro-American Unity that are reinterpreted by contemporary rappers and MCs (masters of ceremonies) sheds light on the progressive potential of the music and the complex interrelationship between Islam, hip-hop, and black nationalism in the late-twentieth and twenty-first centuries.

The university-based hip-hop audience with regard to the influence of Malcolm X is important for several reasons. Malcolm's *Autobiography* is now part of the canon of some university curricula and therefore Muslim and non-Muslim youth in university communities have become sophisticated, critical readers of his religious and political philosophies. February Black History Month activities on college campuses in the United States coincide with the date of Malcolm's assassination and often include events that celebrate his connection to youth culture and hip-hop. Moreover in the late 1980s and 90s, the Malcolm X Work Group, an assembly of New York City–based scholars, developed research projects, conferences, and community programs to commemorate the progressive political and religious legacy that Malcolm created in the last year of his life. The Malcolm X Work Group included Mark Brown, an African American Muslim graduate student in religion at Harvard Divinity School and Temple University, and made a significant impact on the religious and political consciousness of the college-based hip-hop audience in the United States.

The above thesis draws strength from innovative research on hip-hop that traces its musical roots to African diasporic sources in West Africa, Jamaica, and Brazil,[3] and from George Lipsitz's brilliant analysis of popular music in the 1970s as an archive of important "historical changes" in postindustrial United States.[4] In this essay, Malcolm's Pan-African legacy for hip-hop is interpreted as an archive for late-twentieth-century historical changes in American religion, the foundation for the ascendancy of Sunni Islam in black youth culture and in African American politics, and the basis for the rise of black nationalism in a postindustrial/post-civil rights era in American history. What aspects of Malcolm's Pan-African internationalist message are accessed and sustained among black youth and MCs in United States hip-hop? What is the influence of Malcolm X and hip-hop on identity formation among African American Muslim youth on university campuses in the United States? These are the questions that I will attempt to answer.

The Muslim Mosque, Inc. and Pan-African hip-hop

Malcolm X left the Nation of Islam on March 8, 1964, because he opposed Elijah Muhammad's apolitical stance on the Christian-led civil rights movement in the United States. The Muslim Mosque, Inc. and the Organization of Afro-American Unity – the religious and political organizations that Malcolm established before his assassination on February 21, 1965 – became important Pan-African international models for African American Muslim MCs and hip-hop fans on university campuses from the 1970s to the present.[5] I argue first that this major segment of hip-hop's youth culture was the primary successor of his Pan-African religious legacy which is outlined below. Also, I provide evidence that a critical reading of the Pan-African significance of Islam in hip-hop culture is an indicator of the complex transnational interactions between Muslims in America and abroad and a new era of religious pluralism in the late twentieth century, with Islam as the fastest-growing and second largest religion in the United States after Christianity.

The Muslim Mosque, Inc., founded on March 11, 1964, as "a religious base" to end the systemic economic, political, and social oppression of black people in the United States,[6] was one of the African American Sunni groups that foreshadowed the renaissance of Islam among black youth in hip-hop and paved the way for Malcolm's hajj to Mecca, Saudi Arabia, in April 1964. The cosmopolitan, international, and multiracial experience of hajj was spiritually and politically transformative and signaled his abandonment of the Nation of Islam's racial theology and his conversion to orthodox Islam as El Hajj Malik El-Shabazz.[7] Malcolm was the most important African American Sunni Muslim to establish transnational interactions between Muslims in

America and abroad, and his hajj became a Pan-African spiritual model for contemporary African American Muslim MCs in hip-hop. Mos Def, the actor and MC from Brooklyn who converted to Sunni Islam in 1997 and also made the hajj, said: "I took my shahada [Muslim testimony of faith] … and Insha' Allah ['if it be the will of God'] my effort will be accepted."[8] The MC Freeway noted: "I just took a trip to Saudi Arabia … It was beautiful … I've been Muslim all my life and that's one of the pillars you're supposed to do it because that's where everything started."[9]

As we shall see, Muslim MCs in hip-hop draw inspiration for their powerful rapping against racism in the United States from the transnational Pan-African "hip hop *umma*,"[10] a version of the Muslim *umma* – the global community of Islam that Malcolm experienced during his hajj. In Mecca, Malcolm was viewed by international Muslim leaders as an ambassador for the African American freedom struggle, and thus he was the first black leader to establish official religious and political connections between the Muslim *umma* and black America.

A Muslim from Algeria, who was a student at the University of Washington at Seattle in the 1990s and is now an American professor of Islamic studies and a hip-hop fan, explains the religious significance of the underground Pan-African movements that Malcolm experienced during hajj:

> They met in Jedda before they came in Mecca and talked about their problems in their home country, and they bring manifestoes, declarations, testimonies, secret letters hand-delivered from the religious authority in their community … seeking solidarity especially with minority Muslims … to further the interest of the abstract community, the *umma*. And that's how the liberation movements and the renewal movements emerged in isolated communities and what the *hajj* provided was the space for them all to network.[11]

After Malcolm's death, the Pan-African "hip hop *umma*" provided new opportunities in both the United States and abroad for consciousness-raising political and religious interactions between African American Muslim MCs and transnational Muslims for several reasons. First, Malcolm X's conversion to Sunni Islam in 1964 was a groundbreaking model for the conversion experiences of several million African American orthodox Muslims in the United States in the late twentieth century and many of these converts were young black men and hip-hop fans in urban communities. Secondly, the US Immigration Act of 1965 brought several million transnational Muslims to American universities and cities, such as New York – the birthplace of hip-hop and home to vibrant African Muslim communities in Harlem, Brooklyn, and the Bronx. These new Muslim communities provided fertile ground for Pan-African political and religious interactions between transnational

Muslims and black youth in hip-hop.[12] Thirdly, Malcolm's Pan-African international model of religious consciousness was reinterpreted and implemented in youth culture in Imam Warith Deen Muhammad's Sunni Muslim American Society and Louis Farrakhan's revived Nation of Islam in the 1980s and 90s. To heal the schism and conflict that developed in the wake of Elijah Muhammad's death in 1975, both of these influential African American Muslim groups developed innovative youth programs that appealed to the hip-hop community at a time when some black church leaders and politicians participated in campaigns to demonize hip-hop.[13] Finally, Muhammad's and Farrakhan's historic public declarations to "work together for the cause of Islam"[14] after years of theological tensions between their communities and the latter's public announcement to move the Nation of Islam "on the path to mainstream Islam"[15] in Chicago on February 28, 2000, mirrored the complex and positive interactions between both orthodox and heterodox religious philosophies in the "hip hop *umma*."

Reinterpreting the model of networking between minority Muslim communities that Malcolm developed during hajj, the Pan-African "hip hop *umma*" encompasses and expresses significant influences from African American Sunni communities, the Nation of Islam, and the Nation of Gods and Earths (also known as the Five Percenters, a splinter group of the Nation of Islam founded by Clarence 13X in New York City in 1964). Theological differences exist among these three communities. Sunni Muslims practice the five pillars of Islam and believe that the Prophet Muhammad in the seventh century C.E. is the final messenger, while the Nation of Islam believes that Elijah Muhammad was a new Messenger of Allah for African Americans and that its founder Fard was Allah in human form. The Five Percenters study the secret literature of Fard and Elijah Muhammad, believe that all black men are gods, and "see themselves as the five percent of African Americans who are the 'poor righteous teachers' of their race."[16]

In spite of the theological differences among the communities that constitute the hip-hop *umma*, there is rich evidence in the most important sourcebook of interviews with MCs and rappers, Joseph D. Eure and James G. Spady's *Nation Conscious Rap*, that Malcolm is the central paradigmatic figure for African American Muslim youth and MCs in hip-hop. Yet he shares that space with Elijah Muhammad and Farrakhan – a trio that inspired hip-hop's youth culture and numerous new converts to Islam from the 1980s to the present.[17] A brief sketch of MCs who rap about Malcolm X in three Islamic communities follows and indicates the profound impact of the "hip hop *umma*" in the religious consciousness of black youth.[18]

Inspired by Malcolm X's Pan-African religious paradigm in the Muslim Mosque, Inc. and Louis Farrakhan's travels to Africa to visit Muammar el-Qaddafi in Libya in the 1980s,[19] several of the early Muslim MCs in the "hip hop *umma*" traveled abroad to connect musically and spiritually to African-descended people in Africa, the Caribbean, and Europe. Doug E. and Daddy-O of Stetsasonic made trips to Senegal. Fareed Kamal traveled to Puerto Rico.[20] In 1982 and 83, Afrika Bambaataa brought the Universal Zulu Nation to France to teach French rappers how to utilize hip-hop to address social and political problems in their nation.[21] Chuck D of Public Enemy said, "As MCs we have young people around the globe listening to our every word" and traveled abroad to disseminate "black news and information" through rap music.[22]

Common, a contemporary Chicago MC whose rapping was popular in a dynamic community of African American Sunni students at the University of Iowa from 2000 to 2004, sums up the interactive Pan-African religious spirit of the "hip hop *umma*" in his rap from *Be*: "I wanna be free as the spirits of ... Malcolm, Coltrane, my man Yusef ... I just wanna be."[23] In the underground hip-hop community at Iowa, MCs such as Chuck D, Mos Def, Nas, and Common are revered. Khalid, a young African American man from Chicago, was influenced both by Muslim rappers in that university community and by Malcolm X's Pan-African religious identity formation during hajj and converted to Sunni Islam in 2000:

> This friend of mine, Amir, used to hang out with Musa who is a Muslim. Then Amir accepted Islam ... He was also a rapper ... Musa had a [rap] group ... One day he invited me to mosque ... I started going to Jumah. Then Ramadan came around. I was reading Malcolm X's autobiography – the part where he went on *hajj* ... There was that point where I was real radical and had that hate going on for what my environment was. But then when Malcolm got to *hajj*, he eventually shed that hatred and I was seeing the same thing in front of my eyes. Seeing these different brothers greeting each other, asking for God's peace to be on you, feeding each other, doing acts of humility to each other. I could relate to Malcolm X's sincerity ... This is internally what I was looking for ... I eventually accepted Islam at the end of 2000.[24]

Eventually, Khalid became the leader of his campus's Muslim Student Association – a group of students that included African American and European American Muslims, as well as transnational Muslims from Asia and Africa. In the aftermath of the terrorist attacks on September 11, 2001 and the passage of the American Patriot Act, these students mobilized with non-Muslims to educate the university community about Islam and about universal social justice and human rights issues. Their political activism on behalf of their religion was influenced both by themes of social justice and human rights in the rapping of Pan-African MCs in hip-hop and by some of the ideas and programs of Malcolm X's Organization of Afro-American Unity. I now turn to a consideration of the impact of this important Pan-African political organization on identity formation among MCs in hip-hop and African American Muslim youth on university campuses.

The Organization of Afro-American Unity and Pan-African hip-hop

Malcolm X held the first rally of the Organization of Afro-American Unity on June 28, 1964 in New York City.[25] Inspired by the Organization of African Unity, his organization's aim was to shift the domestic focus of the civil rights movement in the United States to an international Pan-African movement for human rights that connected the African American freedom struggle to revolutionary, antiimperialist struggles for self-determination in Africa.[26] As we shall see, the Pan-African and worldwide focus of the Organization of Afro-American Unity has had a profound influence on identity formation among both African American and transnational Muslim university students in hip-hop culture. Ahmed, an Algerian Muslim student at the University of Washington at Seattle in the 1990s, saw Malcolm's image as a revolutionary from the news magazine *Jeune Afrique* posted on walls in Algerian and Tunisian homes next to images of Fidel Castro, Nelson Mandela, and Houari Boumediane, the president of Algeria in the 1970s. Ahmed explicates the political potential of the organization's Pan-Africanism for identity formation among Muslim youth in the US and abroad:

> From 1948 until Malcolm X was killed, what was going on was these liberation struggles in the Islamic world. What was impressive for Malcolm X is that all of them succeeded and won independence and Algeria was the last and best example … You look at battered and emerging Islamic identity in this period and the emerging African continent as a whole. Almost every regime there was seen as a radical, militant, revolutionary regime. All of Africa in his eyes with the exception of South Africa was a great example. His argument then became you need to capitalize on the success of the African people and the Islamic world to put pressure on the US government to recognize the rights of the African American people. To do that he needed to work on … the United Nations, the diplomatic track and he was counting on all of these new independent African countries to vote for any initiative.[27]

Malcolm's Organization of Afro-American Unity became the Pan-African model for the Muslim youth culture in hip-hop because he was the first important African American leader to travel to Africa to explain the complexities of US institutionalized racism to their leaders.[28] His ultimate political goals were: to develop international recognition for the organization as a "national liberation organization"; to foster significant interactions between the civil rights movement and the worldwide human rights struggle in Africa, Asia, Latin America, and the Caribbean; and to indict the American government before the United Nations for human rights crimes against black America.[29] To accomplish these goals, he made two trips to Africa in the last year of his life – April 13–May 21 and July 9–November 24, 1964 – and traveled to thirty countries, including Nigeria, Ghana, Egypt, Ethiopia, Sudan, Kenya, and Guinea. Malcolm had official meetings with African presidents and leaders, including Kwame Nkrumah, Gamal Abdel Nasser, Julius Kambarage Nyerere, Jomo Kenyatta, Sekou Toure, Nnamdi Azikiwe, and Milton Obote, and with the Algerian, Cuban, and Chinese ambassadors in Ghana.[30]

Although the original organization did not last long after Malcolm's death, several highlights of its early history continue to resonate with the identity formation of contemporary African American, Arab, and African Muslim youth in university communities and in hip-hop culture.[31] First, Malcolm made a profound and paradigmatic connection to the human rights aspirations of African-descended university students at the University of Ibadan in Nigeria on May 8, 1964, when he argued passionately that African American youth should connect culturally and philosophically to Africa through worldwide Pan-Africanism and that African countries should help African Americans to achieve their human rights through a United Nations case. At the reception, the Nigerian Muslim Student's Society named him Omowale – "the son who has come home."[32] Secondly, in his visit to Ghana during the same trip, Malcolm developed vibrant connections to the African American expatriates such as Julian Mayfield, Shirley Graham Du Bois, and Maya Angelou who resided there, as well as with radical representatives of African nations such as Taher Kaid, the Algerian ambassador who influenced his critical thinking on black nationalism.[33]

Indeed, these transnational political interactions that Malcolm initiated in Nigeria and Ghana were reinterpreted as a Pan-African model for political interaction between an Algerian Muslim student and an African American Muslim student who were hip-hop fans at the University of Washington at Seattle in the 1990s. "Quenton Youngblood changed his name to Amir Rashad," said Ahmed, the Algerian Muslim student:

> He was recruited by University of Washington to play basketball ... Second year of his career he was riding the team bus to Oregon and reading *The Autobiography of Malcolm X.* When the coach saw him and made the comment, "Why are you reading a book about such a racist person?" he was offended by that comment and they argued. After that trip, the coach put him on the bench ... and told him you are not going to start. Then the struggle began.

Quenton and I began talking to community leaders, friends, and relatives and demonstrators protested the decision. Members of the black community in the Central District ... individual Muslim students at the university called the media. Once the movement started it got Quenton's interest in Islam stronger and he officially converted to Islam after the incident. The university in the end fired the coach and hired a new coach who treated Amir fairly. What was amazing is that all these tribulations gave him a new sense of identity. He started seeing Malcolm X in himself. He started volunteering in the Central District and eventually became leader of the team ... He works for a non-profit agency now in the Bay Area to preserve ancient African manuscripts in Arabic in Timbuktu in Mali. He spends a lot of time in Senegal where he met his new wife.[34]

Malcolm was the official representative of all people of African descent in the United States at the Organization of African Unity summit in Cairo, Egypt. On July 17, 1964, he argued for international help for his people when he said, "Since the 22 million of us were originally Africans who are now in America not by chance but only by a cruel accident in our history, we strongly believe that African problems are our problems and our problems are African problems."[35] By delivering this Pan-African human rights appeal for support, he developed new critical thinking about the construction of blackness that would have a significant impact on Pan-African hip-hop in the late twentieth century. The Organization for Afro-American Unity replaced the domestic term "Negro" with the international Pan-African designation "Afro-American." This new expansive construction of blackness connected Afro-Americans to the worldwide black nationalist revolution for human rights: "the black revolution is sweeping Asia, is sweeping Africa, is rearing its head in Latin America. The Cuban revolution – that's a revolution,"[36] said Malcolm X.

Contemporary Muslim MCs, such as Mos Def, have reinterpreted the organization's understanding of Pan-African blackness to reflect the black nationalist orientation of hip-hop in his CDs *Black on Both Sides*[37] and *Mos Def and Talib Kweli are Black Star*: "Black like the veil the Muslim Aminah wear ... Black like the slave ship that brought us here ... Black people unite."[38] The hip-hop scholar Charise L. Cheney developed the term "raptivists" to designate MCs "who fused music and politics" in the "golden age of rap nationalism" from the 1980s to the 1990s.[39] Cheney sees African American youth in hip-hop as a new "revolutionary generation"[40] profoundly influenced in its identity formation by Malcolm X. Perhaps no MC has encompassed and expressed Malcolm's revolutionary construction of blackness more effectively than Chuck D in Public Enemy's 1988 CD, *It Takes a Nation of Millions to Hold Us Back*. In "Party for Your Right to Fight," he raps: "J. Edgar Hoover ... he had King and X set up ... Get back on track ... Know who you are to be black."[41]

Indeed Malcolm's Pan-African construction of blackness in the Organization of Afro-American Unity was also reinterpreted in hip-hop identity formation by DJ Kool Herc, who was born in Kingston, Jamaica, and brought the vibe of Rastafarian blackness and music to establish hip-hop in the Bronx in the 1970s.[42] At the same time, numerous adept and talented Puerto Rican break-dancers such as Mr. Wiggles and Fabel of the Rock Steady Crew, Crazy Legs, and Rosie Perez brought the rhythms and percussion of Afro-Latino culture to hip-hop.[43] According to William Jelani Cobb, breakdancing is a Pan-African by-product of Capoeira, the "Afro-Brazilian martial art" of resistance invented by slaves.[44]

A final aspect of Malcolm's influence in youth culture remains for our consideration. His Organization was not a religious movement and was purposely constructed as a Pan-African "united front"[45] of African-descended Muslims and non-Muslims, middle class, working class, and street people, and activists for the equality of women, based in Harlem but interacting with human rights movements through the Third World. This all inclusive united front of "Afro-Americans" resonates with Malcolm's famous words that have inspired the hip-hop community: [to achieve human rights] "by any means necessary."[46]

Malcolm envisioned a Pan-African "cultural revolution" of youth as a primary goal of the Organization of Afro-American Unity. Hip-hop has fulfilled that vision for Muslims and non-Muslims alike as the way that young people "speak to the world"[47] about social justice issues in a post-industrial/post-9/11 United States. The Chicago MC Common raps about the peaceful interaction between Islam and Christianity in hip-hop: "My blood line is one with the divine Quran and the Bible to me they all vital."[48] Ice Cube who is a member of the Nation of Islam highlights systemic racism against black youth in the Reagan/Bush era when he refers to "young black teenagers … as an endangered species" and raps "free Africa cause we ain't got it too good in America" in excerpts from *Amerikkka's Most Wanted*.[49] As a counterpoint to America's war on terrorism after 9/11, the DPZ remind us of the domestic terrorism of police brutality against black people in New York City: "When they murdered Amadou Diallo, that's war!"[50]

Conclusion

The African American university student, Khalid, whose introduction to Sunni Islam came from *The Autobiography of Malcolm X* and two hip-hop musicians provides the most poignant testimony that the struggle for human rights that Malcolm began in the 1960s still continues among contemporary Muslim youth:

[The day after 9/11] I saw more African Americans trying to physically express their religion by wearing hijab in the roughest neighborhoods like the Westside of Chicago ... I took a hard stance on how I felt about Islam; my father and his girlfriend were offended. They thought I had flipped [but] I never felt like I was going to be attacked. I wasn't afraid to proclaim Islam. I am a Muslim; it made me stronger.[51]

Contemporary hip-hop is a complex music culture that disseminates both positive and negative messages to black youth culture. This essay shows that there is still an important Pan-African political core in hip-hop that expresses the resistance strategies of marginalized young people of color across the globe. MCs, such as Mos Def, Chuck D, Common, and many others, reinterpret the powerful internationalist insights of Malcolm X's Muslim Mosque, Inc. and the Organization of Afro-American Unity in their contemporary music which has a unique consciousness-raising appeal to both the Muslim and the non-Muslim college-based hip-hop audience.

My insights here provide evidence of fascinating interactions between Islam, hip-hop, and black nationalism in the youth culture of African-descended Muslim students on university campuses in the United States. Malcolm X's progressive ideas about human rights, reinterpreted in hip-hop culture, are a powerful medium through which global Muslim youth express their counter-conceptions to the hegemonic discourses of oppressive majority communities in a post-9/11 world.

Finally, Malcolm's powerful message about human dignity, expressed so eloquently at the first public meeting of the Organization of Afro-American Unity, continues to resonate with the contemporary human rights struggles of national and transnational youth cultures:

We declare our right on this earth to be a man, to be a human being, to be respected as a human being, to be given the rights of a human being in this society, on this earth, in this day, which we intend to bring into existence by any means necessary.[52]

NOTES

1. William J. Cobb, *To the Break of Dawn: A Freestyle on the Hip Hop Aesthetic* (New York: New York University Press, 2007), back flap.
2. Ibid., pp. 130–7. Eithne Quinn, *Nuthin' But a "G" Thang: The Culture and Commerce of Gangsta Rap* (New York: Columbia University Press, 2005).
3. Cobb, *To the Break of Dawn*, p. 7. Cheryl L. Keyes, *Rap Music and Street Consciousness* (Urbana: University of Illinois, 2002), back flap.
4. George Lipsitz, *Footsteps in the Dark: The Hidden Histories of Popular Music* (Minneapolis: University of Minnesota Press, 2007), p. xv.

5. Richard B. Turner, *Islam in the African-American Experience*, 2nd edn. (Bloomington: Indiana University Press, 1997), pp. 213–14. Clayborne Carson and David Gallen (eds.), *Malcolm X: The FBI File* (New York, Carroll & Graf, 1991), pp. 72–3.

6. Malcolm X, *Malcolm X Speaks*, ed. George Breitman (New York: Pathfinder Press, 1965), pp. 20–1.

7. See Malcolm X and Alex Haley, *The Autobiography of Malcolm X* (1965; London: Penguin Books, 2001).

8. H. Samy Alim, *Roc the Mic Right: The Language of Hip Hop Culture* (New York: Routledge, 2006), p. 20.

9. Ibid.

10. Ibid.

11. Personal interview with Ahmed Souaiaia, June 18, 2008.

12. Turner, *Islam in the African-American Experience*, pp. 234–5.

13. Lipsitz, *Footsteps in the Dark*, pp. 156–7, 168–9.

14. *Chicago Tonight*, WTTW, February 28, 2000.

15. Turner, *Islam in the African-American Experience*, p. xxii.

16. Ibid., p. 279. Michael Muhammad Knight, *The Five Percenters: Islam, Hip Hop and the Gods of New York* (Oxford: One World, 2007).

17. Joseph D. Eure and James G. Spady (eds.), *Nation Conscious Rap* (New York: PC International Press, 1991).

18. Sunni Muslim MCs include: Fareed Kamal (formerly known as Q-Tip) and Ali Shaheed Muhammad, both from A Tribe Called Quest; some of the members of the Roots; Freeway; and Mos Def. MCs who are influenced by or are members of the Nation of Islam include: Afrika Bambaataa, founder of the Universal Zulu Nation; Chuck D, Flava Flav, and Sister Souljah of Public Enemy; Paris; Kam; MC Ren; Ice Cube; Wise Intelligent of Poor Righteous Teachers; Hi-Tek; Talib Kweli; JT the Bigga Figga; Doug E. Fresh; Big Daddy Kane; K-Solo; Shockin' Shawn; Super Jay; Daddy-O (Stetsasonic); Defiant Giant; and Prince Akeem. The following MCs are Five Percenters: Rakim, Big Daddy Kane, Brand Nubian, Lakim Shabazz, Wu-Tang Clan, Poor Righteous Teachers, Busta Rhymes, Doodlebug of Digable Planets, King Sun, and Nas (his name means "human" in African Arabic spoken in Senegal).

19. Turner, *Islam in the African-American Experience*, p. 230.

20. Eure and Spady, *Nation Conscious Rap*, p. 9.

21. Alim, *Roc the Mic Right*, p. 26.

22. Chuck D, *Chuck D: Lyrics of a Rap Revolutionary*, vol. 1, ed. Yusuf Jah (Beverly Hills: Offda Books, 2007), pp. xii, 87.

23. Lonnie Lynn, Kanye West, Caesar Frazier, "Be (Intro)," *Common Be* (Santa Monica, CA: Geffen Records, 2005).

24. Personal interview with Khalid Hudson, October 8, 2004.

25. Malcolm X, *By Any Means Necessary: Speeches, Interviews, and a Letter*, ed. George Breitman (New York: Pathfinder Press, 1970), p. 37.

26. William W. Sales, Jr., *From Civil Rights to Black Liberation: Malcolm X and the Organization of Afro-American Unity* (Boston: South End Press, 1994), p. 27.

27. Personal interview with Ahmed.

28. Sales, *From Civil Rights*, p. 37.

29. Ibid., p. 109.

30. Ibid., p. 100. Kevin Gaines, *African Americans in Ghana: Black Expatriates and the Civil Rights Era* (Chapel Hill: University of North Carolina, 2006), p. 201.
31. Sales, *From Civil Rights*, p. 160. Gaines, *African Americans in Ghana*, p. 182.
32. Turner, *Islam in the African-American Experience*, pp. 217–18.
33. Gaines, *African Americans in Ghana*, p. 181. Sales, *From Civil Rights*, p. 102.
34. Personal interview with Ahmed.
35. Turner, *Islam in the African-American Experience*, pp. 222–3.
36. Ibid., p. 209.
37. Mos Def, *Black on Both Sides* (New York: Rawkus Records, 1999).
38. Ibid., *Mos Def and Talib Kweli are Black Star* (New York: Rawkus Records, 1998, 2002).
39. Charise L. Cheney, *Brothers Gonna Work It Out: Sexual Politics in the Golden Age of Rap Nationalism* (New York: New York University Press, 2005), p. 3, front flap.
40. Ibid., p. 1.
41. Chuck D, *Chuck D*, p. 100.
42. Jeff Chang and DJ Kool Herc, *Can't Stop Won't Stop: A History of the Hip Hop Generation* (New York: St. Martin's Press, 2005), p. 25.
43. Mandalit del Barco, "Rap's Latino Sabor," in *Droppin' Science: Critical Essays on Rap, Music and Hip Hop Culture*, ed. William Eric Perkins (Philadelphia: Temple University Press, 1996), p. 85.
44. Cobb, *To the Break of Dawn*, p. 7.
45. Sales, *From Civil Rights*, p. viii.
46. Spike Lee with Ralph Wiley, *By Any Means Necessary: The Trials and Tribulations of the Making of "Malcolm X"* (New York: Hyperion, 1992), p. 312.
47. Sales, *From Civil Rights*, p. 5.
48. Common, *One Day It'll All Make Sense* (New York: Relativity Records, 1997).
49. Ice Cube, *Amerikkka's Most Wanted* (Los Angeles: Priority Records, 1990).
50. DPZ, *Turn off the Radio, the Mixtape*, vol. 1 (Holla Black, 2002).
51. Personal interview with Khalid.
52. Malcolm X, *By Any Means Necessary*, p. 56.

9

MARK LAWRENCE McPHAIL

Homo rhetoricus Afro-Americanus: Malcolm X and the "rhetorical ideal of life"

The distinction between poetry and rhetoric is as old as Western culture itself, yet attempts to define these two forms of discourse in opposition to each other rarely offer a coherent connection between theory and practice. In theory, poetry is understood in terms of its ability to connect us to an abstract human condition, and is evaluated on the basis of aesthetic quality. Rhetoric, on the other hand, is theorized as the ability to discover the means of persuasion in the context of concrete social situations, and its quality is revealed most powerfully in its ability to produce an observable effect on such situations. Poetry relies upon stylistic devices to move us toward transcendence and being, while rhetoric invokes elements of style to move us toward action and becoming. In theory these distinctions make sense, yet in practice they often break down.

One tradition of discourse in which this is especially true is in the communicative forms and practices of African American culture. Within the realm of black rhetoric and aesthetics, form and function are rarely understood in opposition to one another. Indeed, African American communication offers an integrative vision of style that disrupts the age-old separation of poetry as an art of being and rhetoric as an art of becoming. That vision of style is expressed perhaps most powerfully in the rhetoric of Malcolm X. He was an orator whose use of language reconciled the tensions between poetics and rhetoric, between being and becoming, that lay at the heart of Richard Lanham's "rhetorical ideal of life."[1]

Lanham's view of rhetoric is especially useful when considering the literary qualities of Malcolm's oratory. Though elegant in its use of stylistic devices, it relied upon them as more than mere ornamentation: they were at the root of a discourse of transformation of self, other, and reality. Malcolm's use of figurative language was epistemologically strategic, and reflected an understanding of style that could be reduced to neither quality nor effect, for it was doubly conscious of both: a style peculiarly African American, that relied upon the linguistic resources of each to create something entirely unique: a spiritually inspired rhetoric that expanded the rhetorical ideal of life in powerful and provocative ways.

Malcolm embodied Lanham's conception of *homo rhetoricus*, rhetorical man, but he was also, as Ossie Davis explained in his eulogy for Malcolm X, "bigger than that." Lanham's description of rhetorical man, then, tells only part of the story:

> Rhetorical man is an actor. His reality public, dramatic. His sense of identity, his self, depends on the reassurance of daily histrionic reenactment. He is thus centered in time and concrete local event. The lowest common denominator of his life is a social situation. And his motivations must be characteristically ludic, agonistic. He thinks first of winning, of mastering the rules the current game enforces. He assumes a natural agility in changing orientations. He hits the street already street wise.[2]

Surely this description captures a man whose life took him from streetwise hustler to self-taught master of the English language. What it does not capture, however, is Malcolm X's blackness, the rhetorical ideals of his racial identity, an identity *both* Western *and* non-Western, both American *and* African.

Thus, any discussion of Malcolm X's rhetorical style must consider his reliance upon figures of speech and master tropes, but must also consider the motivation behind his mastery of "*the master's tools*."[3] Although Audre Lorde argues that those tools "will never dismantle the master's house," can only be used to play his game and never to bring about true change, Malcolm X's language, life, and message suggest otherwise. Through his mastery of the master tropes of metaphor, analogy, synecdoche, and irony, Malcolm X changed the rules of the game of race, that "chess game of naked exploitation and power,"[4] transformed "Negroes" into "Afro-Americans," and established the foundations for a politically conscious aesthetic and a revolutionary rhetoric of radical judgment.

Malcolm X inspired his audiences to understand that words were indeed "bullets," potentially more powerful than ballots, though ultimately seeking the same end. For Malcolm X, throughout his life, that end was the demise of white world supremacy, the "burning down" and then the rebuilding of the master's house with new tools, and the articulation of a rhetorical ideal "that amounted to nothing less than dismantling and reconstructing African American identity."[5] Malcolm X's mastery of the master's tools was ultimately an attempt to emancipate American minds, both black and white, from the rhetorical chains that had enslaved them for centuries. He constructed a discourse and a people whom he believed possessed the potential to not only dismantle the master's house, but to rebuild it anew. This was his meaning to his race, *the human race*, and although the seeds he planted have yet to yield new fruit, the effect of his words on the world cannot be denied or diminished.

So, in order to affirm Malcolm's status as *homo rhetoricus Afro-Americanus*, we must first revisit the master tropes of Western rhetoric, and then consider how they intersect with Malcolm's uniquely Africanized style, his signifying and improvising on a discourse that had for centuries denied persons of African descent a sense of place and identity. Malcolm dismantled and then reconstructed the master's house with the master's own tools, first as a spokesperson for the Nation of Islam, and then as an internationalized Muslim. He freed himself and his listeners from the "nightmarish prison of unchanging essence" that rhetoric has always contested and called into question,[6] and offered "a discourse of empowerment," a retooled rhetoric "from which his audience – black or white – might critique any set of rigid categories, any naturalized ideology."[7] Malcolm X articulated a rhetorical vision that challenged the static demarcations of race that defined American institutions and attitudes.

In both his language and his life, Malcolm X embodied the rhetorical ideal of an inclusive vision of humanity, one that drew upon and went beyond the discursive resources of the culture with which he found himself in both debate and dialogue. In order to map out the contours and circumferences of those debates and dialogues, I will begin by first reviewing Malcolm X's stylistic uses of language. By focusing on Malcolm X's use of figures and tropes of Western discourse, we can see how he exploited the resources of the rhetorical ideal to unmask the exploitative pretensions and practices of white supremacy. Next, I will explore the impact that Malcolm's style had on a rethinking of the rupture between rhetoric and aesthetics to illustrate how he himself recognized the potential of a reconstructed rhetoric/aesthetic to bring about individual and social transformation. Finally, I will suggest that Malcolm X's evolution as an orator exemplifies the spiritually inspired impulses of African American rhetoric that embody the most powerful and transformative aspects of Lanham's "rhetorical ideal of life": the ability to not only change one's state of mind, but to also change one's state of being.

Demons and dogs de-essentialized: Making plain the rhetoric of racism

Malcolm X's rhetorical style drew upon the two principles that Lanham suggests have always defined discursive success for *homo rhetoricus* in the West: clarity and sincerity. "When he is communicating facts or concepts, the success with which they are communicated is measured by something we call clarity," he writes. "When he is communicating feelings, success is measured by something we call sincerity, faithfulness to the self who is doing the feeling."[8]

His commitment to clarity was reflected in the directness of his language, his "bold and direct talk of race," that, while embellished with figures and tropes, always aimed at telling what was in his mind, the "plain" truth. His commitment to sincerity was seen in his belief that "the best thing that a person can be is sincere."[9] Malcolm X's oratory expressed the principles of clarity and sincerity in ways that incorporated traditional rhetorical concerns, but by necessity went beyond them to illustrate the limitations of moral suasion when racial difference and identity constrained public discourse.

Race constrained Malcolm X's rhetorical style by virtue of the fact that it demanded always that his discourse be negotiated by two audiences, one white, one black, separate and unequal. Thus, the "plain style" of traditional rhetoric, which Lanham describes as "the transparent style, the style that is looked through rather than noticed, the style which communicates most efficiently either facts, concepts, or imitations of reality,"[10] had a radically different impact on black and white Americans. Black Americans heard in Malcolm X's voice the cold hard facts of their existence in America, while many whites could only hear in his words hatred and violence. Malcolm X's vision of an "American nightmare" possessed a clarity and sharpness for black Americans that few white Americans, who saw only an American dream, could envision. He spoke to white Americans with a directness that called the dream into question and exposed its moral coherence.

Malcolm X's rhetoric challenged the moral authority that white Americans believed they possessed, and exposed the failure of America's professed democratic principles to be realized in practice in the realm of race relations. He also saw clearly the ruptures between Western theory and practice, not only in terms of race, but also in terms of rhetorical style. It was in response to these inconsistencies that he appropriated and exploited the master's stylistic tools: the figures and tropes of rhetoric. Thus, Malcolm X's rhetorical style was a fitting response to a social situation circumscribed by the empty words and broken promissory notes of American politics and law. His call for consistency between principle and practice emerged out of a long tradition of African American rhetoric, yet his direct and uncompromising style differentiated his discourse from all but the most radical black rhetors that had come before him.

Malcolm X's rhetorical radicalism embraced directness as an antidote to the indirection and obfuscation of a society that claimed to be committed to justice and equality, yet refused steadfastly to extend those commitments to its citizens of African descent. Malcolm perhaps saw, as John Illo asserts, that in the America of his time, "[I]ndirection is not workable, for the state has stolen irony; satire is futile, its only resource to repeat the language of the Administration."[11] Malcolm X's message constituted a demand that was uncompromising in its insistence on consistency between principle and practice.

In his rhetoric "figures correspond to the critical imagination restoring the original idea and to the conscience protesting the desecration of the idea. Tropes and schemes of syntax are departures from literal meaning, *abusiones*, 'abuses' of a grammar and semantic that have themselves grown into abuses of original meaning ... Rhetoric, like revolution, is 'a way of redefining reality.'"[12] Malcolm X's rhetoric was "genuine" in the sense that it was a "coherent counterstatement to 'serious' reality."[13] It sought to redefine reality by first rehabilitating discourse, and extending that rehabilitation to the grassroots. Like the rhetorical ideal of life, it made its greatest contribution to the "serious" realities of American society when it refused to compromise its principles, when it insisted "most strenuously on its own coordinates."[14] Its "radical" character was expressed, perhaps most clearly, in its refusal to engage in what Malcolm X referred to as the "sweet talk" that had characterized much African American discourse for centuries.

Malcolm X eschewed the one-sided epideictic insincerity of such talk. He argued that black rhetorics of accommodation and compromise were at the root of America's "Negro problem," and used every opportunity to make that point plain. He refused to invoke those qualities of rhetoric that since Plato have been the basis of its condemnation by critics: he was unwilling to pander to any of his audiences, black or white. He similarly rejected a rhetoric reduced to ornamentation. His use of words was always aimed at creating an effect, an affective yet rational response from his listeners, and he used the resources of figurative language for this purpose. "His speaking style was unique – plain, direct like an arrow, devoid of flowery trimmings. He used metaphors and figures of speech that were lean and simple, rooted in the ordinary, daily experience of his audiences."[15] Malcolm X's plain style was not without ornament, but it deployed its ornamentation for substantive and emancipatory ends; it was never meant to confuse or flatter, but to speak truth to power.

Toward that end, Malcolm X mastered the master's tools and tropes. In his early career he used analogy, metaphor, synecdoche, and irony to challenge the beliefs that held captive the minds of African Americans.[16] Malcolm X criticized mainstream civil rights organizations because the "angels" of those movements, the controlling forces and interests, were invariably white. He once told his sister Yvonne that white involvement in the movement "cooled" the passions that would make those battles successful. "And then he relates it to a cup of coffee: that it's hot, and as soon as you water it, put the milk in it, it cools down. And these analogies Malcolm used sometimes were funny, but they got home. They hit home."[17] Malcolm X used words like weapons, and for his African American audiences his most powerful weapon was the unspoken truths that had circumscribed America's troubling past and present.

Malcolm X's weapons of choice were used to enact rhetorical reversals and transpositions of race and race history. One of his favorite weapons was the metaphor, inherited from the eschatology of the Nation of Islam, and embodied in the phrase "the white man is the devil." Its bold and uncompromising directness shocked his black listeners and frightened his white audiences, and it resonated with all of the master tropes. Its irony was evident in its invocation by a man once himself called "Satan": its accusation of white evil implied the unspoken analogy of black goodness; if the white man was "the devil," then Malcolm X was simply doing the work of Allah in reminding black people of our angelic natures. Finally, the phrase "white devil" was a powerful synecdoche that collapsed individuality into racial identity, implicating the many in the vile and violent behaviors carried out by the few.

A second comparison that Malcolm X exploited often in his early rhetoric was his juxtaposition of white people and dogs. In Malcolm X's time, the word "dog" was an all-purpose pejorative which meant lowly or dirty, and in his early speeches with the Nation of Islam he even suggested that dogs and white people had mated together in the caves of Europe.[18] Malcolm X used other canine metaphors to contest and reverse the dominant white view of African Americans as animals. White Americans were "wolves" in the South, and "foxes" in the North, and by analogy black Americans were "sheep" and "chickens" (perhaps those that had come home to roost?).[19] But he also used canine metaphors to indict his black audience for their failure to act in accordance with their "natures." For Malcolm X, any human being who was treated like a dog had the right to act like a dog, to bite either the hand that ostensibly fed or unabashedly withheld the food of freedom.

Speaking at a rally in Harlem as a representative of the Nation of Islam, Malcolm X invoked the canine metaphor to challenge the complacency of his African American audience and at the same time condemn the savagery of whites:

> When it comes to biting the enemy of America, you'll bite just like that (snaps fingers). Whether he tell you to bite in Korea, or bite in Berlin, or bite in the South Pacific. Soon as he says "sic em," you'll bite anybody he point the finger at. But right here in this country, right in this country, under your nose, with two legged white dogs, sicing four legged dogs, on your and my mother, you and I don't know how to bite. Sicing dogs on your and my sister, and you and I don't know how to bite. Sicing dogs on our children, and dogs on our babies, and you don't know how to bite. You can't bite nor bark until the white man say bark or bite. In the South you are segregated by that dog. In the North you integrated with this dog. And there's no difference.[20]

This critique invokes all of the master's tropes with a devastating double-consciousness. It draws direct comparisons between both blacks and whites and dogs, albeit for competing purposes; it exposes the irony of black men biting and fighting the white man's enemies overseas, of protecting his homes and families but refusing to protect their own; it draws analogies between dogs and men, between faithful companions and guardians of oppression; and it collapses the distinction between the part and the whole, the individual and the collective, to illustrate the collective complicity that sustains and supports racial oppression.

Malcolm X then extends the implied analogy, giving an ironic twist to a popular expression. "The dog is their best friend. The dog is their closest relative. They got the same kind of hair: the same kind of skin: and the same kind of smell. Oh yeah!"[21] Throughout the passage, Malcolm X also plays upon the dual meanings associated with the signifier "dog," an animal that is at one and the same time aggressor and protector. In an interview with two reporters, one black and one white, Malcolm X offered the same message with a slightly different style, changing "from *homo afer* to *homo europaeus* as the ambience and occasion required."[22] "If a dog is siced on a black man, when that black man is doing nothing but trying take advantage of what the government says is supposed to be his, then that black man should kill that dog, or any two legged dog, who sics the dog on him."[23] Malcolm X's rhetorical reversal of black subordination and white mastery revealed his understanding of the double-sided character of the word as weapon, as both an instrument of deconstruction and reconstruction.

After his break from the Nation of Islam and his embrace of international Islam, Malcolm X's critiques became more nuanced and subtle. The devil and dog metaphors disappeared, even though the "white man" remained. Yet even this phrase lost its synecdochal resonance. After his trip to Mecca, "Malcolm X is forced to change his concept of 'white man.' No longer is he able to divide the world neatly between 'white oppressors' and 'black oppressed'; between 'white devils' and 'black angels'; between 'white tyrants' and 'black freedom fighters.'"[24] Unfettered by the constraints of the Nation of Islam's Manichean vision of reality, El-Hajj Malik El-Shabazz was able to reconstruct the rigid oppositionality that had held the vision and voice of Malcolm X in bondage.

This shift was evident in his concluding remarks to a predominantly white audience at the Oxford Union Society shortly before his death. "In my opinion, the young generation of whites, blacks, brown, whatever else there is, you're living at a time of extremism, a time a revolution, a time when there's got to be a change," he remarked. "People in power have misused it and now there has to be a change and a better world has to be built, and the only way it's going to be built is with extreme methods, and I for one will join in with anyone – I don't care what color you are – as long as you want to change this miserable condition that exists on this earth."[25] Malcolm X continued to speak truth to power, yet power was no longer isomorphic with "the white man." His willingness to work with committed individuals on either side of the color line signaled his individual and ideological growth and moral maturity.

From "serious" reality to an Africanized ideal of life: Malcolm X and the rhetoric and aesthetics of blackness

In many ways Malcolm X embodied Lanham's rhetorical ideal: his oratory was performative, agonistic, and ultimately, at the end of his life, critical of any essentializing discourse. But in one important sense he remade that ideal into one that was both pragmatic and aesthetic. "When Malcolm X spoke his images were perfect: the cadence of his sentences were like poetry whose rhythmic structure harked back to the profound African sensibility of a people victorious against a million agonies."[26] Malcolm X's oratory reflected "language styles suitable for poetry," relying on the practice of signifying, the antiphonal response patterns of African cultures, and an emphasis on extemporaneous presentation "akin to the function of improvisation in dance and jazz."[27] These stylistic practices would become central to the vision of black rhetoric that emerged during Malcolm X's lifetime and would significantly influence much subsequent African American communicative theory and practice.

As Molefi Kete Asante (Arthur L. Smith) explains, that vision breaks down traditional distinctions between rhetoric and aesthetics through its recognition of the musicality of black speech: "When the black man speaks from the public platform, he must make his words conform to music." Asante argues that the African-centered concept of *nommo*, the power of the spoken word, was central to the success of African American orators. Writing specifically of Malcolm X, Asante notes that "*nommo* was developed by the paraphernalia of the occasions so that music and speech invoked the cohesion of the audiences. To speak forcefully is to speak poetically, and the speaker who fails to realize that fact, black or white, will not be effective as an orator within the community."[28] Malcolm X's mastery of the master's tools and tropes, combined with his recognition of the centrality of rhythm and the musicality of language, contributed significantly to his success as an orator. His rhetorical style was thus uniquely African American, and in many ways paralleled the stylistic impulses of another African American aesthetic practice: jazz music.

Jazz is recognized as a uniquely African American aesthetic practice that combines the discipline of traditional musical training with the creative freedom of improvisation, which was one of Malcolm X's most compelling stylistic qualities. "He sometimes spoke for hours extemporaneously, but the attention of a standing crowd never faltered."[29] What began for Malcolm as a speaking style, at the end of his life was transformed into a critical strategy: "During the last year of his life, Malcolm's social criticism and political engagement reflected a will to spontaneity, his analysis an improvisatory and fluid affair that drew from his rapidly evolving quest for the best means available for real black liberation – but a black liberation connected to the realization of human rights for all suffering people."[30] Malcolm's synthesis of Western rhetorical principles with an African centered attitude paralleled the innovation and transformation of Western music expressed in African American musical traditions such as jazz.

Jazz is generally viewed as one of the core expressive experiences of African American culture. It reveals an aesthetic sensibility that has powerful emancipatory potential, one which reconciles divisions between art, rhetoric, and politics. Malcolm X clearly recognized that potential when in 1964 he made "an explicit analogy between the black musician's ability to improvise musically and the development of new social and political forms."[31] In a speech that outlined the founding principles of the Organization of Afro-American Unity, Malcolm X juxtaposed the musical skills of white and black musicians in order to illustrate the importance of improvisation in the creation of new meanings:

> I've seen black musicians when they'd be jamming at a jam session with white musicians – a whole lot of difference. The white musician can jam if he's got some sheet music in front of him. He can jam on something that he's heard jammed before. If he's heard it, then he can duplicate it or he can imitate it or he can read it. But that black musician, he picks up his horn and starts blowing some sounds that he never thought of before. He improvises, he creates, it comes from within. It's his soul, it's that soul music. It's the only area on the American scene where the black man has been free to create. And he has mastered it. He has shown that he can come up with something that nobody ever thought of on his horn.[32]

Malcolm X recognized in jazz the improvisational impulses of traditional African and African American culture that had the potential to create new meanings and possibilities. The insoluble fusion of form and content in jazz, the way that it rejects rigid rules at the same time that it maintains a basic sonic shape, was the force that encouraged the invention of new ideas. He saw in jazz not only an aesthetic practice, but a potential political force as well.

Although that recognition came late in his life, before he was able to translate it into a coherent praxis, Malcolm X anticipated and inspired the connection between art and politics that would have an important impact on the study and practice of communication. His influence was clearly felt in the emergence of black rhetorical studies, Afrocentric communication, and in the more traditional study of public address. In each of these, he opened new vistas and visions of what the art of rhetoric could be. Malcolm X made "his audience into rhetoricians,"[33] and an examination of the literary and stylistic aspects of his rhetoric suggest that Malcolm X also made his audiences into *artists*: artists who synthesized art, rhetoric, and politics into *equipment for living together*, equipment that transgressed the limitations of racial identity, and established the discursive means for reconciling racial divisions and differences.

The reconciliation of difference that marked his rhetorical style may be the most potent indicator of Malcolm X's status as *homo rhetoricus Afro-Americanus*, for it illustrates one of the most powerful and persistent dimensions of the rhetorical ideal of life: the ability, provided by a respect and appreciation of the possibilities of discourse, to embrace diverse and sometimes divergent ways of knowing and being. As Lanham explains, *homo rhetoricus* "is not pledged to a single set of values and the cosmic orchestration they adumbrate. He is not, like the serious man, alienated from his own language."[34] Malcolm X was able to redefine what it meant to be white and black in America, moving from the essentialism of the Nation of Islam that saw black people as inherently divine and white people inherently evil, to an ecumenicist vision of Islam which allowed him to see those he once defined as devils and dogs as members of a human family. This willingness to relinquish the racial identities that had shaped his life and language gave him, in Lanham's words, "the tolerance, and usually the sense of humor, that comes from knowing he – and others – may not only *think* differently, but may *be* differently. He pays a price for this, of course – religious sublimity, and its reassuring, if breathtaking unities."[35] Malcolm X paid another price, of course, for the spiritually inspired vision that ultimately defined the man and his message: the price of freedom, which as he once plainly stated, was death.

Yet, even in death Malcolm X left a legacy of language that in all of its stylistic sublimity helped to bring about another type of death: the death of a state of mind that prohibited both black and white Americans from reconciling our rhetorical selves and wrestling with what Abraham Lincoln in his First Inaugural Address called "the better angels of our nature." Like Lincoln, Malcolm X understood the crippling consequences of division, and in response crafted a rhetorical style that was radically integrative, that reconciled the symbolic, social, and spiritual divisions between the angels and demons of race, and that appended to the West's rhetorical ideal of life a uniquely African-centered vision of language. Malcolm X's legacy of language brings us closer to Lincoln's better angels, allows us to see the rhetorical ideal of life in both black and white, and offers students and scholars of rhetoric an opportunity to append to the title *homo rhetoricus*, the unifying and breathtaking appellation, *Afro-Americanus*.

NOTES

1. Richard Lanham, *The Motives of Eloquence: Literary Rhetoric in the Renaissance* (New Haven: Yale University Press, 1976), pp. 1–36.
2. Ibid., p. 4. Ossie Davis, "Eulogy of Malcolm X," in *For Malcolm: Poems on the Life and the Death of Malcolm X*, ed. Dudley Randall and Margaret G. Burroughs (Detroit: Broadside Press, 1969), p. 121.
3. Audre Lorde, *Sister Outsider: Essays and Speeches* (Berkeley: Crossing Press, 1984), p. 112.
4. Malcolm X and Alex Haley, *The Autobiography of Malcolm X* (1965; London: Penguin Books, 2001), p. 272.
5. Keith D. Miller, "Plymouth Rock Landed on Us: Malcolm X's Whiteness Theory as a Basis for Alternative Literacy," *College Composition and Communication*, 56 (2004), p. 200.
6. Lanham, *Motives of Eloquence*, p. 8.
7. Robert E. Terrill, "Colonizing the Borderlands: Shifting Circumference in the Rhetoric of Malcolm X," *Quarterly Journal of Speech*, 86 (2000), p. 80.
8. Lanham, *Motives of Eloquence*, p. 1.
9. Quoted in Peter Goldman, *The Death and Life of Malcolm X* (Urbana: University of Illinois Press, 1979), p. 238.
10. Lanham, *Motives of Eloquence*, p. 1.
11. John Illo, "The Rhetoric of Malcolm X," *Columbia University Forum*, 9 (1966), p. 8.
12. Ibid., p. 9.
13. Lanham, *Motives of Eloquence*, p. 6.
14. Ibid.
15. George Breitman, quoted in John Henrik Clarke (ed.), *Malcolm X: The Man and His Times* (New York: Macmillan, 1969), p. xvii.
16. Bradford T. Stull defines these terms as follows: to use "metaphor" is to claim that something is what it literally is not; to use "analogy" is to construct a comparative relationship between four terms; to use "synecdoche" is to discuss a part as it represent the whole or vice versa; and to use "irony" is to discover or construct the opposite of the apparent meaning. See *The Elements of Figurative Language* (New York: Longman, 2002), p. 4.
17. Quoted in *Malcolm X: Make it Plain*, VHS, directed by Orlando Bagwell (Boston: Blackside Film, PBS Video, 1994).
18. Malcolm X, *The End of White World Supremacy: Four Speeches by Malcolm X*, ed. Imam Benjamin Karim (New York: Arcade Publishing, 1971), p. 63.
19. For further discussion of Malcolm's use of animal metaphors, see Hank Flick and Larry Powell, "Animal Imagery in the Rhetoric of Malcolm X," *Journal of Black Studies*, 18.4 (1988): 435–451.

20. Quoted in *El Hajj Malik El Shabazz: A Like It Is Special Presentation*, VHS, directed by Gil Noble (Prior Lake, MN: MNTEX Entertainment, 1991).
21. Ibid.
22. Illo, "Rhetoric of Malcolm X," p. 11.
23. Quoted in *Malcolm X: Make it Plain*, VHS.
24. Stull, *Elements of Figurative Language*, p. 30.
25. Quoted in *Malcolm X: Make it Plain*, VHS.
26. Molefi Kete Asante, *Malcolm X as Cultural Hero & Other Afrocentric Essays* (Trenton, NJ: Africa World Press, 1994), p. 32.
27. Jeffrey Lynn Woodyard, "Africological Theory and Criticism," in *Understanding African American Rhetoric: Classical Origins to Contemporary Innovations*, ed. Ronald L. Jackson and Elaine B. Richardson (New York: Routledge, 2003), pp. 150, 141.
28. Arthur L. Smith (Molefi Kete Asante), "Theoretical and Research Issues in Black Communication," in *Black Communication: Dimensions of Research and Instruction*, ed. J. Daniel (New York: Speech Communication Association, 1974), p. 139.
29. *El Hajj Malik El Shabazz*, VHS.
30. Michael Eric Dyson, *Making Malcolm: The Myth and Meaning of Malcolm X* (New York: Oxford University Press, 1995).
31. Daniel Fischlin and Ajay Heble, *The Other Side of Nowhere: Jazz, Improvisation, and Communities in Dialogue* (Middletown, CT: Wesleyan University Press, 2004), p. 25.
32. Malcolm X, *By Any Means Necessary: Speeches, Interviews, and a Letter by Malcolm X*, ed. George Breitman (New York: Pathfinder Press, 1970), pp. 63–4.
33. Robert E. Terrill, *Malcolm X: Inventing Radical Judgment* (East Lansing: Michigan State University Press, 2004), p. 191.
34. Lanham, *Motives of Eloquence*, p. 5.
35. Ibid.

10

ROBERT E. TERRILL

Judgment and critique in the rhetoric of Malcolm X

It is possible to judge Malcolm X a failure. His many admirers can point to no law that he changed, to no sustainable movement that he established, nor even to a lunch counter that he desegregated. He never led his followers in large-scale collective political action, never organized a mass protest march, and never was associated with the passage of any piece of legislation designed to improve the condition of African Americans. What Malcolm did do was talk, and both during his lifetime and since, this talk has been criticized as taking the place of real political action. Whitney Young, for example, the head of the National Urban League, once complained that Malcolm "never got anybody a job or decent housing ... but you could find his name in the *TV Guide* program listings more times than Johnny Carson's."[1]

Such assessments stem from assumptions about the function of public address that must be modified before we can appreciate Malcolm's unique contributions to political culture. Because his legacy consists primarily of all those words, in order to assess it in any meaningful way we need first a more robust way to assess the impact of those words. Malcolm did his political work by filling the newspapers and airways with ideas, not by crowding the streets and jails with bodies. As A. Peter Bailey, who worked closely with Malcolm, put it: "When someone asks, 'what did he leave, there are no buildings, no this, no that,' I say, 'Minds. He left minds.'"[2]

This essay is an effort to begin to describe the sort of minds that have been left by Malcolm's speeches and statements. Specifically, I argue that Malcolm's speeches in his last year model empowering tactics of judgment and critique that his audiences are invited to emulate. I do not mean that his audiences necessarily are asked to accede to the specific conclusions that Malcolm reaches, but rather that they are invited to engage in a process of analysis and interpretation analogous to that which he performs. Malcolm's speeches do not encourage his listeners to engage in specific political actions, but rather demonstrate for them tactics of judgment and critique that do not *lead toward* liberation so much as they *are* a liberation from the constraints and norms of the dominant culture.

Witnessing Malcolm's critical performance, therefore, requires close attention to his oratory. In this essay I look very closely at two of his speeches: his
most well-known address, titled "The Ballot or the Bullet," delivered April 3,
1964, and one of the very last speeches he gave, to which he gave no title,
delivered at the Corn Hill Methodist Church in Rochester, New York, on
February 16, 1965. The process may seem tedious, but I believe that tracking
the development of Malcolm's arguments through time, as he developed them
in these oratorical performances, provides insights into his thought processes
that are not otherwise available. These two speeches, one delivered soon after
Malcolm's famous split with the Nation of Islam and the other almost a year
later, only days before his death, allow me to describe some points of evolution
in his thought during the last year of his life. More importantly, when taken
together, these speeches provide a rich and dynamic presentation of the critical
judgment Malcolm was modeling for his audiences.

The Ballot or the Bullet

James Cone calls "The Ballot or the Bullet" "one of his [Malcolm's] best talks,"
Archie Epps concedes that the speech is "now famous," Celeste Condit and
John Lucaites call it "Malcolm X's most well-known speech," and Henry Louis
Gates, Jr. declares it one of Malcolm's "masterpieces of the rhetorical arts."[3]
This speech became the standard text that he delivered many times between his
split with the Nation of Islam and his journey to Mecca, and because Malcolm
generally spoke extemporaneously the specific wording varied. I take as my text
the version included in *Malcolm X Speaks*, delivered to a predominantly black
audience at the Cory Methodist Church in Cleveland, Ohio, at a meeting
sponsored by the local chapter of the Congress of Racial Equality (CORE).
   Structurally, the speech divides into three sections. The first two-thirds
pushes against boundaries that limit African American behavior and self-
evaluation within the dominant white culture, beginning within the United
States and then expanding to an international scope. Then, in the final third of
the speech, working within the broadened circumference that he has established, Malcolm models the anti-foundationalist mode of interpretive judgment that he would have his audience emulate.

Voting or violence

As the speech works to open up a broader perspective, its key terms, "ballot"
and "bullet," shift their meaning and implications. In simplest terms, Malcolm
demonstrates that African American political power is severely limited as long
as it is understood as operating primarily or exclusively within the United

States, and that by expanding affiliations and identifications beyond North America, African Americans can augment their influence. Analyzing the "ballot" in this domestic scene, in other words, entails understanding both the potential political power of the black vote and the structural constraints that are placed on that power.[4] The significant argument in this speech, as in many of the speeches he delivered during his last year, is not only that African American political action might consist of forming international alliances, but that an international perspective should inform *any* political action African Americans might choose to undertake.

Malcolm begins by indicating the potential power of the African American vote, explaining that: "It was the black man's vote that put the present [Kennedy–Johnson] administration in Washington, DC ... Your vote, your dumb vote, your ignorant vote, your wasted vote," he continues, "put in an administration in Washington, DC, that has seen fit to pass every kind of legislation imaginable, saving you until last, then filibustering on top of that." He is referring to the Senate filibuster that was keeping the Civil Rights Act of 1964 from coming to a vote – he calls it "the same old giant con game."[5]

"Look at it the way it is," Malcolm urges his audience. "They have got a con game going on, a political con game, and you and I are in the middle." This introduces one of the key motifs of the speech, and of Malcolm's speeches throughout his last year: recurrent references to *sight*. It is clear that, for Malcolm X, *seeing* things in a certain way is a substantive political act: African Americans, he says, are "beginning to see what they used to only look at. They're becoming politically mature." African Americans need to be able to "let them know your eyes are wide open. And let them know you got something else that's wide open, too. It's got to be the ballot or the bullet. The ballot or the bullet." The "bullet," indeed, might even encompass actions such as those of teenagers in Jacksonville, Florida, "throwing Molotov cocktails" at police officers: "there's new thinking coming in ... It'll be Molotov cocktails this month, hand grenades next month, and something else next month. It'll be ballots, or it'll be bullets. It'll be liberty, or it will be death." This sort of action is justified because of the "Three hundred and ten years we worked in this country without a dime in return – I mean without a *dime* in return."[6]

Malcolm is not telling his audience to throw bottles at the police; he never advocated violence in any of his speeches – though of course he did not endorse nonviolence either. "I don't mean go out and get violent," he tells his audience, "but at the same time you should never be nonviolent unless you run into some nonviolence."[7] He is presenting a concrete visual vignette to illustrate a justifiable possibility, one that lies clearly beyond the norms established by the dominant culture but one that should be included within the widening scope of possible actions contemplated by his audience.

Representation or warfare

The second section of the speech explores the possibilities for the "ballot" and the "bullet" when reframed in an international or global context. "When we begin to get in this area," he says, "we need new friends, we need new allies. We need to expand the civil-rights struggle to a higher level – to the level of human rights." The shift from "civil" to "human" rights is another common theme throughout the speeches of Malcolm's last year, and entails not only taking a broader perspective but transcending the limitations of the domestic political scene. "Whenever you are in a civil-rights struggle," Malcolm argues, "whether you know it or not, you are confining yourself to the jurisdiction of Uncle Sam."[8]

The broader scope of this international perspective would support bringing "Uncle Sam before a world court" represented by the United Nations. Though this plan never came to fruition, Malcolm does exploit the possibilities for more flexible and imaginative identifications within the broader sphere represented by the U.N. He urges his audience, for example: "You'd get farther calling yourself African instead of Negro," because "they don't have to pass civil-rights bills for Africans ... Just stop being a Negro. Change your name to Hoogagagooba." Malcolm also tells about "a friend of mine who's very dark [who] put a turban on his head and went into a restaurant in Atlanta before they called themselves desegregated," and was served.[9]

Again, Malcolm is not advocating that his audience put on turbans and enter segregated Southern restaurants. Rather, his purpose here seems to be to provide an illustration of the sort of thinking and acting that is made possible when drawing upon the resources present in a wider frame of reference. The legal system of the United States is not the only one available; the "Negro" identity is unstable and arbitrary and thus open to subversion; and seemingly impermeable racial barriers are ridiculed when exposed to the light of a broader perspective.

Paralleling the pattern of the first part of the speech, Malcolm next shifts his attention to the "bullet" by approvingly discussing guerrilla tactics. Dark-skinned people "who just a few years previously were rice farmers got together and ran the heavily-mechanized French army out of Indochina," he points out, and the "Algerians, who were nothing but Bedouins, took a rifle and sneaked off to the hills, and de Gaulle and all of his highfalutin' war machinery couldn't defeat those guerrillas. Nowhere on this earth does the white man win in a guerrilla warfare."[10]

Once again, in what by now is a recognizable pattern, it is clear that Malcolm X is not recommending that his audience in the Cory Methodist Church begin a guerrilla war armed only with "a rifle, some sneakers and a bowl of rice."[11] But thinking like a guerrilla, or perhaps thinking that being a guerrilla is a viable potential identity, can show his audiences that the great white nations can successfully be challenged through inventive tactics. Together with the Jacksonville teens throwing Molotov cocktails, the U.N. trial, and the turban-wearing friend, the guerrillas that Malcolm presents as embodiments of the international "bullet" broaden the palate of identities and actions from which his audience might choose.

Ballots and bullets

To this point, Malcolm has stretched the boundaries of the possible and thereby opened up some conceptual space that might allow analytical flexibility, but he has not advocated any specific political action. The emphasis has been on enlarging the perceptual horizon of his audiences, providing the conceptual space they require if they are to become critical interpreters of their political environment. In the final third of the speech, Malcolm rounds out his case for a shift in attitude and perspective as a form of political action.

Near the end of the speech, for example, Malcolm calls for a "black nationalist convention." This never materialized, but its most prominent feature was to have been a radical flexibility. He promises that: "We become involved with anybody, anywhere, any time and in any manner that's designed to eliminate the evils, the political, economic and social evils that are afflicting the people of our community." "We will hold a seminar," he continues, "we will hold discussions, we will listen to everyone," and "at that time, if we see fit then to form a black nationalist party, we'll form a black nationalist party. If it's necessary to form a black nationalist army, we'll form a black nationalist army. It'll be the ballot or the bullet."[12] Thus two key terms of this speech – the ballot and the bullet – mark the extremes of a wide range of options, most of which may be well outside the range accepted by the dominant white culture, but all of which must remain on the table as live possibilities.

In Rochester

Malcolm left for his famous journey to Mecca on April 13, 1964, ten days after delivering "The Ballot or the Bullet." In his autobiography he describes his experiences in great detail, and in one of his well-publicized letters he tells that he has "eaten from the same plate, drunk from the same glass, and slept in the same bed (or on the same rug) – while praying to the *same God* – with fellow Muslims, whose eyes were the bluest of blue, whose hair was the blondest of blond, and whose skin was the whitest of white."[13] Many understood these statements to indicate a softening of Malcolm's previous rigid views.

He returned to New York on May 21, and on June 28, 1964, founded the Organization for Afro-American Unity, which was inspired by the Organization of African Unity and which followed closely the program of black nationalism outlined at the end of "The Ballot or the Bullet." But he left the country again on July 9, so this organization did not and would never receive his full attention. The highlight of this trip was distributing a written appeal at the meeting of the Organization for African Unity, in Cairo, in which Malcolm urged the gathered African heads of state to acknowledge and support the African American freedom struggle. Malcolm returned to New York on November 24, and immediately continued the frenetic speaking schedule that was his norm, including appearances at the Harvard Law School Forum, at a meeting jointly sponsored by the Student Nonviolent Coordinating Committee and the Mississippi Freedom Democrats, at the socialist Militant Labor Forum, at Tuskegee Institute, and in Selma, Alabama.

Five days before he was assassinated, Malcolm X addressed a racially mixed audience at the Corn Hill Methodist Church in Rochester. This speech bears some resemblance to "The Ballot or the Bullet," but while that earlier text seems optimistic that a wider circumference will bring an empowering perspective, in the latter Malcolm portrays the international political arena as nearly as corrupt as the domestic. For example, Africans are just as oppressed as African Americans, and through many of the same tactics, so simply identifying yourself as African and changing your name to "Hoogagagooba" does not offer the critical distance required for the radical judgment that he is advocating. Instead, in this speech, Malcolm invites his audience toward a political stance *between* the domestic and international spheres, so that they might exercise judgment utilizing the potentials of each.

Outward

Early in the speech, Malcolm signals his intention to focus on the relationships between the domestic and the international perspectives, urging his audience that "we have to not only know the various ingredients involved at the local level and national level, but also the ingredients that are involved at the international level," because racial oppression has "become a problem that is so complex … that you have to study it in its entire world, in the world context or in its international context, to really see it as it actually is." Echoing the emphasis on *sight* from "The Ballot or the Bullet," Malcolm warns his audience that "if you only try and look at it in the local context, you'll never understand it. You have to see the trend that is taking place on this earth."[14] "Sight" takes on an added significance, however, because this speech is concerned with the ways that images of blacks are manipulated by whites.

The "racism practiced by America," for example, is the same as that is involved in "a war against the dark-skinned people in Asia ... a war against the dark-skinned people in the Congo, the same as it involves a war against the dark-skinned people in Mississippi, Alabama, Georgia, and Rochester, New York." And a key technique of this practice of racism is, as Malcolm puts it, "a science that's called image making" designed to make it "look like the victim is the criminal, and the criminal is the victim."[15]

Malcolm provides a pair of examples to illustrate this theory, one in the United States and the other in Africa. The domestic example concerns the press coverage of the Harlem riots of the previous summer. "During these riots," Malcolm notes, "the press, very skillfully, depicted the rioters as hoodlums, criminals, thieves, because they were busting up property." But Malcolm invites his audience to "look at it from another angle," and to see that actually the inner-city African American is "a victim of economic exploitation, political exploitation, and every other kind." The apparent victims, on the other hand, are revealed to be "landlords who are nothing but thieves, merchants who are nothing but thieves, politicians who sit in the city hall and who are nothing but thieves in cahoots with the landlords and the merchants."[16]

And "just as this imagery is practiced at the local level, you can understand it better by an international example," such as the US-supported bombing of rebels in newly independent Congo. The American press "refer to the villages as 'rebel held,'" for example, "as if to say, because they are rebel-held villages, you can destroy the population, and it's okay"; the pilots were called "'Anti-Castro Cuban,' that makes them okay"; and "they're able to do all of this mass murder and get away with it by labeling it 'humanitarian,' 'an act of humanitarianism.'"[17] In this way, a criminal act in the international scene – bombing villages – is remade into a heroic act.

Of particular note is the fact that Malcolm's audience is not asked to view one of these examples from the point of view of the other; that is, neither example is privileged, and the audience is not asked to identify with either the domestic or the global position. They are both corrupt. Rather, the audience is invited to view both examples simultaneously, side-by-side. The audience, then, is encouraged to critique each of these two perspectives without becoming aligned with either, and thus is positioned to exploit the interpretive potentials of both perspectives while avoiding the constraints of either.

Inward

The speech proceeds with another pair of parallel examples. This time Malcolm begins with a global perspective and then moves back toward the domestic, but again the lesson is about the methods consistently used by the white oppressor to keep dark-skinned people in check. He begins by noting that at the conference of emerging postcolonial states held in Bandung, Indonesia, in 1955, people found that they were bound together by a common oppressor. As Malcolm tells it, this realization "fed the flames of nationalism" in Asia and Africa, causing the colonial powers to turn to the United States for assistance, and this inspired the United States to develop a new approach to oppression, which Malcolm calls "benevolent colonialism" or "philanthropic imperialism."[18]

The link back to the domestic scene is through a Pan-Africanist militant awakening. Malcolm explains that as "the Black man in Africa got independent" and became "master of making his own image," the "Black man throughout the Western Hemisphere, in his subconscious mind, began to identify with that emerging positive African image." As African Americans were inspired by this new image and began to more closely identify with the Africans, the United States began to use on African Americans the same strategies of oppression that had been developed to deal with the Africans. As Malcolm explains, "just as [the Americans] had to change their approach with the people on the African continent, they also began to change their approach with our people on this continent. As they used tokenism and a whole lot of other friendly, benevolent, philanthropic approaches on the African continent ... they began to do the same thing with us here in the States."[19]

Thus far, then, Malcolm has presented two sets of parallel examples of racial oppression: the "science of image making," used by the white press during the Harlem riots and during the Congo bombing, and the tactic of "philanthropic imperialism" used by the United States both internationally and domestically. As the speech continues, he places these examples into the context of his own conversion narrative, showing how they might contribute to his audience's ability to engage and critique the dominant political culture.

Forward

The Nation of Islam, Malcolm explains as he begins his peroration, offered little opportunity for political engagement. It was "a sort of a religious-political hybrid, all to ourselves. Not involved in anything but just standing on the sidelines condemning everything." This sort of isolation rendered the organization politically mute, "actually alienated, cut off from all type of activity with even the world that we were fighting against." And yet, the Nation of Islam "attracted the activists ... who wanted to do something about the evils that confronted all Black people." Eventually, as Malcolm puts it, "dissension set in and eventually a split." He himself, of course, was one of these activists, who wanted to become politically engaged while also identified as a Muslim. Malcolm's life often is presented as a series of conversions, and here he presents his conversion narrative as a model for his audience. Just as he broke himself out of the voiceless confines of the Nation, so too, through the rhetorical action of speeches such as this one – as a further development of some of the themes in "The Ballot or the Bullet" – he would break out his audience so that they might increase their repertoire of tactics for engaging and critiquing the political world. The motto of his Organization of Afro-American Unity, he reminds his audience, "is 'By any means necessary.'"[20]

Malcolm reviews twentieth-century racial progress, constructing a narrative arc that parallels the gradual enlightenment that he experienced as he outgrew and eventually split from the Nation of Islam. "When we go back to 1939, Black people in America were shining shoes." It was only the advent of World War II that began to open some doors, for "then we began to learn how to run machines, when they needed us." Malcolm's point is that "it was not change of heart on Uncle Sam's part that permitted some of us to go a few steps forward. It was world pressure." Just as the political process could not be understood or engaged in by members of the Nation until they broke free of those constraints, so too the history of racial progress in America cannot be understood until Malcolm's audience has broken free of their limited domestic horizon. As he puts it, again emphasizing *sight* as a metaphor for critical action, "once you properly analyze the ingredients that opened the doors even to the degree that they were cracked open, when you see what it was, you'll better understand your position today … Any kind of movement for freedom of Black people based solely within the confines of America is absolutely doomed to fail."[21]

In this speech, as in "The Ballot or the Bullet," Malcolm again mentions a plan to bring the United States before the World Court of the United Nations. Here, though, it seems clear that the U.N. does not represent a clean break from the domestic sphere, but instead a venue wherein the international and domestic sphere might interact, where the domestic civil rights issues can "be discussed by people all over the world."[22] In other words, Malcolm is working here to position his audience in between the domestic and international spheres, where they can engage in processes of critical judgment unbound by the limitations of the first but yet not so thoroughly absorbed into the second that they lose contact with the United States.

Conclusion

In speeches during his last year, as exemplified by "The Ballot or the Bullet" and the one at Rochester, Malcolm worked to break his audiences free from the limitations of the dominant white culture, to broaden the scope within which they perceived their own situation, and, thus, to bring to their minds and hands resources that would not otherwise be available. He presented to them the audacity to identify with Bedouin guerrillas or to understand violent street resistance as justified, and the perspective to see the absurdity of racial segregation in the United States and the potential leverage available in global forums such as the United Nations. Most importantly, what Malcolm was modeling for his audiences was a *way of thinking* – his point was not that his listeners should now take action based on his analysis, but that they should engage in their own analysis using the interpretive strategies he had performed. Just as Malcolm X is able, at will, to expand or constrict the stage upon which he reasons, just as he is willing to entertain outrageous, unlikely, and even potentially dangerous possibilities far outside the decorous confines of the dominant culture, and just as he is able to critique both the domestic and international spheres without fully rejecting the productive potentials of either – so too should his audiences become similarly perspicacious, unaligned, and fearless.

In some of the speeches Malcolm delivered after he returned from Mecca, he gave this untethered, nomadic critical stance a name: "positive neutrality." On December 20 in New York City's Audubon Ballroom – where he would be assassinated two months later – he explained "what this positive neutrality means:"

> If you want to help us, help us; we're still not with you. If you have a contribution to make to our development, do it. But that doesn't mean we're with you or against you. We're neutral. We're for ourselves. Whatever is good for us, that's what we're interested in. That doesn't mean we're against you. But it does mean we're for ourselves.[23]

An attitude of "positive neutrality" carries tremendous emancipatory potential for Malcolm's audiences. Suspended between dangerous sites of power and oppression, they can engage in practices of judgment and critique that are not otherwise available; under no obligation to become aligned with preexisting norms or categories, they are free to innovate and invent extravagantly. In response to particular situations, they might alter their identities, justify violence, or expand their perspective so as to see the entire globe as under white oppression and their struggle as playing on an international stage. For his listeners, then, the world exists somewhat less as merely an inert array of brutish fact and instead, perhaps, as a resource of inventional opportunity; perhaps less an intractable materiality against which it is easy to feel powerless and more as a constructed world that one might bend, if only a bit, to one's will.

The significance of Malcolm X, then, cannot be divorced from a close analysis of his speeches and statements. This is where he did his thinking;

Peter Goldman notes that Malcolm "did his cerebrating on his feet, in the heat of battle."[24] More importantly, this is where Malcolm did his *performing* – it was through the act of performing his public address that he invented and modeled the modes of critical political engagement that he would have his audiences emulate. He did not lay out a static set of precepts or formulae, and rarely articulated an explicit plan of action; the inventive process that Malcolm sets in motion is never finished, and as a result can never come to rest in a way that might be distilled and disconnected from the dynamic action of his public address. Seen in this way, the significance of Malcolm X lies in the fact that he continues to model these modes of critical engagement each time an audience encounters his words. And to the extent that race continues to be a pivotal element in the contemporary political landscape, the untethered critical space and the radical interpretive tactics that Malcolm X makes available continue to provide his audiences with essential inventional resources.

NOTES

1. Whitney Young paraphrased in Peter Goldman, *The Death and Life of Malcolm X* (Urbana: University of Illinois Press, 1979), p. 8.

2. L. C. Jones, "Talking Book: Oral History of a Movement," *Village Voice*, 26 February 1985, p. 18.

3. James H. Cone, *Martin & Malcolm & America: A Dream or a Nightmare* (Maryknoll, NY: Orbis Books, 1991), p. 194; Archie Epps (ed.), *Malcolm X: Speeches at Harvard* (New York: Paragon House, 1991), p. 11; Celeste Michelle Condit and John Louis Lucaites, "Malcolm X and the Limits of the Rhetoric of Revolutionary Dissent," *Journal of Black Studies*, 33.2 (1993), p. 292; Henry Louis Gates, Jr., "Malcolm, the Aardvark, and Me," *New York Times* (February 21, 1993): sec. 7, p. 11.

4. On "scene," as I am using the term, see Kenneth Burke, *A Grammar of Motives* (Berkeley: University of California Press, 1969), pp. 3–15, 77. "Circumference" is Burke's term for the breadth or scope of a scene.

5. Malcolm X, *Malcolm X Speaks*, ed. George Breitman (New York: Pathfinder Press, 1965), pp. 26–7. To minimize notes, all references to this speech in a given paragraph will be collected into a note.

6. Malcolm X, *Malcolm X Speaks*, pp. 28, 31–2.

7. Ibid., p. 34.

8. Ibid.

9. Ibid., p. 36.

10. Ibid., p. 37.

11. Ibid.

12. Ibid., p. 41.

13. Malcolm X & Alex Haley, *The Autobiography of Malcolm X* (1965; London: Penguin Books, 2001), pp. 454–5.

14. Malcolm X, *February 1965: The Final Speeches*, ed. Steve Clark (New York: Pathfinder, 1992), pp. 144, 147. To minimize notes, all references to this speech in a given paragraph will be collected into a note.

15. Malcolm X, *February 1965*, p. 150.
16. Ibid., p. 153.
17. Ibid., pp. 153–4.
18. Ibid., p. 160.
19. Ibid., pp. 161–2.
20. Ibid., pp. 164–5.
21. Ibid., pp. 165, 167–8.
22. Ibid., p. 170.
23. Malcolm X, *Malcolm X Speaks*, p. 132.
24. Goldman, *Death and Life*, p. 13.

11

JAMES TYNER

Nightmarish landscapes: geography and the dystopian writings of Malcolm X

I have a dream that one day every valley will be exalted, every hill and mountain shall be made low, the rough places will be made plain, and the crooked places will be made straight, and the glory of the Lord shall be revealed ... So let freedom ring from the prodigious hilltops of New Hampshire ... from the mighty mountains of New York ... from the snow-capped Rockies of Colorado ... From the curvaceous peaks of California ... let freedom ring from Stone Mountain Georgia ... from every hill ... of Mississippi ... when we let it ring ... from every state and every city, we will be able to speed up that day when all God's children, black men and white men, Jews and Gentiles, Protestants and Catholics, will be able to join hands and sing ... thank God almighty, we are free at last.
Speech by Martin Luther King, Jr., delivered on August 28, 1963, on the steps of the Lincoln Memorial in Washington, DC

"I see America through the eyes of the victim. I don't see any American dream; I see an American nightmare." So argued Malcolm X in his "Ballot or the Bullet" speech delivered at the Cory Methodist Church in Cleveland, Ohio, just months after King's "I Have a Dream" Speech. Malcolm X explained that he was not an American. Rather, he considered himself to be "one of the 22 million black people who are victims of Americanism. One of the 22 million black people who are victims of democracy, nothing but disguised hypocrisy." Consequently, Malcolm X spoke "not as an American, or a patriot, or a flag-saluter, or a flag-waver" but instead "as a victim of [the] American system."[1]

Malcolm X viewed the American landscape as a nightmare. He did not see a Promised Land; America – at least for African Americans – was not a bright "City on a Hill" illuminating the world in all its glory. Rather, America was a place of dreams deferred and promises not kept. Malcolm X thus spoke to the concept of geographical imaginations, of alternative place-making and place-meaning, and of remaking space. In acknowledgment of these alternative geographies forwarded by Malcolm X, this essay is part of recent spatial turn in the social sciences and humanities.

As Phil Hubbard and his colleagues identify, in disciplines such as sociology, cultural studies, and literary studies, there is evidence of a "spatial turn" wherein researchers have come to appreciate the importance of space in understanding social and cultural phenomena. James Ryan, for example, writes that "geographical metaphors and techniques for 'mapping' the 'topographies' of culture have become incorporated into the language and practice of disciplines such as cultural studies."[2] Mike Crang and Nigel Thrift likewise note that "Space is the everywhere of modern thought. It is the flesh that flatters the bones of theory. It is an all-purpose nostrum to be applied whenever things look sticky," but unfortunately, they note, space "is used with such abandon that its meanings run into each other before they have been properly interrogated." Indeed, as they state, "in literary theory, space is often a kind of textual operator ... [in] anthropology, it is a means of questioning how communities are constituted in an increasingly cosmopolitan world. In media theory it tends to signify an aesthetic shift away from narrative."[3]

This spatial turn – and how we respond to it – has important implications for studies of African American society and, more specifically, black (radical) political thought. Robin Kelley, for example, argues that the conditions and the very existence of social movements enable participants to imagine something different, to realize that things need not always be this way.[4] It is that imagination, that effort to see the future in the present, that Kelley calls *poetic knowledge* and that Derek Gregory terms *geographical imaginations*. These alternative knowledges have a long history among writers and activists, seen most prominently in the genre of dystopian writings. The work of George Orwell and Ray Bradbury, for example, are world writings; they are *geographings*. Moreover, the geographical imaginations of these writers have become exemplars of social justice in that they serve as warnings of oppression and exploitation.

Significantly, many black radical writings and speeches also serve as exemplars of justice and warning. Kelley explains that in the poetics of struggle and lived experience, in the utterances of ordinary folk, in the cultural products of social movements, in the reflections of activists, we discover the many different cognitive maps of the future, of the world not yet born. Indeed, he concludes that the most radical art is not protest art but works that take us to another place, that envision a different way of seeing, perhaps a different way of feeling.[5] Kelley's use of "maps" and spatial analogies extends beyond a mere metaphorical use, for he effectively captures the literal "geo-graphing" of space.

This is a need, however, to direct greater attention to an understanding of "how human geographies – both real and imagined – are integral to black ways of life."[6] In this essay therefore I situate Malcolm X within the genre of dystopian writings as a means to establish his work within a larger tradition of both American and African American political thought.[7] Dystopian literatures have long been recognized as important literary forms of social criticism.[8] The fictional works of George Orwell, Aldous Huxley, and Anthony Burgess, for example, served (and continue to serve) as warnings of totalitarian systems and – crucially – how humanity fits into such draconian systems. Orwell, for instance, was less concerned about the political orientation of abuses of power than he was about the manifestation of power and the loss of humanity – of self.[9] Thus, Keith Alldritt argues that Orwell was concerned "to provide some critical description of the psychological state within the individual which makes the totalitarian state possible."[10] Indeed, Orwell's work disturbs the "modernist" ideas of the constitution of self – of who we are and who we may become – through language. This is perhaps most clearly evident in Orwell's classic *Nineteen Eighty-Four*, in which he offered insights into the necessity of remaining human in a totalitarian landscape, one so disciplined, so controlled, that all semblance of humanity was at risk of being dissolved.

Malcolm X was not a writer per se, and he certainly was not a novelist. Nevertheless, here I blur the traditional boundaries between written text and speech to argue that Malcolm X, similar to Orwell and other dystopian writers, understood that the constitution of self *takes place*: it occurs in a particular landscape. In other words, there is a geography to the idea of self.

The writing of landscapes

When we write our geographies, we are creating artifacts that impose meaning on the world. The moral claims implicit in our descriptions and explanations of landscapes and places are what have determined their choice as subject-matter, controlled the mode of study, produced the story we tell and structured the mode of its telling.   Denis Cosgrove and Mona Domosh[11]

There exist many traditions – and just as many debates – of "landscape" studies in geography and, more broadly, the social sciences and humanities. Hubbard and his coauthors explain that for some, "landscape" denotes a portion of the earth's surface and is effectively synonymous with its shape and form; conversely, others *conceive* of landscape as having a more specific connotation, encapsulating a particular way of imagining and framing space.[12] Richard Schein, for example, finds that landscapes have been conceived as symbolic, representative, and as representation.[13] In this section I follow Robert B. Riley, who advocates an understanding of landscape not simply as something visible (able to be seen) or visual (viewed through interpretation), but as places that convey meaning in everyday life.[14] In other words, places are both visible and visual, but places are also sites of social (re)production and interaction. This conforms with Schein, who argues that the cultural landscape is produced and implicated in the ongoing reproduction of social and cultural life.[15]

Recent work on landscapes has directed attention to the everydayness of the spaces in which we live. The landscapes in which Malcolm X lived (and died) were marked by oppressive living conditions, from the squalid Northern urban ghettos to the segregated Jim Crow South. Malcolm X's landscapes consisted of police dogs tearing into the flesh of African Americans, of African American babies and children being blown up in churches, and of lynchings and beatings of African Americans. These were violent landscapes, scenes of horrible and terrifying events. And it was in these everyday landscapes that discrimination, prejudice, and violence were confronted by African Americans.[16]

Much of African American history, as Mumia Abu-Jamal explains, is rooted in a radical understanding that America is not the land of liberty, but rather a place that is decidedly unfree, a land of repression and insecurity.[17] Indeed, as Manning Marable asserts, "Black consciousness was ... formed in response to the omnipresent reality of racist violence that generations of African Americans experienced in their daily lives."[18] This accounts for the critical commentary of the United States that was expressed so passionately, so forcibly, by Malcolm X. Consequently, a literary engagement with Malcolm X augments the crucial importance of "everyday" landscapes, for it is these spaces – more so than the grandiose monuments with high-styled designs – that are most vital to the formation of human meaning.[19] It is within these landscapes that day-to-day activities occur, and that revolutionary social movements are played out.

The French theorist Henri Lefebvre argues that a "revolution that does not produce a new space has not realized its full potential." He explains that lacking a new space, the revolution has failed "in that it has not changed life itself, but has merely changed ideological superstructures, institutions, or political apparatuses." Lefebvre concludes that a "social transformation, to be truly revolutionary in character, must manifest a creative capacity in its effects on daily life, on language and on space."[20] This conceptualization of revolutionary transformation is immediately apparent in the words of Malcolm X. In confronting a totalitarian state – the American political, social, and economic system – he advocated revolution because he believed that fundamental transformations of racism (and the attainment of "civil rights") were not possible within such a system. To "integrate" or "assimilate" into such a system was to placate a racist hegemony. Malcolm X explained that "it's impossible for a chicken to produce a duck egg ... A chicken just doesn't have it within its system to produce a duck egg ... The system in this country cannot produce freedom for an Afro-American. It is impossible for this system, this economic system, this political system, this social system, this system, period ... And if ever a chicken did produce a duck egg, I'm quite sure that you would say it was certainly a revolutionary chicken!"[21]

Progressive social movements (including revolutionary activities) do not simply produce statistics and narratives of oppression; rather, the best ones do what great poetry always does: transport us to another place, compel us to relive horrors, and, more importantly, enable us to imagine a new society.[22] As David Delaney writes, "If we want to understand the historical construction of geographies of race and racism in the United States, it seems we have to do more than map changing distributions of 'black people' – as if the geographies of race were in principle no different than the geographies of cotton or the blues or the AME Church."[23] Likewise, as Katherine McKittrick and Clyde Woods explain, "identifying the 'where' of blackness in positivist terms can reduce black lives to essential measurable 'facts' rather than presenting communities that have struggled, resisted, and significantly contributed to the production of space."[24]

Unlike the poetic discourses of social movements, the literary construction of alternative geographies in dystopian writings is always related, more or less directly, to specific "real-world" societies and problems. M. Keith Booker, for example, explains that dystopian *fictions* are typically set in places or times far distant from the author's own, but it is usually clear that the real referents of dystopian fictions are generally quite concrete and near-at-hand.[25] The fictional writings of Orwell, to illustrate, are modeled after the Soviet Union. Malcolm X, on the other hand, also attempted to represent an immediate and "authentic" landscape; he did so, however, not from the position of a social scientist, seeking to empirically document, verify, and explain accurately an authentic landscape. Nor did he follow the lead of dystopian writers through the creation of a fictionalized and distant society. Instead, the realism of Malcolm X was used rhetorically. He grounded his political thought on his routine observations, as well as his audience's life experiences. The world-building rhetoric of Malcolm X thus raises interesting ontological and epistemological issues of "truth" in the pursuit of justice.

In his writings and speeches, Malcolm X did not present "truths" to be assimilated, but rather patterns of interpretation to be emulated.[26] Malcolm X did not try to support his assertions with the type of *quantitative* evidence that whites would accept, because he was not trying to convince them; rather, he was speaking from a *black* point of view, and he wanted to identify the enemies of African Americans so that they would know whom they had to fight against in their struggle for dignity. Consequently, Malcolm X constructed composite landscapes, scenes of oppression and exploitation which his African American audiences would readily see and thus could relate to. The writings and speeches of Malcolm X were not meant to be read as fiction; nevertheless, as composite representations of landscapes, the place-making of Malcolm X operated as a powerful tool of social criticism. His narratives were minimalist; detailed, in-depth descriptions were not necessary. The realism – and significance – of his words lie in their personal, experiential basis, one that his audiences would quickly grasp. And it was this construction of concrete landscapes – of places of discrimination, prejudice, and violence with which his audiences were all too familiar – that was most effective. Indeed, Malcolm X crafted his speeches in a way he would have his audiences envision their own everyday lives in everyday places. Consider, briefly, Malcolm X's description of the urban landscape of Harlem, and his theoretical connection between urban politics and "riots." Malcolm X explained:

> It's the city structure that incites [riots]. A city that continues to let people live in rat-nest dens in Harlem and pay higher rent in Harlem than they pay downtown ... Who lets merchants outcharge or overcharge people for their groceries and their clothing and other commodities in Harlem, while you pay less for it downtown. This is what incites. A city that will not create some kind of employment for people who are barred from having jobs just because their skin is black. That's what incites. Don't ever accuse a black man for voicing his resentment and dissatisfaction over the criminal condition of his people as being responsible for inciting the situation. You have to indict the society that allows these things to exist.[27]

For Malcolm X, it was imperative to situate his audiences' understanding of racism within the material landscape. It was about reproducing alternative worlds, of imagining a new society. It was, as Robert Terrill maintains, about "enlarging the perceptual horizon of his audience" and of "encouraging his listeners to become critical interpreters of their political environment."[28]

The inhumanity of American landscapes: three readings

> If we want to understand ourselves, we would do well to take a searching look at landscapes.
> Pierce Lewis[29]

The overarching objective of cultural landscape writing, according to Paul Groth, is to inform the public.[30] It is thus a form of advocacy and, viewed in this manner, sits comfortably within the dystopian genre. In this section, I situate the writings and speeches of Malcolm X within three aspects of dystopian literature. First, dystopian literature makes us ponder how an originally *utopian* promise – such as the "American Dream" – was abused, betrayed, or, ironically, fulfilled so as to create tragic consequences for humanity.[31] Malcolm X, particularly after his split from the Nation of Islam, was exceptionally forthright in his accusations that African Americans had been denied their right to participate in the American Dream. In 1963, for example, Malcolm X assailed President John F. Kennedy for "talking about freedom in

Europe when 20,000,000 black [people] have no freedom" in the United States and noted that "representatives of the American government are in Nazi Germany complaining about the Berlin Wall, but haven't done anything about the Alabama Wall."[32] And in his critique of promises unkept, Malcolm X mirrored the strategies of other dystopian writers by challenging the overall structure of a racist *capitalist* society. In a speech delivered in 1964, Malcolm X asked what type of country was the United States. His response was a series of questions and answers:

> Why should we do the dirtiest jobs for the lowest pay? Why should we do the hardest work for the lowest pay? Why should we pay the most money for the worst kind of food and the most money for the worst kind of place to live in? I'm telling you we do it because we live in one of the rottenest countries that has ever existed on this earth. It's the system that is rotten; we have a rotten system. It's a system of exploitation, a political and economic system of exploitation, of outright humiliation, degradation, discrimination.[33]

What emerged in the speeches of Malcolm X was a powerful critique of capitalism, a critique based on the self-evident contradictions of capitalist accumulation within urban ghettos.[34]

Second, dystopian writings attempt to de-familiarize the familiar. By focusing critiques of society on spatially or temporally distinct settings, dystopian fictions provide fresh perspectives on problematic social, political, and/or economic practices that might otherwise be taken for granted or considered natural and inevitable.[35] To this end, Malcolm X attempted to de-familiarize the ghetto and thus challenge the *public* explanations of poverty disseminated in the media. Malcolm X argued that the living conditions of African Americans were not natural; squalid conditions in the ghetto were neither normal nor inevitable. But as it currently existed, the ghetto was certainly alienating. Malcolm X informed his audiences that, in 1964, there were thirty-five council members in New York City. He asked if they knew how many were black, and then explained:

> there's only one black one, and he's a councilman-at-large ... And many of our people don't even know who the black councilman is. How would you expect to change our miserable situation when we have a council that the black man can't even get into? He's not even represented there. We're not represented in the city government in proportion to our number. We're not represented in the state government in proportion to our number. And we aren't represented in the federal government in proportion to our number.[36]

In his critique of the political landscape, Malcolm X sought to demonstrate that African Americans, through their acquiescence to a racist (but supposedly democratic) system, remained alienated. Furthermore, Malcolm X explained how African Americans were linguistically defined by this undemocratic white society and thus remained marginalized. A first step was to de-familiarize the "Negro" landscape as constructed by white society. Malcolm X began with a simple declarative statement: "One of the main reasons we are called Negro is so we won't know who we really are." He then proceeded to emphasize the geography inherent in the term "Negro." Malcolm X explained, "Negro doesn't tell you anything. I mean nothing, absolutely nothing. What do you identify it with? ... Nothing ... It's completely in the middle of nowhere. And when you call yourself that, that's where you are – right in the middle of nowhere."[37] Reminiscent of Franz Fanon's rhetorical question, "Where am I to be classified? Or, if you prefer, tucked away?", Malcolm X understood the interconnections of self and place.[38] "Negro," for him, was a term used to negate, to alienate, the physical presence of African Americans. This is made possible because, according to Malcolm X, "Negroes" do not exist as people. Rather, they "were scientifically produced by the white man."[39] In other words, we would say that "Negro" is a social as well as spatial construction, one perpetuated through the reiteration of the term "Negro" in our academic studies, classroom teachings, and other activities. Malcolm X clearly understood the linkage between "self" and landscape: it is a matter of *who* we are through a concern of *where* we are.

Third, and related, dystopian literatures highlight the sense of alienation, the dehumanizing experiences, that emerge within totalitarian systems. This idea conforms readily with Malcolm X's spatial understanding of the term "Negro." Within a racist totalitarian system that was the United States, Malcolm X implored his listeners to make the connection between institutional racism and the suppression of African American individuality and humanity. Malcolm X explained that "Negro" "doesn't give you a language, because there is no such thing as a Negro language. It doesn't give you a country, because there is no such thing as a Negro country. It doesn't give you a culture – there is no such thing as a Negro culture, it doesn't exist. The land doesn't exist, the culture doesn't exist, the language doesn't exist, and the man [sic] doesn't exist. *They take you out of existence by calling you a Negro*."[40]

African Americans, defined by others as "Negroes," were existentially removed from the American landscape. They became, to paraphrase Orlando Patterson, socially *and* spatially dead.[41] Accordingly, the segregated landscapes of the Jim Crow South and the concentrated urban ghettos of the North were sites emptied of humanity, a dark void on the mental map of a racist society.

To counter these representations Malcolm X attempted to cultivate in his African American audiences a sense of self. The crux of his view was his insistence that African Americans were worthy independent of their association with whites. Both socially and spatially, whites were not required as yardsticks by which to measure the self-worth of African Americans. He used the geographic example of school desegregation to make his point: "If we can get an all-black school, that we can control, staff it ourselves with the type of teachers that have good at heart, with the type of books that have in them many of the missing ingredients that have produced [an] inferiority complex in our people, then we don't feel that an all-black school is necessarily a segregated school." This comment was made in response to debates regarding the earlier Supreme Court decision of 1954 (*Brown v. Board of Education*), and specifically King's comments that it was important for black children to interact with white children. From Malcolm X's perspective, black children should not be defined by their relation to white children; nor should the sense of self-worth of black children be based on an association with whites. He concluded: "I just can't see where if white people can go to a white classroom and there are no [African Americans] present and it doesn't affect the academic diet they're receiving, then I don't see where an all-black classroom can be affected by the absence of white children. If the absence of black children doesn't affect white students, I don't see how the absence of whites is going to affect the blacks."[42]

For Malcolm X, black liberation would result only when African Americans were seen as equals. This was not to be accomplished through integrationist practices. Integration was a technique of cultural genocide and economic imperialism, one that favored the status quo. Integration policies, as well as assimilation and acculturation beliefs and practices, deprived African Americans of their fundamental right of self-determination. Simply put, to integrate into a white supremacist society would negate the spaces of African Americans. To adopt the norms, values, and nomenclature of the dominant society, African Americans would cease to exist as a people. As such, integrated landscapes contributed to the dehumanization and displacement of African Americans just as strongly as segregation policies. In neither case were African Americans in control of their own communities and, hence, their self-determination.

Conclusion

Geography has always been a part of the struggle for political, economic, and social rights. The literary critic Edward Said, for example, argued that "Just as none of us is outside or beyond geography, none of us is completely free from the struggle over geography."[43] Consequently, as Ruth Wilson Gilmore writes, some geographic imperative must lie at the heart of every struggle for social justice.[44] Moreover, that these struggles are manifest on the landscape should be immediately obvious. Consequently, this essay is part of a larger spatial turn within the social sciences and humanities. Specifically, I situate Malcolm X, a radical *orator*, within the *literary* tradition of dystopian writings. I do so from the standpoint that both Malcolm X and many dystopian writers sought to discursively produce alternative geographies in the minds of their audiences.

Much dystopian literature has focused on various political forms of totalitarian states, such as socialism and fascism. A reading of Malcolm X, however, directs attention to the racial underscoring of dystopian landscapes and the interconnections of self and place. Malcolm X encouraged his (African American) audiences to resist the dehumanizing tendencies of a racist and undemocratic capitalist society. The social revolution he advocated was not, as commonly and erroneously characterized, reducible to violence. Rather, Malcolm X forwarded a transformative revolution in thinking and learning. He encouraged his audiences, and especially the younger members, to observe their landscape and to draw insight and awareness into the workings of society. Malcolm X, in this respect, was a landscape geographer, one who understood that landscapes say much about how people behave and interact.

For Malcolm X there was an immediate and practical dimension to the reading of landscapes and the production of knowledge. As he explained in a 1965 interview, students must learn to think for themselves. He said:

> if the students in this country forgot the analysis that has been presented to them, and they went into a huddle and began to research this problem of racism for themselves, independent of politicians and independent of all the foundations (which are a part of the power structure), and did it themselves, then some of their findings would be shocking, but they would see that they would never be able to bring about a solution to racism in their country as long as they're relying on the government to do it.[45]

Malcolm X did not want his students to memorize what was there but to *re*read it, against the grain, simultaneously learning from and critiquing the materials.[46] Consequently, the teaching and learning approach advocated by Malcolm X falls in line with that of many other dystopian writers. Orwell, for example, explained that "Every line of serious work that I have written since 1936 has been written, directly or indirectly, against totalitarianism and for democratic socialism, as I understand it ... I write ... because there is some lie that I want to expose, some fact to which I want to draw attention, and my initial concern is to get a hearing."[47] Malcolm X sought to expose the "lie" of the American Dream, to highlight the oppressive and exploitative landscapes of a racist society. And it is because of this form of social criticism that I situate Malcolm X within the genre of literary geography and dystopian writings.

NOTES

Epigraph: Martin Luther King, Jr., *I Have a Dream: Writings and Speeches That Changed the World*, ed. James M. Washington (New York: Harper Collins, 1992), p. 105.

1. Malcolm X, *Malcolm X Speaks*, ed. George Breitman (New York: Pathfinder Press, 1965), p. 26.
2. James Ryan, "Introduction: Cultural Turns, Geographical Turns," in *Cultural Turns/Geographical Turns*, ed. Ian Cook, David Crouch, Simon Naylor, and James R. Ryan (Harlow: Prentice Hall, 2000), p. 10.
3. Mike Crang and Nigel Thrift, "Introduction," in *Thinking Space*, ed. Mike Crang and Nigel Thrift (London: Routledge, 2000), p. 1.
4. Robin D. G. Kelley, *Freedom Dreams: The Black Radical Imagination* (Boston: Beacon Press, 2002), p. 9. See Derek Gregory, *Geographical Imaginations* (Oxford: Blackwell Publishers, 1994).
5. Ibid., pp. 9–11.
6. Katherine McKittrick and Clyde Woods, "No One Knows the Mysteries at the Bottom of the Ocean," in *Black Geographies and the Politics of Place*, ed. Katherine McKittrick and Clyde Woods (Cambridge, MA: South End Press, 2007), pp. 6–7.
7. For a fuller development of these arguments, see James A. Tyner, *The Geography of Malcolm X: Black Radicalism and the Remaking of American Space* (New York: Routledge, 2006); and James A. Tyner, "Nightmarish Landscapes: The Orwellian World of Malcolm X," in *Race, Ethnicity, and Place in a Changing America*, ed. John W. Frazier and Eugene L. Tettey-Fio (Binghamton, NY: Global Academic Publishing, 2006), pp. 25–31.
8. M. Keith Booker, *Dystopian Literature: A Theory and Research Guide* (Westport, CT: Greenwood Press, 1994); and Erika Gottlieb, *Dystopian Fiction East and West: A Universe of Terror and Trial* (Montreal and Kingston: McGill-Queen's University Press, 2001).
9. James A. Tyner, "Self and Space, Resistance and Discipline: A Foucauldian Reading of George Orwell's *1984*," *Social & Cultural Geography*, 5 (2004), p. 581; see also James A. Tyner, "Landscape and the Mask of Self in George Orwell's 'Shooting an Elephant,'" *Area* 37.3, (2005), pp. 260–7.
10. Keith Alldritt, *The Making of George Orwell: An Essay in Literary History* (New York: St. Martin's Press, 1969), p. 156.
11. Denis Cosgrove and Mona Domosh, "Author and Authority: Writing the New Cultural Geography," in *Place/Culture/Representation*, ed. James Duncan and David Ley (London: Routledge, 1993), p. 37.
12. Phil Hubbard, Rob Kitchin, Brendan Bartley, and Duncan Fuller, *Thinking Geographically: Space, Theory and Contemporary Human Geography* (London: Continuum, 2002), p. 139.
13. Richard H. Schein, "The Place of Landscape: A Conceptual Framework for Interpreting an American Scene," *Annals of the Association of American Geographers*, 87 (1997), p. 660.
14. Robert B. Riley, "The Visible, the Visual, and the Vicarious: Questions About Vision," in *Understanding Ordinary Landscapes*, ed. Paul Groth and Todd W. Bressi (New Haven: Yale University Press, 1997), pp. 200–9.

15. Schein, "Place of Landscape," p. 662.
16. The violence to which I refer is both structural (or systemic) and direct. Structural violence refers both to material inequalities that are embedded within a society, such as differentially-based access to education, healthcare, employment, or housing, as well as socio-symbolic practices (i.e. discrimination, racial slurs). Direct violence refers to specific events, such as beatings, lynchings, rape, and murder. Within the spaces of the *everyday* it is generally assumed that structural violence becomes routine or "normal." However, for many African Americans, direct violence was also a "fact" of life – the threat or actuality of physical violence was an everyday occurrence.
17. Mumia Abu-Jamal, *We Want Freedom: A Life in the Black Panther Party* (Boston: South End Press, 2004), p. 14.
18. Manning Marable, *Living Black History: How Reimagining the African-American Past Can Remake America's Racial Future* (New York: Basic Civitas Books, 2006), p. 16.
19. Paul Groth, "Frameworks of Cultural Landscape Study," in Groth and Bressi, *Understanding Ordinary Landscapes*.
20. Henri Lefebvre, *The Production of Space*, trans. Donald Nicholson-Smith (Oxford: Blackwell, 1991), p. 54.
21. Malcolm X, *Malcolm X Speaks*, pp. 68–9.
22. Kelley, *Freedom Dreams*, p. 9.
23. David Delaney, *Race, Place, and the Law, 1836–1948* (Austin: University of Texas Press, 1998), pp. 9–10.
24. McKittrick and Woods, "No One Knows the Mysteries," p. 6. AME Church is the African Methodist Episcopal Church.
25. Booker, *Dystopian Literature*.
26. Robert E. Terrill, *Malcolm X: Inventing Radical Judgment* (East Lansing: Michigan State University Press, 2004), p. 124.
27. Quoted in Louis E. Lomax, *To Kill a Black Man: The Shocking Parallel in the Lives of Malcolm X and Martin Luther King, Jr.* (Los Angeles: Holloway House, 1968), p. 239.
28. Terrill, *Malcolm X*, p. 129.
29. Pierce Lewis, "Axioms for Reading the Landscape: Some Guides to the American Scene," in *The Interpretation of Ordinary Landscapes: Geographical Essays*, ed. Donald W. Meinig (New York: Oxford University Press, 1979), p. 11.
30. Groth, "Frameworks of Cultural Landscape Study."
31. Gottlieb, *Dystopian Fiction*.
32. Quoted in John H. Cone, *Martin & Malcolm & America: A Dream or a Nightmare* (Maryknoll, NY: Orbis Books, 1991), p. 113.
33. Malcolm X, *By Any Means Necessary: Speeches, Interviews and a Letter by Malcolm X*, ed. George Breitman (New York: Pathfinder Books, 1970), p. 46.
34. James A. Tyner, "Urban Revolutions and the Spaces of Black Radicalism," in McKittrick and Woods, *Black Geographies and the Politics of Place*, pp. 218–32.
35. Booker, *Dystopian Literature*.
36. Malcolm X, *By Any Means Necessary*, pp. 94–5.
37. Malcolm X, *Malcolm X on Afro-American History*, ed. Stere Clark (New York: Pathfinder Press, 1967), pp. 24–5.
38. Frantz Fanon, *Black Skin, White Masks* (New York: Grove Press, 1967), p. 113.

39. Malcolm X, *Malcolm X on Afro-American History*, p. 24.
40. Ibid., p. 25, emphasis mine.
41. Orlando Patterson, *Slavery and Social Death: A Comparative Study* (Cambridge, MA: Harvard University Press, 1982).
42. Malcolm X, *By Any Means Necessary*, p. 17.
43. Edward Said, *Culture and Imperialism* (New York: Alfred A. Knopf, 1993), p. 7.
44. Ruth Wilson Gilmore, "Fatal Couplings of Power and Difference: Notes on Racism and Geography," *Professional, Geographer*, 54.1 (2002), pp. 15–24.
45. Malcolm X, *Malcolm X Talks to Young People: Speeches in the US, Britain, and Africa* (New York: Pathfinder Press, 1991), p. 89.
46. Terrill, *Malcolm X*, p. 7.
47. George Orwell, *A Collection of Essays* (New York: Harcourt, 1981), p. 314.

12

MOLEFI KETE ASANTE

Afrocentricity and Malcolm X

Afrocentricity, as an intellectual idea, owes much of its popularity to the political trajectory charted by Malcolm X. This is not to claim that he was an Afrocentrist for clearly there were elements of Malcolm's life that were not strictly Afrocentric. Indeed the Afrocentric paradigm, as conceptualized by Ama Mazama, declares that Africans' liberation "rests upon the ability to systematically replace European ways of thinking, being, consciously replace them with ways that are germane to the African cultural experience."[1] One could argue that Malcolm's attachment to Islam in many ways mirrored that of other Africans to Christianity and that the latter was problematic from an Afrocentric perspective. Although Malcolm was clearly on the road toward a full appreciation of the subject position of Africans within our own history, he was not sufficiently knowledgeable of historical processes to incorporate information about the role of Africans in African or world history in his discourse. He was, on the other hand, devoted to seeking the rise of a black nationalist consciousness, which in itself was a major step toward the idea of mental liberation.

Afrocentricity is a paradigmatic intellectual perspective that privileges African agency within the context of African history and culture transcontinentally and trans-generationally. This means that location is essential to any analysis that involves African culture and behavior whether literary or economic, political or cultural.[2] The term "African" in an Afrocentric framework refers to people of African descent who may live in Africa, the Caribbean, and North and South America. It is a term that has diasporan aspects as well.

However, because Afrocentricity is preeminently a cultural paradigm that affects all aspects of African life, from this perspective of Malcolm X as a cultural hero is directly related to his emphasis on cultural transformation. What he disliked were African people who appeared to be beggars, dressing themselves in the robes of inferiority, and praying for a deliverance that only they could bring about. His rejection of this beggarly stance was the turn, the pivot that was necessary for a radically different cultural agenda. Afrocentricity as a mode of consciousness where African agency is front and center in interpretation, critique, development, and action grows from this pivot much like Kawaida philosophy[3] found its source in the same Malcolmian moment. Culture may be viewed as a product of the historical processes which lead to self-conscious recognition of defining characteristics in the social, political, and economic arenas; Malcolm X was preeminently a cultural spokesperson, an analyst and theorist of culture, and a revolutionary cultural scientist. Thus, when he is examined within the context of his own community and within the framework of the African American situation generally, he emerges as a concrete example of the cultural hero.

Malcolm's identity as an intellectual and an organizer must be seen in the light of his emphasis on people in transformation. He wanted Africans in America to be transformed, changed, and perfected in resistance to oppression. He expressed this in his concept of the radically different type of African American who was not afraid to speak up and stand up for legitimate rights. This was the key to what Harold Cruse would see as the responsibility of the mature, independent-thinking African American's response to the crisis in culture and leadership.[4]

Malcolm X radically changed the political discourse in the United States around African American rights in that he was not speaking merely a discourse of integration into the white society but rather demanding human rights as an African person. This was un-King-like, unique, creative, and so fundamentally authentic that the masses found his rhetoric compelling. Malcolm was never an apolitical public intellectual; he always addressed issues within a context informed by the resistance to oppression. His public stance was inevitably a very real demonstration of his passionate commitment to freedom.

Thus, his oratory was comprehensive, tight, sharp, unrehearsed, from an intellectual genius who felt one with his people in that his experiences had made him understand the self-hatred, docility, and self-degrading activities of many Africans. He rejected the condition of servitude and expressed himself as a conscious, historical being committed to the ultimate liberation of African people by any means necessary. This was new, in sharp contrast to the previous approaches of negotiation, petition, and prayer.

Malcolm taught that Africans in America had been badly taught. Most African Americans did not know their names and the names they wore were not their African names. Malcolm's idea was that Africans had allowed the white man to dictate terms of existence: indeed, it was impossible for them to express concerns for liberation except in terms that had been determined by whites. Here was an example of blacks seeking freedom from oppression but going to whites to ask them to approve the rules of discussion or, in some cases, even to provide the rules. Malcolm rejected this procedure and advanced what became a model for Afrocentric scholars who understood the dimensions of the servility and sought to assert political, economic, cultural, and moral authority based on a clear reading of African history, past and present. It is the tendency toward seeming like a junior brother or sister that Malcolm struggled against, and he demonstrated in his public and private discourses a way to articulate new visions and new agendas. It is this stance that was so productive and generative in the launching of youth movements and passionately cultural and political institutions such as the Black Panthers and the Us Organization and new philosophies including Kawaida and Afrocentricity. Each proponent of transformation saw in Malcolm's rhetoric and life a way to be; thus, it was his boldness that alerted the white opposition that racism was threatened.

While he was a minister of the Nation of Islam, Malcolm was influenced by the Honorable Elijah Muhammad and held to the nationalist positions that were expected of him, but he became disenchanted with the overall thrust of that movement and emerged as a seminal thinker himself. As Malcolm came to stand alongside Muhammad, then, Afrocentrists can stand alongside other theorists and say that their own work, with its boldness, courageous attitude toward domination, posture of African agency, and cultural reconstruction, is analogous to the Malcolmian project itself.

Culture has the ability to pull behaviors, symbols, customs, motifs, moods, and icons together into a single comprehensive affirming presence. It is Malcolm's stance toward self-hatred, culturicide, and menticide that governs his cultural ideology. Malcolm recognized that the real enemy of the African in America is white racism and its attendant manifestations in the society's institutions, which is one reason that he rejected the white man's Christian religion. Malcolm explains that the African American often thinks his friend is his enemy and his enemy is his friend.[5]

A concept of culture

Malcolm X suggested that there were three overarching political lessons that the African had to understand about America: (1) American society could not be redeemed on the basis of its present institutions, (2) whites would not agree to share power with Africans committed to social justice, and (3) Africans had to accept their Africanity as a basis for political, economic, and moral actions. Of course Malcolm X thought that the issue of Africanity is that African Americans, as people with an African narrative based on traditions and values inherited from experience and history, could reinterpret American life and bring about a new dispensation of freedom and justice. This, however, depended upon a concept of culture.

With the Age of Malcolm a new epoch began in the conception of a national culture or cultural nationalism which caused a far-reaching revolution in the traditional views held by members of African American institutions. He was not merely the keeper of African America's manhood, but of the ancestral flames of a proactive response to the human condition. His own life represented the rebirth of the extensive African American commitments to cultural reconstruction that would be seen in the extensive philosophical contours of Maulana Karenga's Kawaida movement.

What is necessary still is the consistent and persistent dissemination of the ideas Malcolm espoused in regard to culture, essentially a "pattern or the habit of seeing for ourselves, hearing for ourselves, thinking for ourselves, and then we can come to an intelligent judgment for ourselves."[6] Malcolm saw that the adaptation of our ideas, attitudes, language, and history to the social and cultural imperative of the African people was the first requirement for a comprehensive transformation. There could be no other interface with our historical destiny; we had to center ourselves in our African reality.

A long list of precursors contributed to Malcolm's pattern of growth. For example, his father had been a member of the Universal Negro Improvement Association led by Marcus Garvey. One can say that the Garvey movement prepared Malcolm for the more personal and concrete teachings of Elijah Muhammad. These doctrines deeply impacted his thinking, of course, and later he was significantly influenced by the richly textured words of Paul Robeson.

African culture, already present in the thinking of the nationalists, gained respectability with Malcolm's pronouncement that we were African people despite all of the claims to the contrary by the African American establishment. He knew that the word "African" had come to have a negative meaning to most African Americans, which he explained as a cultural misorientation. He said, "The word 'African' was used in this country in a derogatory way. But now, since Africa has gotten, is getting, its independence and there are so many independent African states, the image of the African has changed from negative to positive."[7]

The recuperation of African culture was pregnant with cultural possibilities inherent in the historical ground of our social and political reality. Others before Malcolm had recognized the power of this truism, but never had it been expressed with so much force by an African American who understood the implications of cultural revolution. Garvey, Edward Wilmot Blyden, and Martin Delaney, all in a chain, were the progenitors of Malcolm's maturity on the cultural question. For the first time since Garvey had used the express symbol of Africa as a powerful instrument in cultural awakening, the cultural attitude was revived in the rhetoric of Malcolm. Here it came as a torrent, breaking the shackles of a genuflected people and announcing a new more aggressive approach to cultural reconstruction. As we heard him and sat at his feet, it was inevitable that his faith would be reflected in numerous attempts to restructure our response to America. Thousands of urban Africans reached toward Malcolm's vision and when it was comprehended they preached in Shangoan voices the truth they had seen.

Furthermore, with Malcolm's challenge – that we were Africans – it became clearer "Negro," as a word and a concept, was dead. In the struggle of ideas where cultural considerations were seen as primary, that is, fundamental, the old Negro Order, hailed in its day by Alain Locke and others as the "new Negro," was permanently laid to rest by Malcolm. No one could be taken seriously without a response to the Chakan posture of this radical discourse. Malcolm brought discontent within the old order, creating, by the power of his logic, schisms in the conservative body politic of African America. It is easy to understand the preeminent position of Malcolm as a cultural figure when we consider in addition the intense reaction of the white American establishment to his call for black cultural nationalism. He was considered an extremist and a militant by most of the white press. Of course, the African American press, itself often tied to the white corporate structure, was hardly better on Malcolm. In fact the black church that had at moments seemed interested in Martin Luther King, Jr.'s movement found Malcolm too strong for their liking.

The cultural epoch of Malcolm is multifaceted, of course, a sort of umbrella under which walks a new woman and man born of cultural struggle and understanding Karenga's notion of "history as the struggle and record of humans in the process of humanizing the world, i.e., shaping it in their own image and interests."[8] Even now the legacies African Americans have inherited from Malcolm are the most dominant motifs of our approach to humanity. Since culture involved struggle and this process was at the core of developing a cultural tradition, Malcolm X, preeminently a struggler against racism, under-stood the necessity for the African American to recognize value in *our* traditions.

Malcolm made an end to the apologia of the *Negro* and declared that African Americans should gain freedom by any means necessary, which we often understood to include self-defense. But we know from his teachings that he was committed to changing the way we *thought* about ourselves and Africa. Planting the seed of an affirming African presence, his cultural project was the foundation from which African Americans could grow strong, vital, positive sentiments and attitudes. Malcolm's project gave incentive to the rampant and rambunctious cultural nationalism which always existed just below the emotional surface of every conscious African American.

Along with this impulse to cultural nationalism, for someone to be cultured in the traditional African manner carries with it the responsibility to use the language effectively. In his heroic persona, Malcolm was the master of this. Numerous studies of his ability to communicate suggest that his power was so elemental and essential that his voice remained unanswerable: fluid, pure, and fundamental. The best oratorical genius converged in his heroism, and Africans were always left with the feeling of having been in the presence of the purest self of the race. When Malcolm X spoke his images were perfect; the cadence of his sentences were like poetry whose rhythmic structure harked back to the profound oratory of a people long tired of suffering and struggling to regain historical footing.

In effect, he was the sensibility of millions of Africans ready to rise up against all forms of persecution. If death was the price of freedom, then death would be the price of African freedom in America. So full of his culture, it was as if he knew everything about his people and wanted to teach by sharing the depth of the experience. Malcolm could juxtapose "singing" and "swinging," "landless" against the "landlord," "grass roots" versus "grass leaves," "house Negro" versus "field Negro," and a "Black March on Washington" versus a "Negro March on Washington."

While the philosophical core of the African's relationship to reality is not an antagonistic duality, Malcolm demonstrated that the African condition in America was fraught with extreme danger. Therefore, he positioned the one against the other, the good against the evil, and the African versus *diablo blanco* as an instructive device rather than a philosophical statement. In the end, it is natural for him to show us the unreality of Hollywood and the basic reality of Harlem. The point is not lost on an audience of true votaries.

Perhaps the principal clue to Malcolm's understanding of culture emerges when he demonstrates his rationale for action: the struggle against the condition of oppression. For us, culture has no other practical end. It must be the regaining of freedom in order to be truly effective as humans in history.

Malcolm X had arrived at his analysis of the role of culture through testing the historical choices made by African Americans. The civil rights movement came under extremely close scrutiny since it had galvanized thousands and had captured the imagination of the black establishment. What Malcolm discerned, however, was the ineffectiveness of a movement which did not address the cultural question. He spent his life asserting this idea and the varied implications of it. If some found his theses violent, it was because he laid them down without excuse, and because the system of white domination of African Americans was itself vile, violent, and brutal in its execution of power. In this situation defense was not meanness of spirit but the magnificent nobility of African American culture derived from traditional African philosophical roots.

As an African person I can say that Malcolm resembled us at our best, in our most authoritative manner, in our humanity, in our oratorical style, in our humor, in our nuances, and in the manner of our relationships, and our treatment of each other. In these things collectively, and with specific qualities, we each could individually admire Malcolm's life as a testament to African American culture.

Conclusion

Malcolm resembled African Americans in the highest cultural reality; he was also a cultural teacher with lessons on self-consciousness, respect, and dignity for all humans, African history, and moral uprightness. Creating a curriculum of his own history, he elevated the art of instruction by serving as the model for what he taught. If he taught that courage was more rewarding than cowardice, he demonstrated by his own life that he believed what he taught. If the government was full of "tricksters," then African American leaders should not have coffee with the tricksters. He met the protectors and defenders of the establishment only to tell them of the grievances Africans rightly held. Thus, culture, for Malcolm, was proactive and he promulgated the view that Africans had an obligation to advance from the oppressed state to freedom. The broad dissemination of this message alone was sufficient to create for him a place in cultural history because no one had ever taught quite so effectively, or so directly, to the oppressed Africans in America.

Malcolm's cultural path will not be complete until it is fully realized in the active political and social lives of African Americans. In the end, that is the only authentic test for his conception of a centered, agency directed, and determined Afrocentric culture. He becomes a figure transformed in the actuality of historical experiences; thus, to live Malcolm, is to see him as an *orisha* of power and purpose, a true aspect of Afrocentric culture. He is represented now by some with a string of solid black beads, an *aleke* of strength.[9] Afrocentricity as an intellectual idea has the aim of fulfilling the Malcolmian project of removing African self-hatred and restoring African self-confidence.

NOTES

1. Ama Mazama (ed.), *The Afrocentric Paradigm* (Trenton, NJ: Africa World Press, 2003), p. 5.
2. Molefi Kete Asante, *An Afrocentric Manifesto* (London: Polity Press, 2008), p. 6.
3. Kawaida is a cultural and social philosophy expounded by Maulana Karenga and founded on the principles called the *Nguzo Saba*, seven principles (unity, self-determination, collective work and responsibility, cooperative economics, purpose, creativity, and faith).
4. Harold Cruse, *The Crisis of the Negro Intellectual* (New York: Quill, 1984).

5. Malcolm X, *The Last Speeches*, ed. Bruce Perry (New York: Pathfinder, 1989), p. 39.
6. Ibid., p. 156.
7. Ibid., p. 95.
8. Maulana Karenga, *Kawaida Theory* (Los Angeles: Kawaida Publications, 1990), p. 29.
9. *Orisha* is a Yoruba term that refers to spiritual entities that have the possibility of becoming the "ori" or "head" of a living person. *Aleke* is also Yoruba, and refers to qualities represented by necklaces of beads that are often worn by the spiritual leaders of Yoruba.

13

KEVIN GAINES

Malcolm X in global perspective

In August 2008, S. Shankar wrote in the *Hindu* newspaper, "Now the world is full of Barack Obama, but 50 years ago another young, charismatic Black American filled the world in his own way." That precursor was Malcolm X, who had filled the world with his indictment of US racism and empire. Shankar invoked his memory to argue that the rise of Obama did not signal, as some would have it, the arrival of a "post-racial" American society. Obama had just captured the nomination of the Democratic party (months before his election as the first African American president in US history). To Shankar, the federal government's shocking negligence in the face of the massive suffering wrought by Hurricane Katrina in 2005 revealed the persistence of racism in American social and political life. "In celebrating Obama, there is no need to forget either Malcolm or Katrina," Shankar concluded.[1]

That Obama transcends race is an article of faith among his supporters; his approach could not be further in temperament from Malcolm's confrontational stance on racism. To be sure, when Malcolm was alive, Southern white extremists could brutalize blacks with impunity. Still, Shankar's comparison reminds us that Obama is a product of the history of the black freedom movement in the United States. That history belongs to the world, due in no small part to Malcolm X's travels to Europe, Africa, and the Middle East, and the importance of his Islamic faith to his rejection of the Nation of Islam's antiwhite doctrine. The African American struggle for equality, which for some, like Shankar, was embodied by Malcolm, inspired people all over the world, throughout Africa, Asia, the Middle East, and Eastern Europe. During the last year of his life, Malcolm represented the black freedom movement, from his pilgrimage to Mecca to his travels throughout Africa and Europe.

As Farah Jasmine Griffin has observed, "The image of Malcolm X refuses to die and remains a space where contemporary urban black men can create their own sense of identity in contrast to the construction of them by the dominant society."[2] Although he is remembered by overseas audiences as a key figure in the US black struggle for equality, in the country of his birth the image of Malcolm X remains deeply contested, a continuation of the controversy and vilification that surrounded him during his lifetime. A measure of acceptance is evident in the postage stamp bearing his image issued by the US Postal Service in 1999. For some conservatives, however, Malcolm X's influence on a suburban white youth, John Walker Lindh, the American convicted of treason for taking up arms against US forces with the Taliban in Afghanistan, confirms their view of Malcolm as a dangerous figure.

The meaning of his image and legacy is often in the eye of the beholder. The popular narrative of Malcolm's prison conversion from criminality and nihilism to Islamic faith and exploder of America's racial illusions (including those he himself had harbored as the Nation of Islam's national spokesman) has become the stuff of myth for many who discover him today. Immediately after his death, black activists sought guidance and inspiration from his fearless example. For many, Malcolm's global reframing of African Americans' struggles for human rights was the central lesson of his life, and, arguably, the cause of his untimely death. In 1968, Patricia Robinson described Malcolm's legacy as "a brilliant Black humanist" who awakened African Americans "to the wider factors in our oppression, the international oppression by the US of poor dark people and their rising revolt." He had "[given] us back our roots, our history, and he connected us with the world revolutions," producing a generation more historically aware and critical of America's counterrevolutionary opposition to global human rights struggles.[3] Robinson's tribute, undoubtedly a rejoinder to the postmortem condemnations of Malcolm that filled the news media, is a serious attempt to give him his due, but it also shows our indulgence toward martyrs. Robinson avoids the complicated story of Malcolm's political evolution. She cannot begin to acknowledge his decidedly mixed legacy.

Malcolm X was a deeply tragic figure. Many look to his spiritual redemption from a life of crime and nihilism and to his hunger for education as the paramount lessons to be drawn from his life. Yet in hindsight, Malcolm's rise within an authoritarian religious movement was both his salvation and his downfall. The Nation of Islam gave him a voice and public platform from which to indict white America for its crimes, but he also used that voice to proselytize the twisted racial doctrines of the Nation, damaging his credibility. Malcolm's penchant for inflammatory rhetoric too alienated potential allies in the movement. In the end, he was trapped by his notoriety. Finally, Malcolm committed a fatal error in choosing to go public with allegations of Muhammad's extramarital affairs. What if Malcolm had chosen to remain in exile, deferring for an indefinite period his return to the United States? And if exile in some African nation had been an option for him and perhaps his family, why did he return to the United States knowing that death stalked him?

Malcolm's sojourn and the newly acquired political insights on US racism and global imperialism he shared with audiences are central to the narrative of his posthumous vindication. During the 1960s, as African Americans and their allies waged a bitter and bloody struggle against the final throes of Jim Crow segregation and the violence waged by white supremacists, Malcolm X did perhaps more than any other African American leader to link the civil rights movement with the cause of African liberation in the hearts and minds of African Americans and Africans.

By many accounts, Malcolm did a lot of listening, was willing to question old assumptions, and was committed to intellectual growth. In Jedda, Saudi Arabia, Malcolm was so humbled by the hospitality of "white" Muslims that he began to understand the peculiar socialization and racial arrogance of the American "white man" in relation to the color-blind demeanor of men with white complexions in the Muslim world.[4] At Oxford, Malcolm discussed Islam with Tariq Ali, listening attentively as the nonpracticing Muslim scorned all faiths. When Ali paused, expecting a stinging rebuke, Malcolm said, "it's good to hear you talk like that ... I'm beginning to ask myself many of the same questions."[5] In Ghana, Malcolm impressed the expatriates with his boundless energy for political discussion, and the humility with which he approached it. After his lecture at the University of Ghana, he solicited his hosts' criticisms of the speech. According to Preston King, Malcolm "wasn't full of himself, there was no pulpit manner ... I found him very likeable, not just impressive."[6]

Malcolm was making the transition from the parochial value system of the Nation of Islam to a sound political grasp of the workings of American power and propaganda in the United States and the world. His openness to observation, debate, and dialogue reflected his commitment to presenting his audiences a more persuasive analysis of global imperialist forces, particularly US interventions against national liberation forces in Vietnam and the Congo. Formulating his views against the backdrop of events in Africa and the United States, including the 1964 presidential campaign, Malcolm promoted among African Americans an expansive vision of US citizenship grounded in an identification with the democratic aspirations of African and "Third World" peoples.

Malcolm Little was born a black nationalist, to borrow I. F. Stone's pithy phrase,[7] by virtue of his parents' active membership in the Garvey movement. Marcus Garvey, the Jamaican-born founder of the Universal Negro Improvement Association, had preached the slogan: "Africa for the Africans." Malcolm's youth in Lansing, Michigan and elsewhere was traumatic; his father was brutally slain possibly by a white supremacist group; by this thirteenth birthday, after struggling to support Malcolm and his seven siblings, his mother was committed to a state mental hospital. Malcolm was also shaped by a burgeoning global consciousness among people of African descent over the course of the twentieth century. Historian Nikhil Pal Singh has characterized this formative conjuncture as a culture of black worldliness advanced by African American intellectuals whose discussions of race and democracy in the mid-century United States were informed by the anticolonial revolt of Afro-Asian "darker races," as best exemplified by the historic Bandung conference of nonaligned nations in Indonesia, in 1955.[8]

Malcolm's conversion to the Nation of Islam reflected this global political imagination, but his prison conversion also indicated the limited opportunities available for an intellectually gifted working-class black youth unable to pursue a university education, and thus ineligible for training for leadership in the institutions of the African American establishment. Instead, the Nation, promising a way out of the poverty and alienation faced by African Americans in Northern ghettos, rescued Malcolm from the criminal underworld.

As its national spokesman, Malcolm extolled the Nation's success at redeeming African American men and women from the temptations of the streets. But by mid-1963, he had grown impatient with the organization's avoidance of political activism. Before his break with Muhammad, Malcolm chose his political forays carefully, engineering the stay of Fidel Castro and the Cuban delegation in Harlem during the General Assembly of the United Nation's Security Council in October 1960. Malcolm was at the center of the excitement and visibility accorded to Harlem by the presence of Castro, Soviet premier Nikita Khrushchev, and such stalwarts of anticolonial resistance as Kwame Nkrumah, and Egypt's Gamal Abdel Nasser. Malcolm met with Castro, and gained the confidence of secular African American progressives, including John Henrik Clarke, John O. Killens, and Maya Angelou.

The Congo, and the emergence of the new Afro-American nationalism

By communing in Harlem with Castro, Nkrumah, Nasser, and other anti-imperialist icons, Malcolm X forged a tangible connection with a global Afro-Asian anticolonial movement. Months later, however, at the behest of the Nation of Islam, he met secretly with representatives of the Klan, seeking to negotiate land for a separatist Nation settlement. Malcolm, whose street rallies and speeches in Harlem were popular with secular, Africa-conscious Harlemites, would emerge as the most prominent exponent of Northern African American radicals critical of racism at home and US policy toward Africa. By the time Malcolm visited Ghana in May 1964, at the invitation of Mayfield and other African American expatriates there, he shared with his hosts a commitment to forging operational linkages between US black struggles and African liberation movements. Before that, Malcolm could only watch from the sidelines as a new political formation of Harlem blacks emerged, mobilizing against the West's resistance to African liberation and the very terms of African American civic identity and participation.

On February 3, 1960, British Prime Minister Harold Macmillan addressed the South African Parliament in Cape Town. He acknowledged the inevitability of nationalism in Africa: "The wind of change is blowing through this continent." Macmillan's view was not shared by conservatives who feared that violence would accompany decolonization. Partly in response to such skeptics, and despite the violence wielded by his political opponents, Ghana's Prime Minister Kwame Nkrumah had embraced nonviolence. In 1958, he had supported the direct action campaign of an international pacifist group (including African American activists Bayard Rustin and Bill Sutherland) seeking to prevent France from conducting nuclear testing in the Sahara. Nonviolence, as deployed by this Sahara Protest Team, served for Nkrumah the dual purpose of opposing France's continued imperial designs and distancing Ghana from the hysteria that surrounded the Mau Mau resistance in Kenya.[9]

On March 21, 1960, the wind of change elicited a brutal response in South Africa. In the township of Sharpeville, police fired on unarmed demonstrators opposing pass laws designed to maintain segregation under the apartheid system, killing 69 and wounding over 180, with scores of women and children among the victims. Many of the dead had been shot in the back while fleeing. If independence was said to result in chaos, events at Sharpeville indicated that actual violence would be deployed by colonial and white minority governments opposed to African independence.[10]

The year 1960 was widely heralded in the US press as the year of Africa: over thirty new African nations were expected to gain independence. One such nation was the Congo, whose people had endured almost eighty years of tyrannical Belgian rule. Immediately after the independence ceremonies, Belgian officials engineered the secession of the Congo's mineral-rich Katanga region, subverting the new nation's sovereignty. The Congo's democratically elected Prime Minister, Patrice Lumumba, appealed for support to the United Nations and the US government. The Eisenhower administration, convinced that Lumumba would become an African Castro, authorized the C.I.A. to assassinate him.[11]

Lumumba was not felled by the poisoned toothpaste shipped by the C.I.A. to its operative in the Congo, but US intelligence worked assiduously behind the scenes in the ouster of his government. The announcement of Lumumba's death by Belgium in February 1961 met with worldwide condemnation, including demonstrations in London, New York, Chicago, and Moscow. Lumumba was

executed while in the custody of Belgian troops a month before the announcement of his death and was portrayed in the Western press as a pro-Communist
upstart, as if to offer justification for his removal. So it seemed to many,
including African Americans already frustrated by the slow pace of desegregation in the United States and outraged by racial discrimination against visiting
African diplomats.

In Harlem, Lumumba's death was the last straw for a group of African
American visitors to the United Nations Security Council, including LeRoi
Jones and Maya Angelou, who, along with members of several black nation-
alist and cultural organizations, staged an angry demonstration in the gallery,
replete with shouted denunciations of the crime, and physical skirmishes with
U.N. guards. Afterward, Adlai Stevenson, US Ambassador to the United
Nations, insinuated that the demonstration had obviously been "organized."
Stevenson's accusation of Communist influence echoed the Western media's
scapegoating of Lumumba since the secession as a vicious firebrand and left-
wing agitator.[12]

Just as the Italian invasion of Ethiopia in 1935 had galvanized an earlier
generation of Pan-African nationalists, Lumumba's death and the protest
at the United Nations were a turning point for a generation of young
African American and African intellectuals and activists, including
Malcolm X. Rejecting allegations of Communist influence in the press following the U.N. protest, these activists identified themselves as representatives of a
new independent Afro-American nationalism.[13]

Advocates of this position were critical of Cold War liberalism and a US
foreign policy bent on thwarting the self-determination of Africans in the
Congo and South Africa. Based largely in the urban North, Afro-American
nationalists advanced the cause of African freedom, but also strove to make
the plight of Northern urban blacks visible to the larger society. Malcolm,
along with his counterparts on the black cultural left, including Lorraine
Hansberry, James Baldwin, Julian Mayfield, and John O. Killens, had voiced
the disappointment of the many blacks enduring slum conditions, police
brutality, and inferior education. Within recent memory, many of these
people had fled the South for what they had once looked upon as the
"Promised Land." Rather than identify themselves with a flawed American
nation whose mass media demeaned Africa and Africans and whose political
life was still defined by Jim Crow segregation, Malcolm and many Harlemites
looked to their African heritage as a more appropriate foundation for civic
and political identification.

What was at stake for African American expatriates in Ghana and their
allies back in Harlem and throughout the United States was nothing less than
the meaning and content of African American citizenship and activism. For

their part, US officials who viewed the protest at the U.N. through the prism of Cold War anti-Communism, worried about a potentially uncontrollable black militancy, almost certainly an instrument of the organized left. They equated black nationalism with subversion. They sought to prevent future disruptions such as the one that erupted at Security Council.

Malcolm X was part of the sizable contingent of African Americans well-versed in African affairs who objected to two articles that appeared in the US press shortly after the U.N. demonstration. By Harold Isaacs and Russell Warren Howe, these essays asserted the cultural and political incompatibility of African Americans and Africans. From Ghana, Julian Mayfield disputed such journalistic statements about discord between African Americans and Africans. Black radicals such as Mayfield agreed on this question with such liberal and moderate counterparts as St. Clair Drake and Horace Mann Bond, who were members of the establishment-oriented American Society of African Culture. Bond was far from alone in believing that the intent behind these anecdotal claims of tension between African Americans and Africans was to discourage cooperation and solidarity between the two groups. His critique appeared in the *Journal of Negro Education* after mainstream periodicals rejected it. Acutely aware of their lack of an equal voice within an ideologically segregated print media, Mayfield and the African American expatriates understood that from Ghana, they were free to develop critiques of US policy that exceeded the bounds of permissible debate in the United States.[14]

In August 1963, the black expatriates in Ghana staged a demonstration at the US Embassy in sympathy with the massive March on Washington, and took issue with the Kennedy administration's slowness to intervene on behalf of civil rights demonstrators. The Ghanaian demonstrators also denounced US foreign-policy makers' hostility toward Cuba and their tolerance of the apartheid regime in South Africa. There were other such demonstrations in sympathy with the March on Washington all over the world, including Paris, Oslo, Munich, and Tel Aviv. But the one that garnered the most official concern and scrutiny was that in Ghana.

Although Malcolm had bitterly opposed the March on Washington, he was potentially the most renowned exponent of the new "Afro-American nationalism," exemplified by those who revolted at the U.N. and their allies. Malcolm had cited Lumumba's death in the Congo as part of his controversial (and largely ignored) political argument that Kennedy's assassination represented the "blowback," so to speak, of his administration's tolerance of violence to achieve its foreign policy objectives. This political argument was obscured by his gratuitous coda describing Kennedy's death as a matter of chickens coming home to roost. Malcolm's gaffe provided Elijah Muhammad with the pretext for his suspension from the Nation of

Islam. When the finality of that separation became clear, Malcolm sought to reinvent himself through his travels throughout the Middle East, Africa, and Europe. As part of their strategy of forging connections with the US black movement, Mayfield and the African American expatriates invited Malcolm to Ghana.

Malcolm X in Ghana

Malcolm arrived in Ghana in May 1964, having already visited Egypt, Saudi Arabia, and Lebanon. Not surprisingly, through the novelty of his travels, and with his cultural immersion into orthodox Islam and the hajj, Malcolm was strongly compelled to rethink his political convictions. He had rejected religion as the basis for the new political organization he would head. With the group of secular black progressives, activists, and former Muslims who followed him out of the Nation of Islam, Malcolm founded the Organization of Afro-American Unity in Harlem, inspired by the Organization of African Unity. Before and during his trip to Ghana, Malcolm described his economic, political, and social philosophy and program as "black nationalism." But Malcolm reconsidered his adherence to this when a member of the Ghanaian diplomatic corps pointed out its inherently exclusionary character.

In Ghana, a seemingly tireless Malcolm continued to conduct an intense dialogue with the African American expatriate community and members of the Ghanaian diplomatic corps. The expatriates, eager for news of the latest developments in the United States, welcomed Malcolm's intention to solicit support from African heads of state in advance of his plan to charge the United States with the violation of the human rights of African Americans before the United Nations. Seeking official recognition of their solidarity with Ghana and Africa, the expatriates lobbied hard for a summit between Malcolm and Nkrumah. But the latter faced political pressures of his own amidst deteriorating relations with the United States, and reluctantly agreed only to a brief, inconclusive meeting. In the end, Malcolm was unable to persuade African states to join his challenge to the legitimacy of the United States. He never got the chance to bring his grievances before the U.N., an action which, to be sure, had already been done by the African American leftists Paul Robeson and William L. Patterson of the Civil Rights Congress in 1951. And while Malcolm established an Accra branch of the Organization of Afro-American Unity, back in Harlem the organization languished in his absence.

Yet in many respects, Malcolm's trip to Ghana, and his tour throughout Africa, was a ringing success. Armed with a clearer conception of the ideological and military conflict pitting the United States and its Western allies against Afro-Asian national liberation struggles, Malcolm made favorable impressions among the audiences of students he addressed in Africa and Europe. The enthusiasm of his listeners hints at what Malcolm might have achieved in forging the global culture of opposition he envisioned, including Africans on the continent, people of African descent in the diaspora, and student activists in Europe's metropoles. (On February 9, 1965, Malcolm was barred from entering France to address student activists.) As historian Gerald Horne has suggested, whatever impact the hajj had on Malcolm's racial consciousness, his visit to Ghana and his interaction with European as well as African revolutionaries enabled him to imagine coalitions with whites and to reject the Nation of Islam's parochial black nationalism. Some of Malcolm's followers were not receptive to this change. According to Peter Goldman, after his return to the United States, Malcolm constantly wrestled with his black separatist followers over the terms and extent of nonracialism.[15]

Malcolm's Oxford Debate Union address

On foreign soil, Malcolm's criticisms of US foreign policy received a more favorable hearing by audiences than was possible in the United States and its media. Arguing on behalf of African national liberation forces waging armed struggle against white minority regimes, Malcolm accused the Western powers of hypocrisy in denying the right of self-defense to oppressed peoples. The Congo crisis had impressed upon Nkrumah and other supporters of African liberation, including Malcolm, the irrelevance of hopes of nonviolent change. Appearing before the Oxford Debate Union on December 3, 1964, Malcolm defended the motion, recently taken from Barry Goldwater, that "Extremism in the defense of liberty is no vice, moderation in the pursuit of justice is no virtue." Malcolm deplored the Western media's contempt for such African leaders as Nkrumah and the cause of African liberation. He argued that armed self-defense was a necessary and justifiable response to the organized violence of the Ku Klux Klan at home and the state-sanctioned violence employed by Western neocolonial powers and white minority regimes in Africa. To claim otherwise, he contended, was to fall prey to a racial double-standard. Malcolm highlighted two recent events that exposed US complicity with violence as a tool of political repression. In November 1964, Belgian forces, acting with US military assistance, invaded the Stanleyville region of the Congo on the humanitarian pretext of rescuing European hostages held by Congolese rebels against the central government led by Moise Tshombe. The purported humanitarian intervention led to the slaughter of some 3,000 Congolese civilians. The second event Malcolm referenced was the dismissal of charges by authorities in Meridian, Mississippi against the accused killers of three civil rights workers. Malcolm was not the only one to link these two events. Noting the lack of condemnation in the Western press of the massacre in the Congo by right-wing mercenaries, Guinea's U.N. representative inquired, "[w]as it because the thousands of Congolese citizens murdered by the South Africans, the Rhodesians, the Belgians, and the Cuban refugee adventurers had dark skins just like the colored US citizens murdered in Mississippi?"[16]

For Malcolm, extremism was epitomized by the Belgian/US intervention in the Congo, which he called "cold-blooded murder." The real extremists were the vigilantes in Mississippi and throughout the South who terrorized blacks with impunity, knowing that local courts would exonerate them in the unlikely event that they were brought to trial. Such violence, unchecked by the federal government, justified self-defense. Malcolm noted the double standard by which the State Department and the Western press condoned the slaughter of Congolese under the cover of humanitarianism, yet condemned the rhetorical advocacy of self-defense by blacks as a means of protest against unredressed white violence in the South.

Malcolm remained unmoved by the recent passage of the Civil Rights Act in light of the unpunished murders of civil rights activists. Racism, he argued, was entrenched in the US political system, with congressional committees chaired by powerful Southern segregationists whose seniority was founded on the denial of voting rights to most of the region's blacks. With avowed white supremacists so integral to the business of government, Malcolm was deeply skeptical that meaningful change was possible. Given these structural constraints on the enforcement of the law on behalf of black citizens, he argued they would be justified "by any means necessary to bring about justice where the government can't give them justice."[17]

Malcolm's critique of the use of violence for achieving US foreign policy objectives violated the expectation among its officials during the Cold War that black leaders refrain from criticizing US foreign policy. His use of the phrase "by any means necessary" met with willful distortion in the press. (In his speech in Detroit on February 14, 1965, one week before his death, Malcolm insisted that he had never advocated violence, only self-defense in the face of white violence.) Back in the United States, Malcolm sought to mend fences with civil rights leaders. His frustration with federal passivity in the face of antiblack violence resonated with similar sentiments among the young militants in the Student Nonviolent Coordinating Committee.

Weeks before his death, Malcolm advised "Afro-Americans" to return spiritually, culturally, and philosophically to Africa. That statement was his rejoinder to the ongoing struggle over the terms of African American identification and political consciousness. Malcolm and his followers insisted on the legitimacy of black and African heritage as the basis for full participation in American life. This oppositional self-naming of the "Afro-American" was a defiant assertion of the expansiveness of blackness as the basis for demands for national citizenship, for international affiliation, and ultimately, for a radical democratic politics universal in its applicability. It was an implicit acknowledgment of the pluralism, cosmopolitanism, and indeed, universality inherent in the black freedom movement. Nothing in Malcolm's understanding of solidarity with the cause of African peoples restricted that vision to black people. In practical terms, "Afro-American" entailed an obligation to engage issues of US foreign policy alongside the local concerns of African Americans. In speaking of the "Afro-American," Malcolm had signaled anew the importance of being black *and* American, with no contradiction between the two. In eulogizing Malcolm, the actor and civil rights activist Ossie Davis stressed the importance of "Afro-American": "Malcolm had stopped being a Negro years ago ... Malcolm had become an Afro-American, and he wanted – so desperately – that we, that all his people, would become Afro-Americans too."[18]

Malcolm's untimely death in 1965 at the hands of assassins was a devastating blow to the African American expatriates in Ghana, and their transnational political vision. The expatriates had envisioned Ghana as a refuge and think tank for US black leaders of the movement, a place where they could rest and reassess their ideas and strategy, much as Malcolm X did while in the country. He was widely praised as a martyr, an African American Lumumba, transformed into an immortal symbol of resistance for black and African peoples worldwide. Malcolm's recasting of the black freedom movement as a global struggle for human rights influenced the turn to anti-imperialism of the Student Nonviolent Coordinating Committee. In apartheid South Africa, Malcolm's autobiography was essential reading for student activists in the black consciousness movement, including Steve Biko, who died in 1977 while in prison after being tortured and beaten by his jailers.[19] Malcolm's influence is also evident in the spread of Islam among African Americans. However, Malcolm's belief that African American Muslims are oppressed because of their race rather than their religion could not have imagined the extent to which post-9/11 fears would lead many Americans to conflate religious and racial intolerance during the Obama campaign.

Any assessment of Malcolm's legacy must foreground his engagement with global affairs. Malcolm had taken on the mission of bridging African American and African struggles for human rights. In doing so, he attempted to operationalize the formation of Afro-American nationalism that burst forth on the American scene with the demonstration at the United Nations. For all of his iconic visibility, Malcolm is central to an all but forgotten tendency of black politics – a transgressive internationalism that pursued an independent critique of US foreign policy. By bringing that critique of US imperialism, in Vietnam, the Congo, and Southern Africa, to audiences in Africa, Europe, the Middle East, and finally in the United States, Malcolm challenged the American exceptionalism that sought to preserve the myth of American innocence.

Barack Obama, the forty-fourth president of the United States, seems an unlikely heir to Malcolm X and the formation of Afro-American nationalism and global citizenship that Malcolm projected at home and abroad. Obama was a product of the social and cultural changes of the 1960s, the son of a Kenyan father, an exchange student whose own improbable rise was made possible by education and the hopes of the era of decolonization. Obama's electoral prospects were strengthened by his courageous and early opposition to the 2003 US invasion of Iraq. His emergence on the national scene coincided with a neo-conservative US foreign policy that had unapologetically embraced the project of empire. As is often true during a time of war, there seemed to be little tolerance in the public sphere for historical assessments, let alone a critical perspective, on the role of the United States in the world.

With the ubiquitous broadcast of statements critical of US domestic and foreign policy from excerpts of videotaped sermons by Obama's then pastor, Reverend Jeremiah Wright, the Obama campaign faced perhaps its most serious obstacle. His response, a thoughtful, measured, and intensely personal speech drawing on his biracial family history, placed his pastor's angry outbursts in the context of an enduring legacy of racism and segregation.[20] Few, if any, compared Obama's speech to Malcolm X's legacy. But Obama's willingness to educate the American public on the sensitive issue of race was reminiscent of Malcolm at his best. And Obama's argument that his pastor had erred by assuming that Americans were incapable of change, unable to shake off traditions of racial prejudice, it might be argued, resonated strongly with Malcolm's own change of heart, and his appeals for reconciliation between blacks and whites.

Obama's triumph suggests that perhaps Malcolm's influence on American history is even more profound than we had previously imagined.

NOTES

1. S. Shankar, "Post-racial America?" *Hindu*, Chennai, Tamil Nadu, India, August 4, 2008, www.hindu.com/mag/2008/08/24/stories/2008082450130500.htm.
2. Farah Jasmine Griffin, *Who Set You Flowin'?* (New York: Oxford University Press, 1995), p. 135.
3. Pat Robinson and Group, "Poor Black Women's Study Papers by Poor Black Women of Mount Verson, New York," in *The Black Woman: An Anthology*, ed. Toni Cade Bambara (New York: Washington Square Press, 2005), p. 243.

4. Malcolm X and Alex Haley, *The Autobiography of Malcolm X* (1965; London: Penguin Books, 2001), pp. 454–5.

5. Tariq Ali, *Street Fighting Years: An Autobiography of the Sixties* (New York: Citadel Press, 1987), p. 42.

6. Kevin Gaines, *American Africans in Ghana: Black Expatriates and the Civil Rights Era* (Chapel Hill: University of North Carolina Press, 2006), p. 197.

7. I. F. Stone, "The Pilgrimage of Malcolm X," *In a Time of Torment* (New York: Random House, 1968), p. 110.

8. Nikhil Pal Singh, *Black Is a Country: Race and the Unfinished Struggle for Democracy* (Cambridge: Harvard University, 2004).

9. Gaines, *American Africans*, p. 103.

10. Ambrose Reeves, *Shooting at Sharpeville* (Boston: Houghton Mifflin, 1961).

11. Scott Shane, "Memories of a C.I.A. Officer Resonate in a New Era," *New York Times*, February 24, 2008.

12. Gaines, *American Africans*, p. 127.

13. Ibid., p. 136.

14. Ibid., pp. 128–30.

15. Peter Goldman, *The Death and Life of Malcolm X* (Urbana: University of Illinois Press, 1979), pp. 179, 189.

16. Gaines, *American Africans*, p. 202.

17. Ibid., pp. 201–4.

18. Ibid., pp. 205–6.

19. N. Barney Pityana, Mamphela Ramphele, Malusi Mpumlwana, and Lindy Wilson, *Bounds of Possibility: The Legacy of Steve Biko and Black Consciousness* (Cape Town: Zed Books, 1991), p. 29.

20. Barack Obama, "A More Perfect Union," www.americanrhetoric.com/speeches/barackobamaperfectunion.htm.

14

WILLIAM W. SALES, JR.

The legacy of Malcolm X

Malcolm X is important because his experiences are typical of the experiences that transformed African Americans in the twentieth century – the move from rural peasantry to industrial proletariat to postindustrial redundancy – all of which prepared them for a truly revolutionary role. He is one of the two most important black leadership figures in the second half of the twentieth century. Along with Dr. Martin Luther King, Jr., Malcolm X clarified the alternatives facing black people in the postindustrial period. Malcolm's intervention into the movement was primarily ideological. Tens of thousands of black people were energized by him to take action. He rearticulated their moods, feelings, and sensibilities in ways that helped them gain greater clarity as to who they were, what their problems were, and how they might go about building a movement to liberate themselves. He did this not through innovative thinking and ideas but through a down-to-earth rearticulation of the black radical tradition.

Exponent of the black radical tradition: ideology, culture, and class

The black radical tradition had roots in nineteenth-century Pan-Negro nationalism, twentieth-century Pan-Africanism and Garveyism,[1] and the class struggle approach of the African Blood Brotherhood. Malcolm X came to understand more perfectly this black radical tradition in the last eleven months of his life. At the time of his death, he was advancing a synthesis of the revolutionary Pan-African internationalist tradition with the more conservative elements of black economic and cultural-religious nationalism that he had inherited from the Nation of Islam, and this was further impacted by the need of Malcolm X to be responsive to constituencies with strong proletarian traditions in cities such as Detroit, Cleveland, Philadelphia, and his base in Harlem.[2]

Malcolm X recognized that black liberation had to begin with the psychological emancipation of black people from the internalized self-concept of racial inferiority. This "unbrainwashing of an entire people" required a psychological rapprochement with Africa and an embrace of the entire history of people of African descent before and after the holocaust of the slave trade and slavery. Malcolm X often reminded his audiences of this when he intoned, "Why you say you're no African! You left your mind in Africa."[3]

Malcolm X argued for a reconstruction of black cultural identity that explicitly recognized not only African roots and identity but the class character of the two contradictory cultural tendencies among black people as well. Malcolm argued that the culture and mentality of the "House Negro" was false consciousness, based on assimilating the worldview and culture of the white supremacist as a condition of survival. Rather, he opted for a cultural frame of reference based on the worldview and experiences of "Field Negroes," whose emancipation was based only on the "destruction of the master and all his works."[4]

Malcolm X was central to the restoration of the resistance tradition in African American religious life. James Cone, the leading scholar of black liberation theology, argues that it was Malcolm X's harsh criticism of the accommodationist orientation of church-based civil rights leadership that was a major impetus which forced the black church to question what had become of the prophetic role of the black church.[5] Garaud Wilmore observed that Malcolm X "brought Black religion and Black politics together for the spiritual edification and political empowerment of black people."[6] While Malcolm X in his last months emphasized that religion was a personal matter and built a secular organization, the Organization of Afro-American Unity, as his political vehicle, he deepened his study and involvement in Sunni Islam. Malcolm X was committed to believing in a religion that would help him fight back against oppression. He believed Islam was that religion.[7] Subsequent generations of African Americans have taken a serious look at Islam as an alternative to Christianity, and today it is the fastest growing religion among them.

From civil rights to human rights and black liberation

Moving away from determinations based on skin color in the final months of his life, Malcolm X categorized friends and enemies on the basis of behavior alone.[8] He asserted that the enemy confronting the world's people of color was the white supremacists and colonialist governments organized politically and militarily as the North Atlantic Treaty Organization (N.A.T.O.). Thus the struggle against this enemy was an international anti-imperialist, antiracist struggle for national liberation and human rights. The natural allies of African Americans were all of the nations and peoples of color who had experienced racist western imperialism. Malcolm X was hopeful that this group of nations and people could be an effective counterweight to the tremendous power of N.A.T.O. for two reasons: first, it constituted a majority of the world's people; and secondly, it was achieving national liberation and state power and consequently represented a growing power bloc within international institutions including the United Nations and the World Court. African Americans could get recognition and support from this majority of color if they reconstituted their movement not around the principle of civil rights but as a legitimate national liberation struggle.

The Organization of Afro-American Unity in the thought of Malcolm X: the Black United Front

One of the most important of Malcolm's realizations in his two trips to Africa in 1964 was that the struggle of black people in the United States lacked an international identity that would encourage and facilitate international organizations, nations, and movements to come to its defense. He envisaged the Organization of Afro-American Unity established on June 28, 1964, as the vehicle around which the national identity of black people could be consolidated. The ability of the African nations to give African Americans a platform for indicting the US government in international forums such as the U.N. and the World Court for its treatment of black people was a key ingredient in the platform of Malcolm X's organization. Malcolm X saw this organization as a North American affiliate of the Organization of African Unity. In the summer of 1964, he was given diplomatic status at the Heads of State Meeting of that organization in Cairo, and on July 20 he submitted a memorandum to it outlining the treatment of US blacks by their government.

Martin R. Delany, the nineteenth-century black abolitionist, considered by many to be the father of black nationalism, said that the first order of business was to present the demands of the African American people in their "national" capacity.[9] Malcolm X believed that to do this required the construction of a Black United Front and the Organization of Afro-American Unity was to be that front. He articulated the principles upon which such a Black United Front should be constructed. It had to be democratic by which Malcolm meant that it had to give a voice to the most oppressed and exploited segments of the black community and to be accountable first and foremost to them. The Black United Front had to make space for the poor and the *lumpen* elements to articulate their agenda and assume leadership positions in the struggle.

The nature of leadership in the Black United Front

Malcolm did not desire a charismatic form of leadership. Rather, he preferred a style which was more in the tradition of cadre development which Ella Baker promoted among young Student Nonviolent Coordinating Committee workers in the Deep South. That model encouraged those who had never seen themselves as leaders and decision makers to recognize that potential within their collective selves. Malcolm X was such an organic intellectual, a leader who was from the masses and molded by the masses as they experienced struggle. Malcolm X told his close associate Earl Grant that "I do not want an organization that depended on the life of one man. The organization must be able to survive on its own."[10]

Malcolm X's conception of leadership confronted the question of the role of women head on. He made special efforts to put them in leadership roles in the Organization of Afro-American Unity. In this, he departed from his practice during his tenure in the Nation of Islam. Lynn Shiflett, Gloria Richardson, Fannie Lou Hamer, and others had demonstrated to Malcolm X the capacity of women to lead. His experiences in Africa in 1964 showed him that it was essential for women to assume leadership positions if national liberation were to be achieved. Cadres of the organization were instructed by Malcolm X that "Africa will not be free until it frees its women."[11]

Electoral politics: Malcolm and the "ballot or the bullet"

The Black United Front had to assume responsibility for the defense and welfare of the entire black community in the United States. The "Organization of Afro-American Unity Statement of Principles" clearly accepts this responsibility.[12] In electoral politics, the Black United Front would function independently of the Democratic and Republican parties as Malcolm X saw them as two factions of a single white supremacist party.[13] The Black United Front would test the limits of the effectiveness of the electoral arena for black liberation or as Malcolm X put it "the ballot or the bullet." Its politics would not be limited to the electoral arena nor constrained by nonviolence but would draw upon the experience of national liberation struggles throughout the world to resist "by any means necessary." Malcolm X's politics of black liberation was prepared to legitimize tactics from the vote and nonviolent direct action to urban guerilla warfare.[14]

Self-defense and violence in the thought of Malcolm X

Malcolm X spoke frankly about the role of violence in four areas of social conflict. First, he affirmed the right of self-defense as a fundamental human right. In this, he is actually joined by King and Gandhi despite much misinformation on this point.[15] Secondly, Malcolm recognized a psychological need to be able to respond to the violence of the oppressor as a fundamental condition of manhood and self-respect. One could not claim to be fully human while accepting passively the brutalization of one's women and children. In this,

Malcolm opens up the discussion more fully explored by Franz Fanon in the opening chapter, "On Violence," in *Wretched of the Earth*.[16]

> If violence is wrong in America, violence is wrong abroad. If it is wrong to be violent defending black women and black children and black babies and black men, then it is wrong for America to draft us and make us violent abroad in defense of her. And if it is right for America to draft us, and teach us how to be violent in defense of her then it is right for you and me to do whatever is necessary to defend our own people right here in this country.[17]

Thirdly, he saw nationalist struggles as necessarily violent. According to Malcolm the essence of the oppression of nations worldwide was the usurpation of their sovereign control of their own national territory. Since this process was violent, its restoration would necessarily also be violent. Moreover, the actual observable process of national liberation was everywhere a violent one. If black people saw themselves as a nation desiring liberation, then they must be prepared to do what history mandates in terms of national liberation. They must be prepared to wage a violent fight for it.

> He [the White man] knows that the black revolution is worldwide in scope and in nature. The black revolution is sweeping Asia, is sweeping Africa, is rearing its head in Latin America ... All the revolutions that are going on in Asia and Africa today are based on what? – black nationalism. A revolutionary is a black nationalist. He wants a nation.[18]

After reviewing the various anticolonial uprisings, Malcolm X said: "I cite these various revolutions, brothers and sisters, to show you that you don't have a peaceful revolution. You don't have a turn-the-other-cheek revolution. There is no such thing as a non-violent revolution."[19]

Lastly, if individuals have a fundamental human right of self-defense, do peoples have a collective right of self-defense? Malcolm answered affirmatively and moved on to ponder how it might be most efficiently exercised. Here he feels a serious look at urban guerilla warfare is in order. Everywhere where strong imperialist armies are being confronted in the world some form of guerilla warfare is being used by the forces of national liberation. If black people in the United States have a collective right to self defense, then is some form of urban guerilla warfare in order?[20]

Taking up the legacy of Malcolm X

The violence directed at the civil rights movement forced its organizations to confront its implications in their work. The question of self-defense was taken up by the Revolutionary Action Movement, the Black Panther Party, the

Republic of New Africa, and a host of kindred groups. If reform tactics within the established social order, including nonviolent direct action, produced no change, then what options did black people have? For some, Malcolm X's catchphrase "by any means necessary" meant resort to urban guerilla warfare. To others, especially those in the radical left tradition such as James Boggs, it signified working-class revolution led by street youths organized into a vanguard party. For the Republic of New Africa, it required relocation and concentration of black people in a national homeland in the Southern United States which could be liberated by revolution. There was much rhetoric about revolution, and organizational developments which embraced that notion explicitly, but little was done concretely, however, to develop a military alternative within the black liberation movement.[21]

The Federal Bureau of Investigation's counter intelligence program (COINTELPRO) was a preemptive strike at the legacy of Malcolm X to prevent the transformation of the civil rights movement into a viable movement of national liberation. On July 2, 1964, J. Edgar Hoover in a memo to the New York and Philadelphia field offices of the FBI ordered the destruction of Malcolm X and the Organization of Afro-American Unity.[22] COINTELPRO formally came into existence in August 1967 with goals directly addressed to nullifying the legacy of Malcolm X:

1. Prevent a coalition of militant black nationalist groups.
2. Prevent the rise of a "Messiah" who could unify, and electrify, the militant black nationalist movement.
3. Prevent *violence* on the part of black nationalist groups ... Through counterintelligence it should be possible to pinpoint potential troublemakers and neutralize them before they exercise their potential for violence.
4. Prevent militant black nationalist groups and leaders from gaining respectability.
5. A final goal should be to prevent the long-range *growth* of militant black nationalist organizations, especially among the youth.[23]

By the end of the 1970s, the Student Nonviolent Coordinating Committee, the Revolutionary Action Movement, the Black Panthers and the Republic of New Africa were either repressed into nonexistence or rendered impotent with large numbers of their cadre incarcerated as political prisoners or at least disillusioned and no longer active. By 1980, those who had avoided the dragnet were deep underground in a small *ad hoc* grouping of fugitives known as the Black Liberation Army. Many among the generation of black youth who came of age in the 1980s initially had little or no knowledge of Malcolm X. His legacy was in danger of being lost, but survived and he was rediscovered by a new generation of youth.

Preserving the legacy of Malcolm X into the twenty-first century

The legacy of Malcolm X has flourished in four major areas of black life: in academia, in archival library and museum institutions, in popular culture, and in political thought and action. Malcolm X's method was to verify truth with reference to the facts of history. In this he reinforced the tradition of socially relevant scholarship associated with the fathers of black studies, Carter G. Woodson, W. E. B. Du Bois, and Arturo Schomburg. In the decade after Malcolm's death, black activist-scholars formed two professional organizations in black studies that reflected the influence of Malcolm X as well as the foregoing fathers of the discipline: the African Heritage Studies Association and the National Council on Black Studies. The Malcolm X Workgroup came into existence in 1987 with the purpose of networking with those involved in major research and publication efforts on Malcolm X, and was the initiative of Abdul Alkalimat of Peoples College Press, and included myself, James Cone of Union Theological Seminary, and Alem Habtu of Queens College, CUNY. Working with other scholars and activists, the Malcolm X Workgroup was able to facilitate the organization of two major international conferences on Malcolm X. The first, entitled *A Symposium on Black Liberation and the Cuban Revolution: "Malcolm X Speaks in the 90's,"* involved Cuban and African American scholars and activists, and took place in Havana, Cuba in May 1990. In November of that year, the largest conference held to date on Malcolm X was convened at the Borough of Manhattan Community College, CUNY. Entitled *Malcolm X: Black Tradition and a Legacy of Struggle* it attracted more than 3,000 people from twenty-five countries. Another initiative launched in 1990, the Malcolm X Commemoration Commission was the brainchild of activists Ron Daniels and Dr. James Turner of Cornell's Africana Studies and Research Center.

The most extensive website resource on Malcolm X, Brothermalcolm.net, was another initiative of Dr. Alkalimat and was followed in 2001 by the Columbia University–based research website associated with the Malcolm X Papers Project under the direction of Manning Marable. F. Leon Wilson of St. Johns University, Queens, New York, has established the online Malcolm X Discussion Forum. While not yet digitized, the late social work scholar, Preston Wilcox, creator of the Malcolm X Lovers Network, had the most extensive clipping files on him. Major additional archival resources on Malcolm X have been established at Emory University, the New York Public Library's Schomburg Center for Research on Black Culture, and the Malcolm X Papers Project at Columbia University already mentioned. These projects are but a sample of a plethora of scholarly efforts to preserve Malcolm X's legacy.

Major commemorative museums and centers dedicated to Malcolm X's legacy have emerged in the last twenty years. The Malcolm X Memorial Foundation founded by the late Rowena Moore is dedicated to preserving his homestead in Omaha, Nebraska. In Harlem, New York, the Malcolm X Museum has worked for almost a decade to create a living legacy of memorabilia, audiovisual and written resources, and public programs and commemorations of his life and death. At the site of Malcolm X's assassination, the Audubon Ballroom in Washington Heights, New York City, the Malcolm X and Dr. Betty Shabazz Memorial and Education Center has been established, after intense community protests, through a cooperative venture of Columbia University and the Shabazz family.

Several excellent documentary films have been produced on the legacy of Malcolm X. The earliest, *El Hajj Malik Shabazz*, was from Emmy award-winning producer Gil Noble of WABC-TV, New York. Warner Brothers also distributed a feature-length documentary on Malcolm, and more recently Blackside produced *Make It Plain*.[24]

Malcolm X has had a noticeable impact on popular culture in the United States. By the early 1990s, Malcolm X had become an icon of the hip-hop culture.[25] Malcolm X saw a special role for youth in our community in the struggle for black liberation. The rise of the hip-hop generation was a product of social conditions which first emerged during Malcolm X's youth. Their experiences in the late twentieth-century postindustrial ghettos were quite similar to his youthful experience. Malcolm thus became an icon not only of their anger and alienation but of their political aspirations for resistance and liberation.

During the anti-apartheid upsurge in the middle of the 1980s, African American youth were inspired by their counterparts in South Africa. Rap music videos like Eddie Murphy's *When I Was King* exploited the image and words of Malcolm X. Building on this developing rediscovery of him by a new generation of young people, Spike Lee produced and directed the feature-length blockbuster *Malcolm X* starring Denzel Washington. The movie gave rise to an explosion of "X" logos on caps and clothing and even a brand of potato chips. The classic music genre made room for the idolization of Malcolm with the New York City Opera debut of Anthony Davis's opera, *X*, in 1986.

Malcolm X's political legacy was preserved by a number of groups. Immediately after his death the Student Nonviolent Coordinating Committee continued his representations in the international community. They were joined in 1967 by the Black Panther Party, which in its Ten-Point Program demanded international recognition of the peoplehood of African Americans, their right to self-determination, and a plebiscite to determine the black community's future relationship to the United States. The Republic of New Africa, formed in 1968, established a kind of black government in exile. In that same year, the Black Economic Development Conference took up the demand for reparations and James Foreman indicted the white Christian church by tacking a demand for over $600,000,000 on the doors of Riverside Church in New York City. Black power conferences in Newark in 1967 and Philadelphia in 1968 resurrected a renewed quest for the Black United Front, first seen in the antebellum Negro Conventions. At the beginning of the 1970s, the search for the Black United Front was reflected in the formation of the Congress of African People, and in 1972 by the National Black Political Convention in Gary, Indiana. The latter was an attempt to give organizational substance to the idea of independent black electoral politics. It met again in Little Rock, Arkansas, and in Youngstown, Ohio, but by the end of the 1970s there was little to show for these United Front efforts.

In the area of African-liberation support work, major efforts were made to support the liberation and nation-building project in Africa by activists in the Black Liberation movement. The Pan-African Skills Project sent hundreds of African American teachers and professionals to Tanzania and Zambia in the 1970s. Starting with the Pan-African Solidarity Committee in 1970, a United Front effort emerged around support for the liberation struggle against colonialism and apartheid in Africa. In 1972, African Americans created the African Liberation Support Committee. It sent tens of thousands of dollars of aid to the liberation movements in Africa over the next three years and held demonstrations that involved over 100,000 people in more than twenty North American Cities. It also debated about the interaction of race and class and introduced the serious study of Marxism. Unfortunately, the effort to build a Black United Front seems to have been spent by 1980, although an organization with that name was constituted at a national gathering in New York and, though reduced in influence, remains active today.

Recent black political initiatives in the spirit of Malcolm X

The 1990s saw renewed interest in Malcolm X's political views. This reflected the successes achieved by the liberation struggles in southern Africa, the apparent renewed militancy of black youth as reflected in the disturbances attendant on the verdict in the Rodney King police brutality case in Los Angeles in 1992. By 1998 the generation of the 1960s, now in their mid-fifties, made another attempt to fulfill Malcolm X's dream of a Black United Front. In June of 1998, over 800 black radicals met in Chicago to form the Black Radical Congress. It is a coalition of individuals and groups with local organizing committees in a number of important metropolitan centers and with high profile leadership with impeccable movement credentials. While it continues to exist, its influence has been weakened by a lack of inclusiveness, ideological disagreements, and limited resources.

At the other pole in this struggle are popular forces and African American nongovernment organizations such as the December 12th Movement, the National Coalition of Blacks for Reparations in America (N'COBRA), and the National Reparations Congress. They have acted on Malcolm X's admonition to take the African American human rights struggle and demand for reparations to the United Nations. After many years of patient lobbying in Geneva, links were forged with other nongovernmental organizations in Africa and its diasporas which by the beginning of the millennium had achieved notable breakthroughs. Four of these reflect Malcolm X's legacy in this area: first, the achievement of nongovernment-organization status with the United Nations; secondly, the establishment of an international network of such organizations engaged in antiracist, pro-reparations advocacy; thirdly, the convening under U.N. auspices of an International Conference on Racism, Xenophobia and Other forms of Oppression in Durban, South Africa in August 2001 at which the slave trade, slavery, and colonialism were recognized as crimes against humanity; lastly, the appointment of a special U.N. Rapporteur on Racism, who reports periodically to the United Nations on his investigations of the treatment of racial and ethnic communities and minorities throughout the world.

The most important demographic trend in the early twenty-first century is the significant growth of diasporic African communities in the United States and Europe. Immigrants from West Africa and the Horn of Africa as well as large Caribbean communities present a challenge to more traditional conceptions of African American identity as African communities in England, France, and Germany force redefinition of what it is to be European. Throughout the Western hemisphere, Afro-Latinos are now challenging stereotypes about racial harmony in Latin American society and seeking the right to take their place as constituents in the African diaspora. While these diasporas look to become Americanized, the reality is that the most immediate issue confronting them is their relationship to the established African American community. Tensions based on class as well as culture and the divide-and-rule tactics of political entrepreneurs make the contemporary urban terrain a crucial arena of potential conflict as well as cooperation.[26] Here Malcolm X's hemispheric conception of Afro-American identity may offer a process for transcending internecine divisions and facilitating the kind of united front which he felt could be an important Western hemispheric complement to the Organization of African Unity.

Challenges confronting the legacy of Malcolm X

Black bourgeois leadership has risen to challenge Malcolm X's model of militant Pan-African internationalism. The rise of the black bourgeois political and economic stratum reinforces the model of assimilation based on achievement which had been at the center of the neoconservative resurgence in the late twentieth century. At the political level, thousands of black elected officials hold office throughout the United States, and Barack Obama has been elected as the first African American President of the United States. In economic life there has been an unprecedented expansion of senior black executives in corporate board rooms. In the field of independent entrepreneurship stands the example of Oprah Winfrey, the CEO of Harpo Productions, and Robert L. Johnson, the creator and first chairman of Black Entertainment Television.

The faith-based initiatives of the Bush Administration have been a major stimulus to the mega-church phenomenon among African Americans. On balance the political orientation of their leadership is conservative, and they often seek to replace an explicit commitment to revolutionary social change with a Booker T. Washingtonesque exhortation to pursue the gospel of individual wealth and the Protestant ethic. It may seem sometimes that these church leaders intend for this gospel to replace an explicit commitment to revolutionary social change.

The US government's reaction to the attacks on the World Trade Center in New York City and the Pentagon on September 11, 2001, has led to the drastic curtailment of civil liberties and the fatal compromising of the Bill of Rights. COINTELPRO-like methods, which used to be clandestine, are openly embraced and legitimized by the US government, and are directed at anyone who attempts to operationalize the militancy associated with Malcolm X. In addition, the events of 9/11 have produced a backlash against Islam and American Muslims.

These challenges to the legacy of Malcolm X fail because of the persistence of what Michael Omi and Howard Winant call the "racial dictatorship" in America.[27] Huge gaps persist between whites and blacks in median per-capita family income and wealth, in indices of health, unemployment, business ownership, and political representation. Incarceration, racial profiling, and police violence are virtually black experiences. Over half the prison population in the United States is African American. In the 1990s, the prison population of black women increased by over 800 percent. Today it has been estimated that it would take under the best assumptions 525 years for African Americans to close the wealth gap with their white counterparts. This figure will have to be recalculated given the hugely disproportionate impact on black wealth caused by the bursting of the housing bubble.[28]

Summary: Malcolm X, a model of personal transformation in the service
of the movement

Malcolm X was, as Antonio Gramsci would say, an organic intellectual, not
formally trained as an intellectual but a working-class, self-taught scholar
whose insights develop in the arena of social contestation.[29] Malcolm's
example challenges the traditional notions of who can speak. It was, in
part, through his leadership that unemployed and underemployed black
workers and street people announced themselves prepared to play their role
on the American and world stage. For black activists, Malcolm set the
standard of commitment, service, and integrity against which all subsequent
militants have been measured. He left us a model for personal development,
rooted in the recognition that it is possible to change for the better and
make a contribution to the liberation of our community through constant
study, the development of a critical stance toward all knowledge, and the
commitment to test one's beliefs in the crucible of practice. Malcolm taught
us to be heroic, to face all of the implications of facts as they are revealed,
and to change, no matter how painful, on the basis of these facts.

NOTES

1. Pan-Africanism is a social movement among continental Africans and people of
   African descent with nineteenth-century roots founded in 1900 by a West Indian
   barrister resident in London, Henry Sylvester Williams. In its early decades it was
   led by the African American scholar-activist, Dr. W. E. B. Du Bois. After 1945,
   leadership passed to African nationalist leaders, most prominently, the Ghanaian
   Kwame Nkrumah. As an ideology, Pan-Africanism shares many of the characteristics of black nationalism as it is concerned with race unity, racial pride and
   uplift, racial equality, self-determination, and the liberation of Africa from external control. Garveyism is the black nationalist ideology of Marcus M. Garvey,
   a Jamaican journalist and union organizer, who founded the Universal Negro
   Improvement Organization in 1914, the largest organization of people of African
   descent to emerge in the twentieth century. Garveyism advocated the organization of the Negro race around the principles of racial unity and uplift, race pride,
   and the redemption of Africa from European control. It centered its activities on
   establishing a base area in Africa to be manned by repatriated black people from
   the western hemisphere, but this was unsuccessful. Garveyism had a profound
   influence on later black leaders in the Western hemisphere and in Africa, most
   notably Malcolm X and Kwame Nkrumah.
2. Rod Bush, "The Civil Rights Movement and the Continuing Struggle for the
   Redemption of a People," *Social Justice*, 30 (2003), p. 47.
3. Malcolm X, *By Any Means Necessary*, ed. George Breitman (New York: Pathfinder
   Press, 1970), p. 146.
4. Malcolm X, *Malcolm X Speaks*, ed. George Breitman (New York: Pathfinder Press,
   1965), pp. 10–11.

5. James H. Cone, *Martin & Malcolm & America: A Dream or a Nightmare* (Maryknoll, NY: Orbis Books, 1991), p. 296.

6. Gayraud S. Wilmore, *Black Religion and Black Radicalism: An Interpretation of the Religious History of African Americans* (Garden City, NY: Doubleday, 1972).

7. Louis A. DeCaro, Jr., *On the Side of My People: A Religious Life of Malcolm X* (New York: New York University Press, 1996), pp. 246–7.

8. Ibid., p. 232.

9. Wilson J. Moses, *Classical Black Nationalism: From the American Revolution to Marcus Garvey* (New York: New York University Press, 1996), pp. 120–1.

10. Earl Grant, "The Last Days of Malcolm X," in *Malcolm X: The Man and His Times*, ed. John Henrik Clarke (New York: Collier Books, 1969), p. 91.

11. Personal interview with Benjamin Karim, February 15–16, 1998, in Richmond, Virginia.

12. Malcolm X, *By Any Means Necessary*, p. 110.

13. *Malcolm X Speaks*, ed. George Breitman (New York: Pathfinder Press, 1965), p. 30.

14. Malcolm X, *Malcolm X Speaks*, p. 37.

15. Upon returning from India where he extensively studied Gandhian non-violence with the Mahatma's disciples, Dr. King was thrust into the furor created in the SCLC and the NAACP, when Robert Williams introduced self-defense tactics into civil rights demonstrations in Monroe, North Carolina. In October 1959, Dr. King advanced a nuanced counter to Williams' argument that violence had a positive role to play in the movement. In a speech titled "The Social Organization of Non-violence," King described: "three different views on the subject of violence. One is the approach of pure non-violence, which cannot readily or easily attract large masses, for it requires extraordinary discipline and courage. The second is violence exercised as self defense, which all societies, from the most primitive to the most cultured and civilized, accept as moral and legal. *The principle of self defense, even involving weapons and bloodshed, has never been condemned, even by Gandhi, who sanctioned it for those unable to master pure non-violence.* The third is the advocacy of violence as a tool of advancement, organized as in warfare, deliberately and consciously. To this tendency many Negroes are being tempted today. There are incalculable perils in this approach" [emphasis added] (*I Have a Dream: Writings and Speeches That Changed the World*, ed. James M. Washington [New York: Harper Collins, 1992], p. 51).

16. Frantz Fanon, *The Wretched of the Earth* (New York: Grove Press, 1963), pp. 35–106.

17. Malcolm X, *Malcolm X Speaks*, p. 8.

18. Ibid., pp. 9–10.

19. Ibid., p. 9.

20. Ibid., p. 38.

21. Bush, "Civil Rights Movement," p. 47.

22. Federal Bureau of Investigation, *Organization of Afro-American Unity (OAAU) FBI Surveillance File (100442235)*, unpublished (1964), p. 2.

23. Clayborne Carson and David Gallen, eds., *Malcolm X: The FBI File* (New York: Carroll and Graf, 1991), p. 17. See also M. C. Stanford (Muhammad Ahmed), "Revolutionary Action Movement (RAM): A Case Study of an Urban Revolutionary Movement in Western Capitalist Society" (M.A. thesis, Department of Political Science, Atlanta University, Georgia, 1986), p. 182.

24. *El Hajj Malik El Shabazz: A Like It Is Special Presentation*, VHS, directed by Gil Noble (Prior Lake, MN: MNTEX Entertainment, 1991); *Malcolm X: His Own Story As It Really Happened*, VHS, directed by Arnold Perl (1972; Burbank, CA: Warner Home Video, 1995); *Malcolm X: Make it Plain*, VHS, directed by Orlando Bagwell (Boston: Blackside Film, PBS Video, 1994).

25. Dennis O'Neill, "Malcolm's Message in Rap," *Forward Motion*, 9.1 (1990), p. 22.

26. Kwado Konadu-Ageymang, Baffour K. Takyi, and John A. Arthor (eds.), *The New African Diaspora in North America: Trends, Community Building, and Adaptation* (Lanham, MD: Lexington Books, 2006).

27. Michael Omi and Howard Winant, *Racial Formation in the United States: From 1960s to the 1990s* (New York: Routledge, 1994).

28. Dedrick Muhammad, Attieno Davis, Meizhu Lui, and Betsy Leondar-Wright, *State of the Dream: Enduring Disparities in Black and White* (Boston: United for a Fair Economy, 2004).

29. Antonio Gramsci, *An Antonio Gramsci Reader: Selected Writings 1916–1935*, ed. David Forgacs (New York: Schocken, 1988), p. 301.

The scholarly literature that engages Malcolm X, either specifically or within the context of a broader argument or investigation, is voluminous. The following list is not intended to be exhaustive; it consists primarily of a selection of the materials cited in this volume, together with books by the contributors and a small number of supplemental sources.

The list has been divided under headings to make it easier to locate resources on particular aspects of Malcolm's life and legacy, though the interdisciplinary nature of the scholarship renders these categories somewhat fluid. The first headings contain primary materials – Malcolm's speeches, biographies of Malcolm, memoirs of those who lived and worked with Malcolm, and of course the *Autobiography*. The next sections are scholarly books and monographs, book chapters and essays, and materials related to film adaptations. After that are sections of more general or background information on the Nation of Islam, the 1960s civil rights movement, and African American culture. Within each category the entries are listed alphabetically by author or title; and except where indicated, entries for books, book chapters, and essays are intermixed.

Speeches, biographies, and the Autobiography

Breitman, George, *The Last Year of Malcolm X: The Evolution of a Revolutionary* (New York: Pathfinder Press, 1967).

DeCaro, Louis A., Jr., *On the Side of My People: A Religious Life of Malcolm X* (New York: New York University Press, 1996).

Epps, Archie (ed.), *Malcolm X: Speeches at Harvard* (New York: Paragon House, 1991).

Goldman, Peter, *The Death and Life of Malcolm X* (Urbana: University of Illinois Press, 1979).

Malcolm X, *By Any Means Necessary*, ed. George Breitman (New York: Pathfinder Press, 1970).

Malcolm X, *February 1965: The Final Speeches*, ed. Steve Clark (New York: Pathfinder Press, 1992).

Malcolm X, *Malcolm X on Afro-American History*, ed. Steve Clark (New York: Pathfinder Press, 1967).

Malcolm X, *Malcolm X Speaks*, ed. George Breitman (New York: Pathfinder Press, 1965).

Malcolm X, *Malcolm X Talks to Young People: Speeches in the U.S., Britain, and Africa*, ed. Steve Clark (New York: Pathfinder Press, 1991).

Malcolm X, *The Last Speeches*, ed. Bruce Perry (New York: Pathfinder Press, 1989).
Malcolm X and Alex Haley, *The Autobiography of Malcolm X* (1965; London: Penguin Books, 2001).
Myers, Walter Dean, *Malcolm X: By Any Means Necessary* (New York: Scholastic, 1993).
Perry, Bruce, *Malcolm: The Life of a Man Who Changed Black America* (Barrytown, NY: Station Hill Press, 1991).
Wolfenstein, Eugene V., *The Victims of Democracy: Malcolm X and the Black Revolution* (London: Free Association Books, 1989).

Memoirs

Carew, Jan R., *Ghosts in Our Blood: With Malcolm X in Africa, England, and the Caribbean* (Chicago: Lawrence Hill Books, 1994).
Collins, Rodnell P., and A. Peter Bailey, *The Seventh Child: A Family Memoir of Malcolm X* (New York: Kensington Publishing, 1998).
Karim, Benjamin, *Remembering Malcolm* (New York: Carroll & Graf, 1992).
Mealy, Rosemari, *Fidel and Malcolm X: Memories of a Meeting* (Melbourne: Australia: Ocean Press, 1993).
Shabazz, Ilyasah with Kim McLarin, *Growing Up X: A Memoir by the Daughter of Malcolm X* (New York: Ballantine Books, 2002).

Book-length studies on Malcolm X

Alkalimat, Abdul, *Malcolm X: A Study Guide* (Chicago: 21st Century Books, 1991).
Asante, Molefi Kete, *Malcolm X as Cultural Hero & Other Afrocentric Essays.* (Trenton, NJ: Africa World Press, 1994).
Carson, Clayborne, and David Gallen (eds.), *Malcolm X: The FBI File* (New York: Carroll & Graf, 1991).
Clarke, John Henrik (ed.), *Malcolm X: The Man and His Times* (1969; reprint, New Jersey: Africa World Press, 1990).
Cone, James H., *Martin & Malcolm & America: A Dream or a Nightmare* (Maryknoll, NY: Orbis Books, 1991).
Dyson, Michael Eric, *Making Malcolm: The Myth and Meaning of Malcolm X* (New York: Oxford University Press, 1995).
Lomax, Louis E., *To Kill a Black Man: The Shocking Parallel in the Lives of Malcolm X and Martin Luther King, Jr.* (Los Angeles: Holloway House, 1968).
Perry, Theresa (ed.), *Teaching Malcolm X* (New York: Routledge, 1996).
Sales, William W., Jr., *From Civil Rights to Black Liberation: Malcolm X and the Organization of Afro-American Unity* (Boston: South End Press, 1994).
Strickland, William, and Cheryll Y. Greene, *Malcolm X: Make It Plain* (New York: Viking, 1994).
Terrill, Robert E., *Malcolm X: Inventing Radical Judgment* (East Lansing: Michigan State University Press, 2004).
Tyner, James A., *The Geography of Malcolm X: Black Radicalism and the Remaking of American Space* (New York: Routledge, 2006).
Wood, Joe (ed.), *Malcolm X: In Our Own Image* (New York: St. Martin's Press, 1992).

Articles, scholarly essays, and book chapters on Malcolm X

Condit, Celeste Michelle, and John Louis Lucaites, "Malcolm X and the Limits of Rhetoric of Revolutionary Dissent," *Journal of Black Studies*, 33.2 (1993), pp. 291–313.

Eakin, Paul John, "Malcolm X and the Limits of Autobiography," in *African American Autobiography: A Collection of Critical Essays*, ed. William L. Andrews (Upper Saddle River, NJ: Prentice Hall, 1993), pp. 151–61.

El-Beshti, Bashir M., "The Semiotics of Salvation: Malcolm X and the Autobiographical Self," *Journal of Negro History*, 82.4 (1997) pp. 359–67.

Gates, Henry Louis, Jr., "Malcolm, the Aardvark, and Me," *New York Times*, February 21, 1993, sec. 7, p. 11.

Gillespie, Alex, "Malcolm X and His Autobiography: Identity Development and Self-Narration," *Culture & Psychology*, 11 (2005) pp. 77–88.

Griffin, Farah Jasmine, "Ironies of the Saint: Malcolm X, Black Women and the Price of Protection," in *Sisters in the Struggle*, ed. Bettye Collier Thomas, and V. P. Franklin, (New York: New York University Press, 2001), pp. 214–29.

Horne, Gerald, "'Myth' and the Making of 'Malcolm X,'" *American Historical Review*, 98.2 (1993), pp. 440–50.

Illo, John, "The Rhetoric of Malcolm X," *Columbia University Forum*, 9 (1966), pp. 5–15.

Mandel, Barrett John, "The Didactic Achievement of Malcolm X's Autobiography," *Afro-American Studies*, 2 (1972), pp. 269–74.

Miller, Keith D., "Plymouth Rock Landed on Us: Malcolm X's Whiteness Theory as a Basis for Alternative Literacy," *College Composition and Communication*, 56 (2004), pp. 199–222.

Painter, Nell Irvin, "Malcolm X Across the Genres," *American Historical Review*, 98.2 (1993), pp. 432–39.

Rabaka, Reiland, "Malcolm X and/as Critical Theory: Philosophy, Radical Politics, and the African American Search for Social Justice," *Journal of Black Studies*, 33 (2002), pp. 145–65.

Steele, Shelby, "Malcolm Little," *New Republic*, December 21, 1992, pp. 27–31.

Tyner, James A., "Nightmarish Landscapes: The Orwellian World of Malcolm X," in *Race, Ethnicity, and Place in a Changing America*, ed. John W. Frazier, and Eugene L. Tettey-Fio (Binghamton, NY: Global Academic Publishing, 2006), pp. 25–31.

Feature film and documentaries

El Hajj Malik El Shabazz: A Like It Is Special Presentation, VHS, directed by Gil Noble (Prior Lake, MN: MNTEX Entertainment, 1991).

Malcolm X, directed by Spike Lee (1992; Burbank, CA: Warner Brothers, 2000).

Malcolm X: His Own Story As It Really Happened, VHS, directed by Arnold Perl (1972; Burbank, CA: Warner Home Video, 1995).

Malcolm X: Make it Plain, VHS, directed by Orlando Bagwell (Boston: Blackside Film, PBS Video, 1994).

Screenplays and film studies

Baldwin, James, *One Day, When I Was Lost: A Scenario Based on Alex Haley's "The Autobiography of Malcolm X"* (1972; reprint, New York: Dell, 1992).

Baraka, Amiri, "Spike Lee at the Movies," in *Black American Cinema*, ed. Manthia Diawara (New York: Routledge, 1992), pp. 145–53.

Crowdus, Gary (ed.), "By Any Reviews Necessary: *Malcolm X* Symposium," *Cinéaste*, 19.4 (1993), pp. 4–24.

Doherty, Thomas, "Malcolm X: In Print, On Screen," *Biography*, 23.1 (2000): pp. 29–48.

Lee, Jonathan Scott, "Spike Lee's *Malcolm X* as Transformational Object," *American Imago*, 52.2 (1995), pp. 155–67.

Lee, Spike with Ralph Wiley, *By Any Means Necessary: The Trials and Tribulations of the Making of "Malcolm X" … Including the Screenplay* (New York: Hyperion, 1992).

Norman, Brian, "Reading a 'Closet Screenplay': Hollywood, James Baldwin's Malcolms, and the Threat of Historical Irrelevance," *African American Review* 39.1–2, (2005), pp. 103–18.

Elijah Muhammad, Louis Farrakhan, and the Nation of Islam

Alexander, Amy (ed.), *The Farrakhan Factor* (New York: Grove Press, 1998).

Barboza, Steven, *American Jihad: Islam After Malcolm X* (New York: Doubleday, 1993).

Beynon, Erdmann D., "The Voodoo Cult Among Negro Migrants in Detroit," *American Journal of Sociology*, 43.6 (May 1938), pp. 894–907.

Bracey, John, Jr., August Meier, and Elliott Rudwick (eds.), *Black Nationalism in America* (Indianapolis: Bobbs-Merrill, 1970).

Clegg, Claude A., *An Original Man: The Life and Times of Elijah Muhammad* (New York: St. Martin's Press, 1997).

Essien-Udom, E. U., *Black Nationalism: A Search for an Identity in America* (Chicago: University of Chicago Press, 1962).

Evanzz, Karl, *The Messenger: The Rise and Fall of Elijah Muhammad* (New York: Pantheon Books, 1999).

Gardell, Mattias, *In the Name of Elijah Muhammad: Louis Farrakhan and the Nation of Islam* (Durham, NC: Duke University Press, 1996).

Gomez, Michael A., *Black Crescent: The Experience and Legacy of African Muslims in the Americas* (Cambridge: Cambridge University Press, 2005).

Lincoln, C. Eric, *The Black Muslims in America* (Boston: Beacon Press, 1961).

Lomax, Louis E., *When the Word Is Given* (Cleveland: World Publishing, 1963).

Magida, Arthur J., *Prophet of Rage: A Life of Louis Farrakhan and His Nation* (New York: BasicBooks, 1996).

Marsh, Clifton, *From Black Muslims to Muslims: The Transition from Separatism to Islam, 1930–1980* (Metuchen, NJ: Scarecrow Press, 1984).

Moses, Wilson Jeremiah, *The Golden Age of Black Nationalism, 1850–1925* (New York: Oxford University Press, 1978).

Muhammad, Elijah, *Message to the Blackman in America* (Chicago: Muhammad Mosque of Islam Number 2, 1965).

Turner, Richard B., *Islam in the African-American Experience*, 2nd edn. (Bloomington: Indiana University Press, 1997).

Civil rights and the 1960s

Abu-Jamal, Mumia, *We Want Freedom: A Life in the Black Panther Party* (Boston: South End Press, 2004).

Ahmed, Muhammad, *We Will Return in the Whirlwind: Black Radical Organizations 1960–1975* (Chicago: Charles H. Kerr, 2007).

Ali, Tariq, *Street Fighting Years: An Autobiography of the Sixties* (New York: Citadel Press, 1987).

Branch, Taylor, *Parting The Waters: America in the King Years, 1954–63* (New York: Simon & Schuster, 1988).

   Pillar of Fire: America in the King Years, 1963–65 (New York: Simon & Simon, 1998).

   At Canaan's Edge: America in the King Years, 1965–68 (New York: Simon & Simon, 2006).

Foner, Philip S. (ed.), *The Black Panthers Speak* (J. B. Philadelphia: Lippincott, 1970).

Gaines, Kevin, *African Americans in Ghana: Black Expatriates, and the Civil Rights Era* (Chapel Hill: University of North Carolina Press, 2006).

Stone, I. F., *In a Time of Torment* (New York: Random House, 1968).

Ture, Kwame (Stokely Carmichael), and Charles V. Hamilton, *Black Power: The Politics of Liberation.* (1967; reprint, New York: Vintage, 1992).

African American literature, film, music, and culture

Alim, H. Samy, *Roc the Mic Right: The Language of Hip Hop Culture* (New York, Routledge, 2006).

Andrews, William L., *To Tell a Free Story: The First Century of Afro-American Autobiography, 1760–1865* (Urbana: University of Illinois Press, 1986).

Bogle, Donald, *Toms, Coons, Mulattoes, Mammies, and Bucks: An Interpretive History of Blacks in American Films* 4th edn. (New York: Continuum, 2001).

Chang, Jeff, and D J Kool Herc, *Can't Stop Won't Stop: A History of the Hip Hop Generation* (New York: St. Martin's Press, 2005).

Clegg, Claude A., *The Price of Liberty: African Americans and the Making of Liberia* (Chapel Hill: University of North Carolina Press, 2004).

Cobb, William J., *To the Break of Dawn: A Freestyle on the Hip Hop Aesthetic* (New York: New York University Press, 2007).

Keyes, Cheryl L., *Rap Music and Street Consciousness* (Urbana: University of Illinois, 2002).

Neal, Larry, *Visions of a Liberated Future: Black Arts Movement Writings* (New York: Thunder's Mouth Press, 1989).

Perkins, William Eric (ed.), *Droppin' Science: Critical Essays on Rap, Music and Hip Hop Culture* (Philadelphia: Temple University Press, 1996).

Quinn, Etthne, *Nuthin' But a "G" Thang: The Culture and Commerce of Gangsta Rap* (New York: Columbia University Press, 2005).

Randall, Dudley, and Margaret G. Burroughs (eds.), *For Malcolm: Poems on the Life and the Death of Malcolm X* (Detroit: Broadside Press, 1969).

Reid, Mark, *Black Lenses, Black Voices: African American Film Now* (Lanham, MD: Rowman and Littlefield, 2005).

Smethurst, James Edward, *The Black Arts Movement: Literary Nationalism in the 1960s and 1970s* (Chapel Hill: University of North Carolina Press, 2005).

Stewart, Jacqueline, *Migrating to the Movies: Cinema and Black Urban Modernity* (Berkeley: University of California Press, 2005).

Race, religion, gender, and cultural studies

Cone, James H., *Black Theology and Black Power* (New York: Harper and Row, 1997).

Cruse, Harold, *The Crisis of the Negro Intellectual* (New York: Quill, 1984).

Dillard, Angela D., *Guess Who's Coming to Dinner Now?: Multicultural Conservatism in America* (New York: New York University Press, 2001).

Fanon, Frantz, *Black Skin, White Masks* (New York: Grove Press, 1967).

Gillespie, Alex, *Becoming Other: From Social Interaction to Self-Reflection* (Greenwich, CT: Information Age Publishing, 2006).

Gilmore, Ruth Wilson, "Fatal Couplings of Power and Difference: Notes on Racism and Geography," *Professional Geographer*, 54.1 (2002), pp. 15–24.

Griffin, Farah Jasmine, *Who Set You Flowin'?* (New York: Oxford University Press, 1995).

hooks, bell, *Ain't I a Woman: Black Women and Feminism* (Boston: South End Press, 1981).

Karenga, Maulana, *Kawaida Theory* (Los Angeles: Kawaida Publications, 1990).

Kelley, Robin D. G., *Freedom Dreams: The Black Radical Imagination* (Boston: Beacon Press, 2002).

Keyes, Alan L., and Martin L. Gross, *Masters of the Dream: The Strength and Betrayal of Black America* (New York: William Morrow, 1995).

Leak, Jeffrey B., *Racial Myths and Masculinity in African American Literature* (Knoxville: University of Tennessee Press, 2005).

Leeming, David, *James Baldwin: A Biography* (New York: Penguin, 1994).

McPhail, Mark Lawrence, *The Rhetoric of Racism Revisited: Reparations or Separation?* (Lanham, MD: Rowman and Littlefield Publishers, 2002).

Madhubuti, Haki R., *Black Men: Obsolete, Single, Dangerous?* (Chicago: Third World Press, 1990).

Marable, Manning, *Living Black History: How Reimagining the African-American Past Can Remake America's Racial Future* (New York: Basic Civitas Books, 2006).

Mazama, Ama (ed.), *The Afrocentric Paradigm* (Trenton, NJ: Africa World Press, 2003).

Norman, Brian, *The American Protest Essay and National Belonging* (Albany: State University of New York Press, 2007).

Radford-Hill, Sheila, *Further to Fly: Black Women and the Politics of Empowerment* (Minneapolis: University of Minnesota Press, 2000).

Singh, Nikhil Pal, *Black Is a Country: Race and the Unfinished Struggle for Democracy* (Cambridge: Harvard University, 2004).

Wilmore, Gayraud S., *Black Religion and Black Radicalism: An Interpretation of the Religious History of African Americans* (Garden City, NY: Doubleday, 1972).

INDEX